Rediscovering the Past
at Mexico's Periphery

Rediscovering the Past

at Mexico's Periphery

ESSAYS ON THE HISTORY OF MODERN YUCATÁN

Gilbert M. Joseph

THE UNIVERSITY OF ALABAMA PRESS

All photographs are from
Fototeca"Pedro Guerra" de la E.C.A.U.D.Y.

*An earlier version of certain passages
in this book appeared in Gilbert M. Joseph,
"From Caste War to Class War:
The Historiography of Modern Yucatán (c. 1750–1940),"
HAHR 65, no. 1 (February 1985): 111–34.*

Library of Congress Cataloging in Publication Data

Joseph, G. M. (Gilbert Michael), 1947–
  Rediscovering the past at Mexico's periphery.

  Bibliography: p.
  Includes index.
  1. Yucatán (Mexico)—Historiography.   I. Title.
F1376.J67 1986   972'.65   85–1185
ISBN 0–8173–0268–9 (alk. paper)

Dedicated

---

to the memory of Don Luis López Rivas (1917–1982),
archivist, gentleman, and fellow student
of the Yucatecan past.

Published with support of the Alfredo Barrera Vásquez
Institute for Yucatecan Studies,
The University of Alabama

Contents

Photographs

viii

Foreword

The Yucatán peninsula, shaped like a giant thumb pointing north, was born of the sea, like the goddess Venus. Appropriately, one of our poets has called it "the land of love and legend."

Yucatán is flat and calcareous, without lakes or rivers, where only scrub and agave thrive. Ours is a land where, in certain parts, the hand of man has left no trace; it is a vast surface mirror reflecting the tropical sun's harsh rays back toward the heavens. And yet nature has graced the peninsula with a tranquil sea and sand whiter than ivory; with *cenotes* or grottoes hidden in the earth's crust, through which filters the rain's sweet water; with nights made cool and aromatic by the sea breeze; and with skies so clear and starry that one seems to be inside an immense and wondrous planetarium.

Throughout this land are sown reminders of the magnificent, classic civilization of the Maya. Calling themselves "the chosen ones"—from *ma* (not) and *ya* (many), according to the generally accepted etymology—these ancients, their ruins and culture, and the plight of their modern-day descendants have inspired a copious and distinguished literature, to which not only Yucatecans but also national and international scholars have contributed. Among the latter, North American have joined European and Latin American researchers to produce what seems like an infinity of works over the past hundred years.

Indeed, it was the indefatigable U.S. explorer and scholar, John L. Stephens, who first introduced the world to the treasures of Maya antiquity in the middle of the last century. During the 1920s and 1930s, Sylvanus G. Morley and a team of archaeologists from the Washington-based Carnegie Institution, working closely with Yucatán's revolutionary governor Felipe Carrillo Puerto and his successors, played an instrumental role in restoring the classic sites of Chichén Itzá and Uxmal and in deciphering the character of the civilization that erected them. Another member of the Carnegie generation, colonial historian Robert S. Chamberlain, wrote in the late 1940s what still remains the best history of Yucatán's conquest and early colonization. Currently, a younger generation of North American historians, including Gilbert Joseph, Allen Wells, Nancy Farriss, and Robert Patch, is breaking new ground in the social, economic, and agrarian history of Yucatán and introducing new methods and conceptual frameworks in the process.

North American scholars often have possibilities not available to their Yucatecan and Mexican colleagues. Frequently, they have access to collections not available to us, hampered as we are by insufficient funding and the lack of leave time. For example, Chamberlain and members of the Carnegie generation were able to work for years at a time in the Archivo General de Indias in Seville and in other Spanish and international repositories, and more recently, scholars like Joseph and Wells have profitably consulted the archives of International Harvester and other U.S. corporations in their investigations of modern Yucatecan history.

By and large, North American scholars have demonstrated good faith and scrupulously sought to further the exploration of our region's past. Most have not come to their work with preconceived notions and prejudices which, unfortunately, have occasionally impeded our efforts.

Of course, not all U.S. historians are free of misconceptions; indeed, some writers have come to Yucatán with ethnocentric notions guaranteed to distort their perceptions of our reality. Such was the case, unhappily, with Benjamin Norman's *Rambles in Yucatán,* a book which appeared in the wake of Stephens's writings on the peninsula. Norman's book enjoyed an immediate but short-lived success in U.S. literary circles before fading into much-deserved obscurity. On the other hand, Stephens's insightful volumes still delight readers and have been translated into all of the world's major languages.

The danger also exists that, owing to limited experience, the foreign student of Yucatán is liable to mistake appearances for reality.

Certainly, in our Mexico, things are often different than at first they seem!

Historian Gilbert M. Joseph of the University of North Carolina at Chapel Hill brings to his work the qualities of an experienced researcher: he is hardworking, comprehends the regional milieu and seeks an even better understanding of it, and has few ideological or cultural axes to grind. He is the author of numerous works that explore the social history and political economy of Yucatán. The present work, *Rediscovering the Past at Mexico's Periphery: Essays on the History of Modern Yucatán,* is a pioneering attempt to delineate and interpret the historical contours of our region. Joseph takes as his point of departure the larger social and economic structures that have shaped the peninsular past from late colonial times and incorporates into his synthesis the most important sources available in Mexico and abroad.

By committing himself to the study of our society and to the dissemination of our history in Yucatán, the United States, and throughout the world, Professor Joseph strengthens in a small but important way the bonds of friendship and respect among peoples (for it is impossible to respect what one does not know) and helps to foster more amicable relations in our hemisphere.

Mérida, Yucatán

Rodolfo Ruz Menéndez
Universidad de Yucatán
Academia Nacional de Historia

Preface

Interdisciplinary regional studies have dominated the historiography of Mexico for at least a decade now. Increasingly, Mexican and international scholars are focusing their attention on the modern era (c. 1750 to the present), and significant studies have already appeared on the Bajío, Chiapas, Chihuahua, Coahuila and La Comarca Lagunera, Guerrero, Jalisco (Guadalajara and Los Altos), Michoacán, Morelos, Northern Hidalgo, Nuevo León (Monterrey), Oaxaca, San Luis Potosí, Sinaloa and Sonora, Tabasco, Tlaxcala, Veracruz, and Yucatán. Yucatán, in particular, has generated an unusual appeal and an abundant scholarship. Lured perhaps by the past glories of ancient Maya civilization whose ruins adorn the peninsula, by the fierce resistance of the Maya to their Spanish and, later, Mexican conquerors, and finally by the fabled riches of the henequen boom and its dramatic demise, anthropologists, sociologists, economists, geographers, and demographers have made important contributions along with historians. Of late it must seem to non-*yucatecólogos* as if these specialists are literally swarming over the peninsula.

Nevertheless, this study probably would not have been undertaken without John Johnson's timely encouragement several years ago. Then in the first days of his energetic and innovative editorship of the *Hispanic American Historical Review*, Johnson persuaded me that not only had Mexican regional studies come of age but the time was now ripe to take stock of the historiography of certain key regions like Yucatán. What began as a commission to write an essay for the journal, metamorphosed by degrees into this book. Along the way, I expanded my assignment: in addition to surveying major trends in the modern Yucatecan literature, I relate these to broader

xiii

thematic and methodological currents in Mexican historiography and suggest new departures for regional and local-level research. Since it is likely that regional approaches will continue to produce some of the most vital and innovative work in the Latin American field, it is my hope that this book might prompt comparable studies for other Mexican and Latin American regions that have also begun to generate a mature body of historical writing.

The volume is divided into two sections. In part 1, "Writing History in Yucatán," I examine the dimensions of the current boom in historical research on the region, the reasons behind it, and the long and prestigious social science tradition upon which it builds. Then, in part 2, I detail the major interpretative trends in the new professional work by local, national, and international scholars, giving special attention to the variety of lively debates that have recently emerged. Rather than compiling lists of sources around given subject headings in the manner of many historiographies, I have sought a common ground for analysis in the new literature's preoccupation with changing relations of land, labor, and capital and their impact on regional society and culture. This has suggested a new periodization of modern Yucatecan history and has challenged me to write an integrated series of synthetic essays rooted in regional political economy. Although each chapter identifies specific lacunae, a final epilogue summarizes broad trends and suggests future research priorities. The book concludes with a bibliography which is, to my knowledge, the most comprehensive listing of social science literature on Yucatán to date.

Historiographical works such as this one are inevitably cooperative ventures. Over the course of the past decade, many colleagues in the United States and Mexico helped me to locate specialized materials and hone the ideas found in this book. Mexicanists Barry Carr, John Womack, Stuart Voss, Mark Wasserman, John Hart, William Beezley, Friedrich Katz, Daniela Spenser, and the late David Bailey, and fellow yucatecólogos Allen Wells, Ramón Chacón, Robert Patch, Philip Thompson, Michael Fallon, Graham Knox, Lawrence Remmers, Diane Roazen Parrillo, Laura Batt, Víctor Suárez Molina, Antonio Betancourt Pérez, José Luis Sierra Villarreal, Alejandra García Quintanilla, Carlos Bojórquez Urzáiz, Salvador Rodríguez Losa, Raquel Barceló Quintal, Luis Millet Cámara, Eric Villanueva Mukul, Marie Lapointe, Marie-France Labrecque, Manuel Sarkisyanz, Marta Espejo-Ponce de Hunt, Francisco Paoli, Enrique Montalvo, Jeffrey Brannon, Eric Baklanoff, Edward Moseley, Edward Terry, Grant Jones, Nancy Farriss, Victoria Bricker, Angel Cal, Hernán Menéndez, Miguel Bretos, Juan Valencia Bellavista, James Callaghan, and Mary Murphy have all, in one way or another, provided leads, served as sounding boards, leveled constructive criticisms, and generally furthered my understanding of the region's past. To Allen Wells and Ramón Chacón, I owe a very special professional and personal debt. Beyond their insights into Porfirian and revolutionary Yucatán, which I have enjoyed in sustained dialogues that have now lasted almost ten years, they continue to affirm the potential for warm and open friendship that, unfortunately, is often at a premium given the demands of hectic academic schedules.

Special gratitude is also reserved for *yucatecos* Rodolfo Ruz Menéndez (Universidad de Yucatán), the late Alfredo Barrera Vásquez (Instituto Nacional de Historia y Antropología), Waldemaro Concha Vargas (Fototeca "Pedro Guerra"), Beatriz Reyes Campos, and the late Luis López Rivas (Archivo General del Estado), who have personally guided so many Mexican and international scholars in their historical investigations. The recent surge of professional interest in the Yucatecan past owes more to these modest, courteous individuals than can be expressed here. In a real sense, the production of this small volume is the best tribute to them, particularly the late Don Luis López, who transformed the Archivo General del Estado to facilitate the work of serious researchers in the mid-1970s.

I am also grateful to Malcolm MacDonald, director of The University of Alabama Press, and to Edward Moseley, director of the university's Capstone International Programs Center. Each encouraged this specialized project from its inception, and each in his own way has been instrumental in deepening The University of Alabama's long-standing institutional and intellectual ties with Yucatán.

Rosalie Radcliffe graciously typed the manuscript, and the University of North Carolina provided a leave that enabled me to finish writing the book.

Finally, I owe a great deal to my wife, Alma Blount, who counseled me on maps and photographs. Moreover, in the midst of her own busy career as a photojournalist, she provided an antidote for my binges of compulsiveness, cheerfully bore a succession of late nights, and worked around a dining-room table cluttered with books and scraps of note paper.

Chapel Hill, North Carolina   Gilbert M. Joseph

Abbreviations

AGE	Archivo General del Estado
AGN	Archivo General de la Nación
ANE	Archivo Notarial del Estado
BECA	*Boletín de la Escuela de Ciencias Antropológicas de la Universidad de Yucatán*
CEHSMO	Centro de Estudios Históricos del Movimiento Obrero Mexicano
CIS	Centro de Investigaciones Superiores
CROM	Confederación Regional Obrera Mexicana
DdY	*Diario de Yucatán*
DEES	Departamento de Estudios Económicos y Sociales, Universidad de Yucatán
ECAUDY	Escuela de Cíencias Antropológicas de la Universidad de Yucatán
HAHR	*Hispanic American Historical Review*
IHC	International Harvester Company
INAH	Instituto Nacional de Antropología e Historia
LARR	*Latin American Research Review*
PNA	Partido Nacional Agrario
PNR	Partido Nacional Revolucionario
PRI	Partido Revolucionario Institucional
PSS	Partido Socialista del Sureste
RUY	*Revista de la Universidad de Yucatán*
UAM	Universidad Autónoma Metropolitana
UNAM	Universidad Nacional Autónoma de México
YHE	*Yucatán: Historia y Economía*

Part 1
Writing History in Yucatán

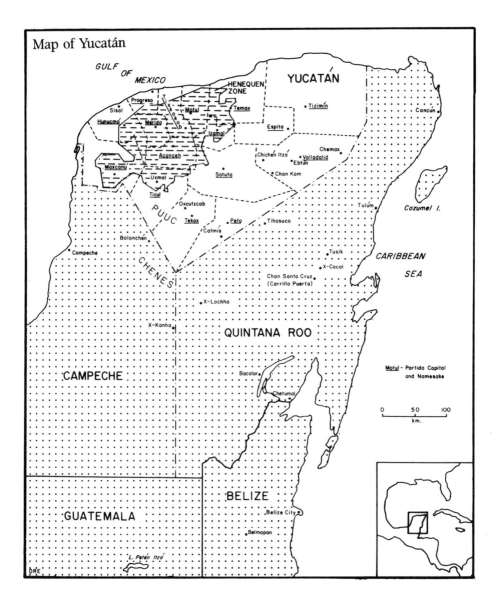

Map of Yucatán

1

The Recent Boom

In the summer of 1973, when I first set foot in Mérida, Yucatán, a callow doctoral student in search of a topic, professional historians were an exotic species in the peninsula. There were no Mexican or international scholars working in the Archivo General del Estado, then housed on the second floor of "La Mejorada," a former Franciscan church built in the sixteenth century. For all of its colonial charm, the AGE lacked electric lighting, plumbing, and any system of classification for its extensive modern holdings. The Universidad de Yucatán, although proud enough of its Escuela de Ciencias Antropológicas to provide it with its own minicampus, lacked a department of history. Nor did the new Centro Regional del Sureste of the Instituto Nacional de Antropología e Historia have a professional historian on its staff; characteristically the director was an archaeologist. Indeed, throughout the duration of my dissertation research, Yucatecan friends persisted in introducing me as an anthropologist, despite my repeated disclaimers and painstaking attempts to explain the nature of my research.

It was not that *yucatecos* had an aversion to the past; on the contrary, they relished it. Yet history was less the province of a trained academic elite than a vibrant pastime practiced in the public domain. Anyone could speculate or write about the region's past, and many did. Every afternoon, intellectuals debated the stuff of regional politics past and present in Mérida's cafes, then committed their opinions, recollections, and occasional researches to print in the local press or in a steady stream of pamphlets, books, and journals published by the university, the state government, or privately. Any number of *meridano* professionals, schoolteachers, party politicians, and sons of the old *casta divina* (divine caste) had expressed a view on the origins of the apocalyptic Caste War of 1847, or captured a grand moment of Yucatán's *belle époque* at the turn of the century, when the export of henequen fiber brought an elegance to the region matched only in the national capital. Many also speculated on the reasons for Yucatán's subsequent precipitous decline in the wake of social revolution and agrarian reform. Heirs to a rich local tradition of literary erudition and rhetoric, such self-styled *pensadores* told (and retold) these stories, passionately contending over the more controversial historical themes. Since I had come, *beca* (fellowship) in hand and "scientifically trained" to investigate Yucatán's past, I must be an anthropologist.

Ten years later, professional history has come of age in Yucatán.[1] The past decade has witnessed an impressive harvest of monographs, anthologies, articles, and dissertations on the region's colonial and modern history by a diverse group of Mexican and foreign scholars. This new literature has been fostered by a more favorable climate for historical research in Yucatán, reflected in the upgrading of archives and libraries; an increased commitment by government, academic institutions, and international foundations to social science training and research; and the creation of several new journals and forums.

The AGE as well as the Archivo Notarial del Estado, the state's Hemeroteca Pino Suárez, and its premier collection, the Biblioteca Crescencio Carrillo y Ancona, have all been moved into larger quarters.[2] The small but hardworking staff of the AGE has now classified the archive's holdings through the Caste War of 1847 and begun the herculean task of ordering the thousands of *legajos* remaining for the nineteenth and twentieth centuries. Local archivists, aided by visiting North American graduate researchers, have taken preliminary steps in organizing the extensive colonial holdings of the Catholic church housed in Mérida's central cathedral, although many of the documents of the national period have yet to be surveyed.[3] The first published guides to regional archives and collections have begun to appear.[4] Researchers based in the United States will be especially interested to learn that the University of Texas at Arlington, aided by a challenge grant from the National Endowment for the

Humanities, has now microfilmed a large portion of the holdings of the AGE, ANE, the state *hemeroteca* (newspaper archives) and the church's historical archives (known by several names, most commonly as the Archivo de la Mitra or the Archivo Histórico de la Arquidiócesis de Yucatán). The university recently published a catalog of its substantial collection (1.5 million pages contained on 1,078 rolls) that includes a description of each of the major archives prepared by Yucatecan archivists.[5]

Finally, students of the regional past received an unexpected windfall when the Universidad de Yucatán recently acquired a significant portion of the extraordinary photographic archives of Guerra and Company, for decades one of Mérida's most prominent commercial studios. Housed on the campus of the university's Escuela de Ciencias Antropológicas, where it is now accessible to researchers, the Fototeca Pedro Guerra contains tens of thousands of uncataloged glass-plate negatives documenting the political, social, and cultural life of the region from about 1880 to 1930.

Within the past seven years, despite recession-induced cutbacks in its budget, the Centro Regional del Sureste of CIS-INAH has sponsored several long-term projects designed to develop the research skills of local investigators and further analysis of the political economy of Yucatán during the nineteenth and twentieth centuries.[6] In 1977 and 1978, anthropologist-social historian Arturo Warman of the Universidad Autónoma Metropolitana directed a team of Yucatecan and visiting UAM researchers in a series of community studies analyzing changes in the social relations of production in the eastern corn and cattle zone.[7] Shortly thereafter, José Luis Sierra Villarreal, the first historian to join the permanent staff of the Centro Regional del Sureste, launched a collective project on the social and economic structures of the region's dominant henequen zone between the Caste War and the Mexican Revolution. Following publication of the results of this study of henequen and the Old Regime, the Centro Regional del Sureste has initiated a new project on the character of the Mexican Revolution in Yucatán, focusing upon questions of political mobilization and leadership.[8]

The Universidad de Yucatán's new Departamento de Estudios Económicos y Sociales (created in 1976), constitutes another focal

point of historical research on the political economy of modern
Yucatán. Research by faculty and students has focused on the evolution of land tenure and labor systems during the nineteenth and
twentieth centuries, popular responses to the expansion of commercial agriculture, and more contemporary questions of rural-urban
migration in the state.[9] In 1977, with financial assistance from the
Ford Foundation, DEES established a Banco de Información specifically to facilitate this regionally oriented research. Among the services offered by the Banco, which has received a commitment of
ongoing support from the Ford Foundation, are a library, a newspaper indexing center, and an archival collection of photographs
emphasizing henequen, rural work, and culture. Using these resources, the DEES has produced useful "bibliografías básicas" for
the study of the henequen industry, the peasant economy, and the
Caste War.

In 1979, the Banco de Información embarked upon a far more
ambitious project: to develop the first database devoted exclusively
to Yucatecan studies. Over the past several years, teams of DEES
faculty and students, under the leadership of Banco director Francisco Anda Vela, have sought to locate, film, and catalog extant
printed literature on Yucatán. Thus far, the most successful aspect
of the project has been the microfilming of private libraries in Mérida. Approximately 2,000 books, pamphlets, and periodicals held
in the personal collections of prominent regional intellectuals have
already been copied. To further a binational approach to mutual
problems of access and preservation, DEES and the Universidad de
Yucatán have graciously consented to make the Banco's growing
microfilm collection available to North American scholars through
The University of Alabama, which is currently seeking funding to
copy and then catalog these materials into this country's OCLC
(Ohio College Library Center) database.

The University of Yucatán's Escuela de Ciencias Antropológicas
(permanently established in 1970) has also increasingly emphasized
history in its curricular and research priorities. Like the DEES, it
has periodically invited scholars from the national capital and
abroad to conduct symposia and teach courses in historiography as
well as other social science theory and methodology. Early in 1981,

the school formally created a Departamento de Estudios Históricos to complement existing specializations in archaeology and social anthropology and added three historians to its staff. By mid-1985, the history faculty had tripled, and the school proudly announced the creation of a master's degree program to commence in 1986.

Equally promising has been the dramatic increase in outlets for the publication and dissemination of the new historical research being undertaken by local, national, and international scholars. Under the leadership of Conrado Menéndez Díaz and Rodolfo Ruz Menéndez, the venerable *Revista de la Universidad de Yucatán,* which traces its lineage back to the early 1920s and the founding of the university by revolutionary governor Felipe Carrillo Puerto, has encouraged professional scholars throughout Mexico and the United States to contribute articles and has occasionally subsidized the translation of English-language pieces. The newer *Boletín de la Escuela de Ciencias Antropológicas de la Universidad de Yucatán,* founded in 1973, although highlighting archaeological and anthropological research, has sometimes published important articles by historians. Within the past five years, the *Boletín* has more than doubled its size and has become perhaps the most prestigious scholarly journal of the region. Newer still is *Yucatán: Historia y Economía,* created in 1977 by the DEES. Like the *Revista* and *Boletín,* the journal has solicited contributions by prominent national and international historians. However, unlike its counterparts, *Historia y Economía* is unabashedly Marxist, is edited by a research collective, and actively concerns itself with the contemporary politics of development and class struggle in Yucatán, Mexico, and Latin America.[10]

Perhaps the clearest indication of the surge of interest in historical research over the course of the past decade is the institution of "history weeks," sponsored by the Universidad de Yucatán. First inaugurated in Mérida in February 1978, the "Primera Semana de la Historia de Yucatán" assembled a diverse group of amateur and professional historians for the purpose of sharing research and cementing collegial ties. In the fall of 1978, the DEES built upon the enthusiasm generated by the first history week, organizing a smaller, exclusively professional symposium entitled "La Hacienda Mexicana en el Cambio (Siglo XIX–XX)." A distinguished panel of na-

tional and international agrarian specialists, including Friedrich
Katz, Marcello Carmagnani, Angel Palerm, and John Coatsworth,
were invited to present papers with a view to their eventual publication in *Yucatán: Historia y Economía,* and the sessions did much to
stimulate local research on the most celebrated Yucatecan version of
the great estate, the henequen plantation.[11] Then, in February 1980,
a second history week was held, drawing many more national and
international participants—whose local expenses were paid by the
university—and producing papers of substantially higher quality
than its 1978 predecessor.[12] Each of the history weeks attracted
substantial public interest, reflected in healthy attendance of the
sessions and extensive media coverage. Originally, it was hoped that
the history weeks would become a regular feature of the region's
cultural life, providing historians with a larger, more public version
of the Palenque *mesas redondas* that have long served archaeologists of the lowland Maya area. Unfortunately, Mexico's current
economic crisis has put the continuing existence of the history
weeks in jeopardy.[13]

What has produced this historiographical renaissance at Mexico's
periphery? Why have an increasing number of Mexican and North
American scholars chosen to work in Yucatán, establishing it, along
with the northwestern states and Oaxaca, as one of the three Mexican regions of greatest interest to the new generation of local historians?[14] To begin with, one cannot ignore the economics of contemporary Yucatecan development. While it has not promoted balanced
growth, tourism has dramatically altered the face of the region over
the past decade, stimulating a long-term commitment by both the
federal and state governments to historical conservation and promotion which, it is hoped, Mexico's current recession will not
jeopardize.[15]

Beyond a materialist explanation, current trends within the historical profession and the larger social science community must also
be considered. A generation ago, Harry Bernstein criticized fellow
Mexicanists for the creation of a "centralist historiography," an exaggerated tendency to concentrate almost exclusively on events in
Mexico City and "the Core," or to interpret events elsewhere only in

the context of the center. This was because most Mexicanists—like their counterparts in other fields—generally assumed that all meaningful ideas and forces for change ultimately radiated outward from the central heartland to the remote regional peripheries.[16] The current generation of historians has reacted against this approach. Mexican historian Luis González would argue that the new generation of yucatecólogos is merely obeying what he calls the "regionalist impulse of our times," a search for identity in the authentic world of local, often rural, traditions in the face of disorienting modernization and stifling centralization. Such an impulse often instills in investigators—even in many who are "outsiders"—a warm, almost personal attachment to their "terruño."[17] Other historians regard this predilection for "microhistory" as part and parcel of a broad movement which has swept up much of the current, methodologically sophisticated, generation of professionals. Dissatisfied with existing generalizations, particularly about socioeconomic phenomena, many younger historians have sought to test those generalizations at the local level. The result has been hailed by some as a "historiographical revolution," a shift in the locus of historical initiative from the institutional superstructure to the level of local regions, communities, and interest groups; a move away from political and institutional history in and from the perspective of the metropolis to social and economic history in and from the perspective of the periphery.[18]

This "revolution," in overflowing disciplinary boundaries, has pointed up their artificial nature. The best historical studies of peripheral areas have necessarily been interdisciplinary in scope, obliging students of local regions and communities to integrate political, economic, social, and cultural levels of activity into a complex whole. This has often involved historians in borrowing methodological and interpretative tools from anthropologists, economists, sociologists, and increasingly, from political economists working within the Marxist paradigm. As we shall see, the process of cross-fertilization between history and anthropology has been especially productive for the study of modern Yucatán. If, in their observation of (and occasionally, participation in) the affairs of local communities, microhistorians have become more like anthropologists, the converse has also been true. The mid-1970s and the early 1980s have witnessed a variety of efforts aimed at integrating ethnographic and archival approaches to the study of lowland Maya society and culture which have contributed significantly to a new regional historiography.

Relatively speaking, however, the "new regional history" took its time getting to Yucatán. Luis González's clarion call—or "invitación"—to do microhistory was issued to Mexicanists in 1973, four years after John Womack's classic study of Morelos had already begun showcasing the exciting possibilities of regional historiography as well as revolutionizing work on the Mexican Revolution.[19] Still, although local amateur historians remained active, professionals outside the peninsula kept their distance, seeking the meaning of the modern Mexican past elsewhere. In bypassing Yucatán, they seem to have concurred with the assessment of Yucatán's revolutionary poet, Antonio Mediz Bolio, that national events took on an "exotic and strange" cast in the peninsula.[20]

Such assumptions regarding the uniqueness and marginal significance of Yucatecan history were likely based upon the region's remote location and its exaggerated reputation for regionalism and separatism, which has become firmly rooted in the national mind. Even if, as has often been said, there is *no* Mexico but *many* Mexicos, the Yucatecan variant is generally regarded as more marked in its regional identity than any other entity within the republic.[21] It was not until the end of World War II that yucatecos were even connected by land with the rest of Mexico. Before that, communication by sea with the port of Veracruz often took longer to reach the peninsula than from many points in the United States. In fact, as recently as 1914, Yucatán's ruling oligarchs petitioned to become a protectorate of the United States, arguing plausibly that they had more in common, geographically and economically, with the North Americans than they did with the Mexican republic.[22]

It is not surprising, then, that Yucatán's traditional isolation was for a long time extended to the academic realm as well. Much of the historiography of post–Caste War Yucatán that has begun to emerge since the late 1970s, however, seems to rest on a basic assumption that great heuristic value may lie in the study of "exceptional regions." In Yucatán and the southeast, and in certain other peripheral regions, such as the northwest, regional society developed with a degree of autonomy unmatched elsewhere in Mexico. It was precisely this degree of autonomy that made such regions the kind of exceptions that bring common historical experiences into focus and enable us better to appreciate the dynamics of nineteenth- and twentieth-century Mexican history as a whole.[23]

In other words, the Yucatecan case facilitates regional analysis under two major categories: (1) the region as a variant case of a larger historical problem; and (2) the region as a dynamic component of the larger whole.[24] It is with both of these categories in mind that my discussion of Yucatán's historical literature proceeds. My tasks will be to chart the progress of this emerging regional historiography and offer suggestions regarding future research priorities. In the process, the characteristic elements in Yucatán's historical evolution will be identified, but the reader will also notice that the contours of the Yucatecan past encompass many of the themes which characterize other regions of Mexico and Latin America as well. Perhaps most prominently, these include the political and economic struggle between peripheral regions and the central state; the development of the export economy and the partnership between local elites and foreign investors in that process; and the expansion of commercial agriculture and its agrarian consequences.

2

Principal Currents in the Early Development of Yucatecan Historiography

For most of the twentieth century—certainly since the 1920s—the writing of Yucatecan history roughly proceeded along two parallel tracks. Occasionally drawing upon rich though poorly documented sources, local amateur historians collectively produced a lively *histoire évènementielle* (narrative history) of modern, predominantly Creole, Yucatán—a historical tradition which their professional colleagues might more attentively mine for both factual content and interpretation.[1] Meanwhile, a cohort of North American and Mexico City scholars, affiliated with the Carnegie Institution of Washington, D.C., was presiding over a golden age of Maya studies.[2] These outsiders—mostly archaeologists but with a strong representation of anthropologists and colonial historians—dramatically advanced our understanding of Maya society before and during the Spanish conquest and produced the first analyses of the impact of the colonial regime. Indeed, much of the illustrious early chapter of North American anthropology, particularly in the subfields of archaeology, linguistics, ethnology, and even physical anthropology, was written by this distinguished generation of regional specialists.

If it is true, as one anthropologist has put it, that archaeology is "the zone of refuge for those in search of the exotic," then many have sought a haven in the Yucatán peninsula.[3] The North American John Lloyd Stephens and his British artist friend, Frederick Catherwood, were perhaps the first Anglo-Saxons to explore and evoke, in word and drawing, the splendor and complexity of Mayan antiquities.[4] Their celebrated explorations in the mid-nineteenth century attached an aura of prestige and mystery to the region that attracted later generations of travelers and scholars, most notably, the Carnegie researchers who began to arrive in the early 1920s. From the inception of its work in Yucatán, the Carnegie Institution's funding for archaeological excavations far outstripped its support for ethnographic and historical investigations; in fact, the latter developed largely as an offshoot of the former. Thus, in 1931, Robert Redfield and Alfonso Villa Rojas began their ethnographic work at Chan Kom, only twenty kilometers from the pyramids of Chichén Itzá, the most prestigious site of its day, where excavations had already been under way for seven years. The landmark Chan Kom study was originally conceived by Carnegie as part of a larger interdisciplinary project on the region surrounding the Chichén site. Had it not been for these archaeological excavations, neither Chan Kom nor the other villages that Redfield ordered on his "folk-urban continuum" would probably have been studied in the 1930s.[5]

As a result of this larger commitment by the Carnegie Institution, a number of classic studies emerged during the 1930s, 1940s, and 1950s by scholars such as Redfield and Villa Rojas, Ralph Roys, France Scholes, and Robert Chamberlain—studies that would lay the foundation for all future work on the history and anthropology of the Yucatec Maya.[6] Owing particularly to the efforts of Roys, Scholes, and Eleanor Adams, a rich collection of Indian and Hispanic documents were found, analyzed, and published.[7] Indeed, the focus of the Carnegie Institution's historical work remained riveted on the historiography and historical ethnography of the early contact and conquest periods and of the first two hundred years of colonial rule.[8] The late colonial period and the important century separating it from the ethnographic present which Redfield and Villa Rojas were investigating at Chan Kom remained a great void; ironically, they knew virtually nothing of the terrible devastation which the nineteenth-century Caste War had visited on the very area in which Chan Kom had recently been founded by migrants—an area which not long before had been a depopulated no-man's-land.[9]

This lacuna did not seem particularly to bother Redfield. For while he occasionally paid lip service to the importance of history, he largely ignored historical phenomena and evidence in explaining contemporary social change. Redfield's work on Yucatán epitomized the tradition of structuralist social anthropology, which limited itself to strictly synchronic investigations of nonliterate peoples.[10] This

"synchronic bias" was most painfully evident in his "folk-urban continuum," which attempted to reconstruct the history of cultural
change in the Yucatán peninsula, not by directly consulting historical documents and informants, but by "translat[ing] space into time
and differences between communities into history."[11]

Redfield freely admitted that his "historical method" was indirect,
comparative, and diffusionist; in fact, "certainly a crude way to
derive even the most tentative historical conclusions."[12] Yet on the
basis of it, he hypothesized that during the course of the peninsula's
history, increasing contact between the capital city, Mérida, and the
outlying communities hastened a process of acculturation to "city
ways," diffusing "Euro-Mexican culture" and concomitantly reducing the traditional or "folk-like" characteristics of the Maya communities in direct proportion to each's distance from the capital city.[13]
According to Redfield: "Even where confirmation is lacking as to the
earlier presence [of traditional cultural traits] in a less-peripheral
community, the different forms of custom and institutions may be
arranged in an order consistent with the spatial order of the communities so as to suggest an actual historical sequence."[14] Interestingly,
Redfield took pains to suggest that although his model was dualistic,
the diffusion of culture from urban to rural communities did not
proceed in a simply mechanistic fashion; rather, the process of diffusion had to be viewed within the context of the "total situation."
Unfortunately, Redfield never explained exactly what he meant by
"total situation," nor did he specify what the historical determinants
of such a larger context might be.[15]

Although the ethnographic work of Redfield and Villa Rojas still
has value for an understanding of "traditional" Yucatec Maya communities, the folk-urban construct, which during the 1940s and
1950s served to discourage historically oriented anthropological
studies of Yucatán's recent past, would be relegated to the intellectual scrap heap by the late 1960s. Ironically it was Redfield's own
restudy of Chan Kom (1950) which first called into question the
simplicity of the original model for anthropologists.[16] By then, a
spate of articles on the social and economic origins and consequences of the 1847 Caste War by historian Howard Cline, by highlighting the chaotic, violent condition of Yucatecan society since

independence, had already begun to undermine Redfield's central premise that postcolonial change represented little more than "ripples of progress" emanating from an increasingly modern Mérida and other urban centers.[17]

Synchronic, diffusionist anthropology was dealt a mortal blow and the case for a more historical approach convincingly established in the middle and late 1960s. Based on his own fieldwork in Chan Kom during the early 1960s, anthropologist Victor Goldkind challenged Redfield's and Villa Rojas's studies of the community on much the same grounds that Oscar Lewis had previously taken issue with Redfield's interpretation of Tepotzlán.[18] According to Goldkind, Redfield and Villa Rojas had been so heavily influenced by evolving ideas of capitalist modernization and the Mexican Institutional Revolutionary Party's own notion of "progress" based on consensus, that they had factored out of their ethnographic work historically conditioned questions of stratification and class. Most conspicuously absent from the Chan Kom studies of the 1930s (and the 1950 restudy) was a recognition of the glaring socioeconomic conflicts attending the rise of *caciquismo* (bossism), an informal political institution that grew out of the local revolutionary process and came to serve as an important pillar of the increasingly centralized, postrevolutionary bourgeois state.[19]

Still, it was the critique of Redfield by a fellow anthropologist, Arnold Strickon, which appeared almost simultaneously with Goldkind's studies, that constituted a true frontal assault on the synchronic approach. Strickon attempted to reexamine the development of Yucatecan society and culture from a different perspective, offering a broad "historical-ecological framework" of analysis which, he contended, would more closely approximate a grasp of the "total situation" than Redfield's dualistic "folk-urban continuum." For example, Strickon found it remarkable that, in addition to neglecting current issues of class, Redfield's "quasi-historical" model had all but ignored such important watersheds as the Caste War and the subsequent rise of the monocrop fiber industry, centered on the henequen plantation.[20] Strickon built on Cline's historical studies of early nineteenth-century Yucatecan society and economy, which tied the origins and consequences of the Caste War to the development of commercial agriculture in the region and the evolution of various forms of the large estate. Since it was patent that, following the Caste War, the export of henequen fiber played a preponderant role in the peninsular economy, society, and polity, Strickon argued that the henequen plantations of Redfield's time had to be central to an understanding of the culture which Redfield observed in the 1930s. Relying upon direct historical data and delineating broad environmental subregions within the peninsula in order to examine the changing "cultural ecological adaptations" made in these subregions throughout the course of modern Yucatecan history, Strickon further contended that the great estate in one or another of its typological forms—for example, cattle *estancia*, maize and livestock haciendas, sugar estate, and henequen plantation—had conditioned the development of social and cultural change in Yucatán since the conquest.[21] Modern Mérida's development, as well as that of the other communities comprising Redfield's folk-urban continuum, was tied to the henequen plantation and the fluctuating needs and fortunes of the global economy. Strickon concluded that the spatial distribution or "historical sequence" of communities on Redfield's 1930s continuum represented just one historical moment in the ongoing adaptation of Yucatecan culture, in both its Maya and ladino (Creole) aspects, to the ever-changing demands of the large estate, which, in turn, tied Yucatán into the world economic system. The social and cultural development of the region was therefore conditioned by much more than the distance or relative isolation of local communities from the big city. All regional centers and settlements had a specialized, dynamic role to play in the larger system of political economy during the 1930s, just as they had in the historic past and have at present. Moreover, the changes that took place in Redfield's communities did not occur serially but coordinately, as each, governed by its particular ecological possibilities, continually adjusted to the changing requirements of the larger system.[22]

More than a compelling critique of Redfieldian structuralist social anthropology, Strickon's 1965 essay must also be regarded as a milestone in the evolution of historical writing on modern Yucatán. Its compelling, jargon-free theoretical framework was accessible to both anthropologists and historians and suggested broad new avenues of research on the region's past. Strickon's conceptualization of the impact which the great estate's relationship to the international economy had on social relations and the process of Yucatecan development was ahead of its time, and it no doubt inspired as well as foreshadowed many of the interdisciplinary studies in modern Yucatecan political economy which have been published within the past decade by economic anthropologists, historians, and other social scientists.[23]

If Strickon's theoretical essay legitimized the search for direct historical data in the eyes of social scientists, Nelson Reed's popular narrative history of the Caste War—published the year before—revealed the rich rewards of such a search.[24] Consulting contemporary periodicals, combing documentary and secondary sources in Mérida and Belize, and (aided by Villa Rojas's ethnography) literally tracking down ancient informants in the Quintana Roo bush, Reed, a St. Louis lawyer and amateur archaeologist-turned-historian, produced an account that is dramatically rendered—as befits its epic theme—and generally accurate, although without the usual scholarly appurtenances. Like Strickon, Reed built upon the solid foundation provided by Howard Cline's early historical articles, and in many respects Reed's well-circulated history has rescued from oblivion Cline's own extensive research on the war, which was originally published in a form that made widespread dissemination difficult.

While *The Caste War of Yucatán* has probably been sold mostly on the basis of its lively battle scenes and grisly *machetazos* (machete blows), its major intellectual contributions lie in the field of ethnohistory. Reed feels compelled to confess to the reader that "the shooting doesn't start until Chapter Three," but no apology is needed for the two succinct literary gems which masterfully evoke the contrasting worlds of ladino and *mazehual* (Indian) and set the stage for violent conflict. Then, following a narration of the major military phase of the war, Reed again shifts gears to analyze the ideology of religious revitalization (the cult of "the Talking Cross") and the sociopolitical organization of the independent rebel Maya state whose headquarters were established deep in the Quintana Roo jungle at Chan Santa Cruz (now Felipe Carrillo Puerto). Despite a flurry of recent publications on the Caste War and its legacy by

anthropologists and ethnohistorians, Nelson Reed's work remains
the most ambitious treatment of the subject in English or Spanish,
and notwithstanding some minor factual errors and dramatic over-
embellishments, its main lines of interpretation have not been
superseded.[25]

Reed, the successful amateur who had contributed perhaps the
first important work of ethnohistory in a new post-Redfield era, was
shortly joined by a rapidly expanding cohort of professionals dedicated to the anthropological study of historical process in Yucatán.
Indeed, the interdisciplinary specialty of "ethnohistory" experienced a kind of self-conscious development and promotion during
the late 1960s and early 1970s.[26] With Redfield's ahistorical approach to cultural differentiation in eclipse, anthropologists and social historians more openly sought to borrow theoretical and methodological insights across disciplinary lines, the better to reexamine
their own materials. What began largely for pragmatic reasons has
over the course of the last decade given way to genuine collaboration
and interchange. Since both disciplines share a common concern
with processes of change and adaptation in society and culture, each
has much to learn from the other. The historical approach provides
anthropologists with a bridge between the archaeological past and
the ethnographic present. The anthropological perspective gives social historians better insight into native American societies, laying
bare social dynamics and cultural adaptations, rejections, and syn-
cretisms which have developed over long periods of time.[27]

Ethnohistorical studies of the lowland Maya area encompassing
Yucatán, like the new regional historiography in general, were
rather late to emerge. Research carried out in the late 1960s and
early 1970s began to appear in print in the mid- to late 1970s, most
notably in a diverse collection of essays broadly, if unceremoniously,
titled *Anthropology and History in Yucatán* (1977).[28] The an-
thology—and a prolific article and monograph literature that has
developed around it—demonstrate how, despite the fragmentary
and often uneven nature of the manuscript sources, it has increasingly become possible to substitute knowledge for speculation
in spanning the gap between archaeological reconstruction and contemporary fieldwork on the Maya.[29] The volume's contributors

bring a wide variety of methodological orientations to this effort. Colonial Spanish and lesser-known British imperial documents (the latter located in Belize and London) are employed in the task of social and cultural reconstruction. Innovative use is made of both written Maya documents and oral tradition, which are frequently used as a counterweight to more standard "externally" produced histories by ladino writers. In order to explore the problem of demographic change, ethnohistorical and ethnographic sources complement an analysis of census data and parish registers.[30] Unfortunately, no attempt is made in the selection of case studies to provide representative regional coverage of the peninsula; on the other hand, the inadequacy of present knowledge would render any attempt at synthesis premature.

Despite the inevitable limitations attending such a "first attempt," the new cohort of ethnohistorians has reached an important general consensus. Relying on new empirical data and conceptual approaches, they have affirmed a view of the Maya implicit in the work of Ralph Roys, an ethnohistorian of the older Carnegie generation. With Roys, they contend that despite centuries of nearly overwhelming external pressure from powerful outside forces, Yucatec Maya society has, through diverse forms of resistance and adaptation, maintained a remarkable degree of cultural integrity and autonomy.[31] The impact of Roys's contributions was originally limited by the poor understanding of Yucatán's recent historical past that prevailed when he wrote in the 1930s and 1940s, and, of course, by the powerful contemporary influence of Redfield's thought.

Whereas Redfield regarded historical process in Yucatán in linear fashion, as the gradual spread outward of essentially benign and powerful modern forces emanating from the urban northwest, the new ethnohistorical studies present a picture which is far more turbulent and complex. They do not discount Redfield's acculturative forces attending the modernization process but argue that they affected different groups of Maya in varying degrees of intensity, depending on a variety of other historically conditioned factors. Building on Strickon's "historical-ecological model," they draw attention to a welter of dynamic competitive relationships alternately pitting Maya groups against various forces of Spanish and

Yucatecan colonialism, against the agents of British imperial expansion, and against each other.

The new generation of ethnohistorians suggests that in very few cases did the Maya submit passively to the dominant Creole society, as Redfield's diffusionist model inevitably implies. While the ethnohistorical literature is far less developed for the more pacified and tightly controlled area of northwestern Yucatán—which for much of the past century has been known as the "henequen zone"—even here it suggests that forms of cultural resistance may have endured, with contending forms of ritual and belief going underground or surviving in syncretistic guises.[32] Several studies document that even today, regardless of their degree of acculturation or the intensity of their experience with ladino domination, the Maya retain an acute sense of having an independent history. This historical tradition is carefully nurtured and transmitted in elaborate oral and written forms from generation to generation.[33] The literature also suggests that the nature and effectiveness of various types of adaptation and resistance often depended on the degree of physical mobility the Maya displayed. Historical research has yet to determine precisely how many dissatisfied and persecuted Maya drifted or fled into the southern and eastern zones of refuge, yet demographic profiles of certain villages can plausibly be explained only by migrations on a rather large scale.[34]

The dramatically increased interest in Yucatecan ethnohistoriography in the middle 1970s represents but one dimension of the new professional concern with the region's past that is engaging the energies of an increasing number of anthropologists, historians, sociologists, economists, geographers, and demographers. Having sketched the broad contours of the development of historical writing on modern Yucatán, I will now examine the current state of the historical literature, highlighting noteworthy recent contributions by historians and other social scientists.

Part 2
From Caste War to Class War: A Survey of Recent Historical Writing on Modern Yucatán

The customary periodization of Mexico's modern past has never been consistently applied to Yucatán, even in the work of many traditional local political historians. Mexico's three great political benchmarks—or "revolutionary cycles," as they have often loosely been termed in the literature—were not violent episodes in Yucatán and have never been recounted as prominently in the peninsula as elsewhere in the republic. The "Grito de Dolores" generated no immediate echo in the region nor were there any "wars of independence" in Yucatán. Liberal yucatecos carried out a concerted campaign against clerical privilege decades before the "wars of reform" were waged throughout Mexico in the late 1850s, thereby ensuring that bloody partisan conflict was minimized in the peninsula. Similarly, the Mexican Revolution of 1910 was a rather nonviolent affair in the southeast. The Revolution did not even arrive in Yucatán until 1915 and caused that region little loss of life. During the height of factional violence throughout the republic in 1915–16, the U.S. consul in Progreso drolly reported to his superiors, "Peace is raging here as usual."[1]

Yet Yucatán's modern history has hardly been tranquil. If the popular Hidalgo Revolt did not resonate in the peninsula it might have been because, in addition to the peninsula's remoteness, the Maya had anticipated it in a rebellion of their own, led by Jacinto Canek in 1761, which was dealt a severely repressive blow. And although other Mexican regions experienced peasant rebellions and caste warfare during the early national period, nowhere were they so tragic and devastating as in Yucatán. The bloodiest, most militarily successful Indian rebellion in Latin American history, the so-called Guerra de las Castas unleashed in 1847, also had much to do with the muting of Reform Era rivalries in Yucatán. While Creole Liberals and Conservatives fought each other elsewhere in Mexico, the members of Yucatán's dominant class were compelled to submerge, at least temporarily, their ideological differences and regionally based economic rivalries and confront a common Maya enemy who, in 1848, nearly drove them from the peninsula. Indeed, so bitterly contested was the Caste War and so indelible its memory, that it also affected the character of Yucatán's participation in the Mexican Revolution. For in addition to demographic dislocation and the tremendous loss of life and property that made a renewal of hostilities either unattractive or infeasible, the Caste War prompted Yucatán's planter-merchant elite, once it had securely reestablished its control over the region, to implement a series of draconian political and social measures to ensure against the recurrence of another homegrown groundswell. Even today the Caste War remains the central historical event in the popular mind, and many yucatecos (and other Mexicans as well) often assume that when one speaks of the Revolution in Yucatán, one is referring to the Caste War.

Generally speaking, the new historical literature on the Caste War period as well as on other aspects of Yucatán's modern past, has reexamined and often downplayed the traditional connection with national-level political phenomena, such as Mexico's "revolutionary cycles," and focused on the structural bedrock of the region's historical development. Much attention has been given to the changing relations of land, labor, and capital and their impact on socioeconomic, political, and cultural processes and institutions. What has emerged is the foundation for a new periodization of Yucatecan history based upon an analysis of the dynamic process of capitalist development in a dependent economy. Such a historiographical project necessarily involves an understanding of the evolution of systems of production and relations between classes as they are conditioned by the interplay of factors internal and external to Yucatán. The following survey of Yucatecan political economy from Caste War to Revolution, although painted in broad strokes, provides a conspectus of major interpretative trends as well as of the lively debates that have emerged in the recent historical literature.

3

The Early Expansion of Commercial Agriculture and Its Consequences (c. 1750–1880)

By about 1880 Yucatán was transformed from the relatively isolated, marginally productive backwater it had been late in the colonial period into a dynamic commodity-exporting region intimately tied to the United States and the fluctuating rhythms of the world market. Vast quantities of land, labor, and capital were reorganized into agroindustrial enterprises, producing first sugar and then henequen. The dominant Creole class became increasingly capitalist in its orientation and consolidated its control over the system of production within the region.

Caste War or Peasant Rebellion?

It was first the rapid penetration of commercial sugar agriculture into precapitalist areas of production on the frontier that stiffened Maya resistance, which eventually erupted into a full-blown rebellion—the so-called Caste War of 1847. Only recently, however, and after generations of lively debate has this consensus on the origins of the war emerged.

The very challenge of the term *caste war* and the increasing emphasis on establishing the agrarian roots of a "peasant rebellion" is indicative of the new thinking on the causes and character of the struggle.[1] Late nineteenth- and early twentieth-century Creole writers like Eligio Ancona, Serapio Baqueiro, and Juan Francisco Molina Solís were the products of a society that bitterly hated and feared the Maya for the devastation they had visited on the interests of white Yucatán. Collectively they advanced a racial thesis that appealed to their Creole audience, even as it twisted reality. They

25

argued that the outbreak of war owed principally to Indian ethno-centrism, to the well-known Maya "hatred of foreigners," which had been fanned by several centuries of European domination. From generation to generation since the conquest, the Maya had passed on a thirst for vengeance against the *dzules,* their white rulers. Then, owing to a series of internecine political squabbles which shattered Creole unity in the 1840s, the Indians were enabled to vent their dammed-up hate in a race war (*guerra de castas*) that almost drove the whites from the peninsula and restored Maya rule. Within this general framework, ladino writers gave more or less emphasis to the mistreatment of the Maya by the dominant society's institutions of church and state; some flatly refused to acknowledge social and economic discrimination as a factor in the war's outbreak, preferring instead to view it as a barbaric attack on the civilized way of life. Most fixed the blame on Creole politicians who, they accurately observed, recruited the Indians to fight their selfish battles with exaggerated promises and arms, or on equally ambitious Maya ca-ciques, who took advantage of these divisions among the dzules to launch their own political careers.[2]

A subsequent, more progressive generation of traditional histo-rians challenged this interpretation, while accepting certain of its premises. According to their chief exponents, Antonio Canto López and Leopoldo Peniche Vallado, the origins of the conflict were social, not racial, and could be traced back to the beginnings of Spanish colonization, in an unbroken tradition of oppression which pro-duced a continual Maya response, culminating in the apocalyptic peasant rebellion of 1847. Canto López likened the Caste War to the European jacqueries of the Middle Ages: here was a primitive re-bellion lacking an ideological or organizational framework, which only later became a race war. Rather than pinpointing historical grievances and linking them to specific relations of production ac-companying transformations in the agrarian structure, Canto López and Peniche Vallado lumped together centuries of land despoilment, feudal labor obligations, and secular and clerical fiscal assessments in a litany of exploitation "Lascasian" in tone. For them, the war expiated centuries of Creole transgressions; it was "inevitable, the tragic outcome of a social pathology whose origins were simply op-pression and social injustice."[3]

Whatever the force of their moral claim, these Creole revisionists provided an analytical framework lacking fundamental historical precision. More recent work on regional agrarian structures by a new generation of historians and anthropologists, although it has not yet definitively reconstructed the history of the sugar estate, has gone a long way toward refining our understanding of the origins, character, and consequences of the 1847 rebellion.

Agrarian Transformations

Robert Patch's research in agrarian history from the conquest to the Caste War has begun to flesh out the origins of capitalist agriculture in Yucatán. Based largely on his own careful survey of notarial, municipal, state, and church archives that has now lasted a decade, Patch has traced the process of agrarian transition from *encomienda* to plantation, documenting the Creole landed class's progressive control over Maya land and water, labor, and ultimately, the system of agricultural production itself.[4] A thorough examination of the principal watersheds in this process running the length of the colonial period and beyond lies outside the chronological scope of this review; however, a brief synopsis is in order.

With the deterioration of the encomienda in the seventeenth century as a sufficient base for the accumulation of wealth, owing largely to demographic decline, the Spanish settlers increasingly looked to the land as a source of goods for consumption and sale. *Encomenderos* used their institutional base to purchase and seize land, import cattle, and provide tributaries to work their new landed estates. A small number of resident *vaqueros* (cowboys) worked on these estancias for a nominal wage and access to land and water. However, the majority of the Maya population, while obligated to provide encomienda tribute, were peasants living in "free villages," meeting their subsistence needs through traditional maize cultivation and maintaining control of their own *milpa* (cornfields).

By the mid-eighteenth century, the now predominantly Creole landed class markedly increased its control over the system of production by expanding its activities into agriculture. According to Patch, *estancieros* made this decision largely for internal reasons, as

a result of the scarcity of grain in the region, which coincided with a
rapid demographic rise in the population beginning about 1750.
They now introduced corn (and, in certain more fertile localities,
rice) onto their estancias, both for their own consumption and its
commercial profitability. In addition to their small resident force of
vaqueros, proprietors now contracted Maya laborers from nearby
communities to work the estancia's milpa. They increased their lev-
erage over the indigenous labor supply through a variety of means,
most notably by controlling access to scarce land and water resources in times of recurrent famine and drought, offering to pay the
Indian's encomienda tribute and/or church tax if he would settle and
work on the estate. Although diverse forms of service tenantry pre-
dominated, the origins of debt peonage, the predominant labor arrangement on regional estates from the early nineteenth century
until 1915, can be traced to this period. Patch estimates that by 1800,
more than 50 percent of the Indian population in the northwestern
districts (roughly within a radius of seventy to eighty kilometers of
Mérida) had resettled on hacienda land. Significantly, only 25 percent of Maya villagers had become *peones acasillados* (resident
workers) outside this radius in the southern and eastern zones,
where the great estate developed more slowly.[5]

Patch's research on the rise of the hacienda and the structure of
production in the late colonial period suggests that while independence was clearly an important historical benchmark, perhaps a
more significant and profound transformation in Yucatán's political
economy occurred roughly a half century earlier. For through the
new socioeconomic unit of the hacienda, the region's landed rulers
appropriated the primary means of agricultural production—land,
water, and labor. Whereas the indigenous population had been able
to control the productive process from an independent village base
under the encomienda, with their integration into the great estate,
the Maya would gradually lose that control, becoming increasingly
dependent on the proprietor for all of their needs. Finally, Patch's
researches reveal that Yucatán's transition in the late eighteenth
century from the tributary-based encomienda to the classic Mexican
cattle-and-corn hacienda also brought with it a more vital internal
commerce, chiefly in grains, which was centered upon the urban

markets of Mérida, Campeche, and Valladolid. At least in the northwest, haciendas increasingly supplied the cities, which, in turn, made available to the estate's proprietors luxury goods received from Havana and Europe.[6]

Despite these significant late eighteenth-century developments which Patch and various local writers regard as constituting "a transitional stage from a tributary feudal society to a dependent capitalistic one," the dominant landowning class still found its entrepreneurial path blocked by imperial restrictions.[7] Patch demonstrates that with the exception of brief periods during 1813–14 and 1820, when the liberal Spanish Constitution of Cádiz was introduced and an attempt was made to reform the neomedieval notions of corporate and communal property rights which had officially guided royal land policy since the sixteenth century, the principle of unconditional individual commercial rights in property would not govern agrarian policy in Yucatán until the 1840s.[8] However, the impetus to begin removing fetters on private property was provided by the new possibilities for commodity production for domestic and international trade following Mexico's separation from the mother country in 1821. Yucatán simultaneously lost its protected imperial market in Cuba for beef and hides but gained greater access to domestic and foreign markets for a variety of other products, most notably, sugar and rum, logwood, tobacco, rice, and cotton. Capital traditionally earmarked for northwestern cattle and corn haciendas, as well as merchant capital, was now increasingly redirected into sugar and, to a much lesser extent, into these other commercial products.[9] And despite rather modest beginnings in the 1830s, as the world fiber market expanded with each passing decade, ever-greater amounts of local capital were invested in henequen production.

Yet it has only been recently, in the detailed doctoral dissertation of Lawrence Remmers (1981), that a broader economic history of this pivotal postindependence generation has been attempted and the dynamic, multifaceted character of Creole commercial agricultural expansion has been established. Building upon but transcending Cline's venerable articles on specific economic "episodes" during the first half of the nineteenth century—for example, sugar, cotton textile manufacturing, and early henequen production—Remmers integrates all of the peninsula's subregions and their principal lines of economic activity into a coherent analytical framework.[10] Like most writers, he emphasizes sugar's role as the motor force of Yucatán's postindependence economy. Sugar surpassed all other commercial agricultural products in acreage, output, and value, and it yielded by far the highest profits to regional entrepreneurs. Indeed, ninetenths of the value of Yucatán's commercial output prior to 1847 came from the production of sugar and rum. Moreover, the sugar boom played an instrumental role in the redistribution of people and economic activity that occurred in Yucatán between 1821 and 1846. Whereas a late colonial census revealed that only 38 percent of the state's population lived in the southeastern frontier zone in 1794, a half century later an absolute majority of yucatecos (51 percent) lived in the interior. Lured by cane profits and government incentives facilitating the acquisition of cheap, fertile land and labor, Yucatecans migrated to the frontier in steadily increasing numbers after independence.[11]

If sugar was chiefly responsible for the southeast's new prominence as the agricultural center of Yucatán, Remmers argues that sugar's gains did not come at the expense of other commercial enterprises—as would be the case with henequen monoculture later in the century. Sugar cane did not receive disproportionate government favor and never monopolized the land or controlled regional capital and labor markets. Also, unlike henequen, sugar was produced almost exclusively for local and domestic markets, and control of the industry (like that of most other commercial products of the period) remained in the hands of yucatecos.[12]

Remmers makes us aware that the economic history of Yucatán between independence and the Caste War is much more than a saga of sugar's expansion, as many writers have led us to believe. By putting the "sugar episode" into proper perspective, then contrasting the possibilities for regional economic development in this early period with those attending the age of monoculture that followed, he makes perhaps his most original contribution to the economic historiography of modern Yucatán. He shows us that prior to the Caste War, the regional economic matrix was far more complex than we suspected. Whereas at independence commercial production was almost entirely restricted to the northwest and west coast, and a surprisingly small percentage of Yucatán's population participated in the market economy, by 1847 few areas of the peninsula remained outside the market economy. Within the span of a quarter of a century, Yucatecan Creoles had fashioned and begun to reap the profits from a balanced and diversified agricultural economy. Most commercial products came from more or less distinct geographical subregions: henequen and livestock from the northwest; logwood and salt from the west coast; sugar, tobacco, cotton, and rice from the interior; and nascent cotton manufacturing in the eastern city of Valladolid. Moreover, complementing these subregional commercial activities was a healthy subsistence base; indeed, the output of these cash crops paled in comparison to the cultivation of corn and other foodstuffs. In the garden plots of haciendas, *ranchos* (small properties), and urban residences, as well as on Indian communal lands (*ejidos*) and public lands, enough food was grown to ensure that each subregional zone remained largely self-sufficient. Such a healthy economic climate, furthered by the beginnings of a road network in the interior, fostered the development of important new urban centers in the southeast. By 1847 ladino market towns such as Bolonchén, Peto, Tekax, and Tihosuco—all located in the settled area behind the cutting edge of the sugar frontier—had begun to achieve prominence not only in subregional trade, but also in an expanding interregional commerce that embraced the entire peninsula.[13]

Remmers joins other scholars in affirming that such heady economic growth came largely at the expense of the Maya communities. Building upon the broader synthetic treatments of Cline, Strickon, and Reed, recent studies have clarified the strategy employed by Creole entrepreneurs to appropriate communal land and labor and the impact it had on the Indian peasant community. As early as 1825, a law was passed facilitating the acquisition of fertile public lands (*tierras baldías*) in the southeastern sugar zone. Frequently, the state sold these lands cheaply to pay off its debts. As a result, large expanses of baldías—technically public lands but, practically speaking, often the forest lands in which Maya communities rotated their milpa—were released for public sale. Then in 1841, narrow limits were explicitly placed on the legal size of communal lands and the significant cost of surveying and establishing ejidal boundaries was to be borne by the Maya pueblos themselves. And if this was not enough to erode the free village land base, an additional weighty tax was levied on peasant agriculture in 1844, serving the dual purpose of raising money for the depleted state treasury as well as pressing Indian communities to sell out to Creole proprietors with ready cash at hand. Simultaneously, the system of debt peonage was institutionalized through a series of legislative decrees (1823–43), some purportedly to combat "vagrancy" and laziness by bringing all independent Maya under effective municipal jurisdiction, others explicitly guaranteeing the fulfillment of work contracts and the permanence of workers on estates.[14]

In the absence of detailed hacienda records which would facilitate monographic studies of early nineteenth-century capitalist agriculture, scholars have ventured tentative conclusions regarding social relations on sugar estates, based largely on government publications, the local press, and the accounts of contemporary observers.[15] Sugar—and later, henequen—required a more rigid, harsher labor regime than anything the Maya had previously experienced. The high capital risk attending these new commercial ventures compelled the proprietor to take firm measures against fugitivism and lack of productivity which had previously characterized regional cattle estancias and mixed cereal and livestock haciendas. *Hacendados* or, more commonly, their administrators, now assumed full control over the productive process, disciplining their Maya laborers to produce new and unfamiliar crops requiring different work tasks and a more highly structured organization of labor than traditional milpa cultivation. While generally referred to as "haciendas," these sugar (and later, henequen) enterprises more closely resembled "plantations" in their degree of capitalization, production for a large export market, industrial organization of work, and increasingly slavelike relations of production.[16]

The transition from hacienda to plantation did not occur uniformly throughout Yucatán. The northwest quadrant, although soon to be the seat of the henequen boom, was too arid and thin-soiled to nurture sugar cane or other tropical cash crops. Rather, these plantations—the majority of them sugar estates—expanded rapidly throughout the deeper-soiled, more humid regions along the southeastern frontier in a large crescent which extended from the Chenes region, south of the Puuc, eastward to Tihosuco, south of Valladolid. Where the transition did occur, it wreaked havoc with the Maya *campesino's* traditional milpa agriculture. Unlike the northern corn and cattle hacienda, which was labor-, land-, and capital-extensive, and facilitated a virtually identical labor cycle on both hacienda and Maya maize plots, the sugar plantation made intensive use of these factors of production and demanded a work cycle that brought the large estate and the *milpero* into conflict. Thus, whereas the classic hacienda had stripped the Maya of his property, it had not denied him his cornfield, the source of physical sustenance and the locale of a major religious rite: the planting of corn. Access to milpa now became more and more difficult under the new system of production which sugar (and henequen) required. The semisedentary slash-and-burn subsistence agriculture of the Maya no longer complemented the highly integrated and controlled work regime of the ever-expanding plantation.

Thus, unlike the Creole revisionists, the current generation of agrarian and economic historians, most notably Patch, Moisés González Navarro, Víctor Suárez Molina, and Lawrence Remmers, have centered the debate about the war's origins specifically on the struggle for land and a labor force which accompanied the rapid expansion of sugar (and other commercial agricultural) production into "free pueblo" areas on the southeastern frontier between 1821 and 1847.[17] Suárez Molina has sharpened the discussion of labor relations on the frontier of sugar expansion by explicitly challenging the revisionists' notion that the underlying cause of the rebellion was a lengthy heritage of "bad treatment," manifested in feudal-like forms of bondage dating back to Montejo the Conqueror. On the contrary, the Maya's sociocultural adaptation to white domination in the older northwestern corn and cattle zone had been a gradual process over generations, and by the end of the colonial period it had produced a stable, at least outwardly compliant, labor force. It was only on the frontier, where strong market conditions for sugar and other cash crops produced an increased demand for workers, necessitating the rapid subordination of a previously isolated peasant population to a different and harsher labor regime that was now backed by the full power of the state, that armed resistance occurred. Moreover, Suárez Molina argues that although Creole society viewed the rebellion in racial terms from its inception, it was only after negotiations of their land and labor grievances irreparably broke down in 1848 that the rebels' initially economic and agrarian perception of the conflict receded and the struggle assumed a more savage and explicitly racial character.[18]

The recent presentation by ethnohistorian Victoria R. Bricker of the Maya's own account of the Caste War reinforces this emerging view of the rebellion's agrarian origins and character.[19] Unlike partisan Creole writers, whose principal sources were the letters, military reports, and eyewitness testimonies of whites, or unlike more recent professional scholars, who, while trying to be more even-handed, were nonetheless dependent upon sources in Spanish, Bricker has investigated the Maya oral tradition and written record. She argues persuasively that the history of the war (and Yucatecan history in general) has traditionally been written by the dominant society; Indian accounts of the same events have either been inaccessible or regarded as mere legends (*leyendas*) or stories (*cuentos*). In fact, such indigenous accounts are often no less accurate than the "history" written by the victors, which itself is often "simply the folklore of the dominant group."[20] Many of the rebel leaders were literate and wrote eloquently about the struggle. Drawing upon approximately two hundred letters and other documents as well as a rich oral tradition, Bricker reconstructs the Maya's reasons for rebelling, their day-to-day hardships and needs, their military and ideological strategies, and the cultural transformations wrought upon their society by the conflict.

According to Bricker, for the frontier Maya, the 1847 rebellion assumed the dimensions of a social revolution against the encroachment of commercial agriculture, although it was triggered by a series of petty Creole disputes which expediently put guns into Indian hands. Although Maya documents provide little mention per se of the sugar plantation's expansion, they are quite explicit about its effects: increased taxation on peasant agriculture, debt peonage and physical abuse on the great estate, and the loss of accustomed access to milpa land.

Moreover, Bricker's research also helps to clarify the racial or "caste" nature of the war. A dominant theme in the communications of Indian leaders is that laws should apply equally to all peoples, whatever their ethnic background. Hence, the burden of taxation should be borne by all racial categories; land should be available to everyone (and "the forest should not be purchasable"); and no ethnic group should have the right physically to abuse another with impugnity. In this sense, the free Maya clearly made a social revolution to erase caste distinctions. On the other hand, Bricker contends that the fearful, skittish ladinos must bear major responsibility for redefining a social conflict into a brutal race war. Her argument turns on the Creoles' costly decision during the earliest days of the rebellion not to honor the distinction which then existed between rich Indian caciques, or *hidalgos* as they were then called, and the majority of poor, landless Indians. Many of these educated, politically powerful Maya had connections in, and identified closely with, white society and, like Creole hacendados, seem to have obtained their wealth by exploiting Indian labor. Bricker maintains that by persecuting and actually lynching members of this privileged class, the ladinos forced such caciques as Jacinto Pat and Cecilio Chi to identify as Indians and contribute their leadership abilities to the rebel movement.[21]

Another intriguing question which the new literature has reexamined is why the Maya, only kilometers from the gates of Mérida and Campeche, and seemingly poised to drive the dzules from the peninsula in June and July of 1848, halted their drive, and subsequently lost the initiative. Traditional Creole writers praise the bravery of their forefathers in holding their ground in the countryside and resisting further rebel advances.[22] However, even with the provisions of food and ammunition that they received from Havana, Veracruz, and New Orleans,[23] these remaining veteran units could not by themselves have stopped the Maya offensive. Although Bricker has found no relevant letters from Indian leaders to explain the Maya's failure to pursue their advantage, oral tradition recorded several generations after the events indicates that the military campaign was interrupted by the beginning of the planting season. Consequently, Maya ritual and the peasant economy demanded that the rebels return to their cornfields. Bricker also suspects that with victory so close, the rebels may have fallen to quarreling among themselves over the nature and leadership of the new order—a lead that should be explored.[24] Finally, new research suggests that the Creole comeback would probably not have been possible without the support—or at least the acquiescence—of the northwestern Maya acasillados who had long been attached to haciendas. Yucatecan historian Carlos Bojórquez Urzáiz emphasizes the "great ideological control" which ladino hacendados exerted over this group, since "during the most critical periods of the rebellion these acasillados fought the rebels, performed essential tasks for the Creole troops [such as growing food] . . . and received the nominal title hidalgo for their efforts."[25] Anthropologist Philip C. Thompson suggests that in certain cases these acasillados were tenacious auxiliaries, forcing the rebel Maya to contend with Indian as well as ladino armed resistance.[26] While future research must clarify more precisely the role of the northwestern acasillados during the rebellion, it seems likely that had more of them joined the free Maya, the small Creole forces might never have held out long enough later to assume the offensive.

It is precisely this participation of a significant segment of the Maya population on the Creole side that prompts Patch to argue that, even in the most basic sense, the "War of the Castes" is "badly named." Mexican historian Leticia Reina concurs, adding that, conversely, white and mestizo regulars in the Creole army occasionally defected to the Indian side and, in some cases, actually led the rebel Maya or instructed them in military tactics. Remmers, on the other hand, rejects this interpretation, for, while it is "literally" correct, ultimately "the war . . . was fought along racial lines."[27]

The Consequences of War:
Realignment, Recovery, and Regional Disparity

The rash of agrarian revolts and caste wars that erupted in several key Mexican regions in the aftermath of independence points up both the disintegration of the imperial central state and the political and economic disenfranchisement of Indian minorities during the early national period. Other nineteenth-century indigenous peasant rebellions would last longer than the Caste War of Yucatán (e.g., the Yaqui rebellion in Sonora), encompass a greater geographical area (the Sierra Gorda revolt in central Mexico), or range more freely in their depredations against ladino society (the Cora rebellion of Manuel Lozada). Yet none drew upon as many advantages as the rebel Maya: a homogeneous ethnic base still animated by a vigorous pre-Hispanic cultural tradition; the absence of serious natural obstacles (mountains, rivers, etc.), which reinforced this ethnic identity and strategically facilitated mobility across the frontier of white settlement; the proximity of British arms and supplies in Belize; and finally, the weak economic, political, and logistical ties between Yucatán and central Mexico, which permitted the revolt to proceed for a long time without federal intervention.[28]

It is not surprising, therefore, that the Yucatecan rebellion was the most violent of this turbulent age, nor that its regional consequences were likely the most profound.[29] Writers have differed in their attempts to capture its immense significance. Many continue to regard the rebellion as an anticolonial war, the last in a series of failed Maya attempts to cast off Western domination.[30] Four decades ago, Cline viewed the Caste War in ultimately more positive terms, as the killing ground of colonialism in the region: "after [the Caste War] the foundations of modern Yucatán evolved rapidly, serving as a base for new aspirations and outlook."[31] Several local writers later built on this insight, regarding the conflict as essential to the rise of a more durable form of agricultural capitalism, the henequen monoculture that eclipsed sugar during the second half of the nineteenth century.[32] The new historiography has generally stepped back from such broad generalizations and reexamined the war's consequences in the context of more circumscribed historical investigations, usually focusing on specific socioethnic groups, economic sectors and classes, or geographical subregions.

While it is clear that the Caste War had an immediate, devastating impact on Yucatecan society and dramatically altered the peninsula's demographic and economic profile, even today there are few empirical studies of the war's short- or long-term consequences.[33] First of all, fundamental population questions must be resolved.

Yucatecan anthropologist and demographer Salvador Rodríguez Losa has challenged the standard estimates, issued in 1851 by the state government and echoed uncritically since, that in less than four years the war reduced the peninsula's population by more than half. Rodríguez Losa assembles all available census data and population estimates for the period 1846–81 and subjects each finding to a rigorous process of internal and external criticism. He suggests that although the number of persons who died in the fighting or from related causes was probably closer to Reed's estimate of 30 percent of the original population of about 600,000, there is as yet no reliable analysis of the war's casualties or the magnitude of the state's overall population loss. Such a study would have to sort out a number of factors that have previously either been ignored or confused—for example, the number of Indians who rose up in frontier areas beyond the government's control; the number of Indians killed in internal factional struggles; the number of people who fled to central Mexico, Central America, the United States, and Cuba (as well as those captured rebel Maya who were sold into slavery in Cuba); the impact of epidemic disease (principally cholera); and finally, the natural increase of the population. Rodríguez Losa speculates that the state government exaggerated the peninsula's loss of life and property in an effort to gain economic and military aid from the central government in the early 1850s.[34] Working independently of Rodríguez Losa but accounting for many of the key variables he cites, Víctor Suárez Molina has estimated that slightly more than 40 percent of the Yucatecan population perished in this war or left the peninsula because of it.[35]

In perhaps the most authoritative discussion of demography to date, Remmers estimates population decline from 1846 to 1850 at between 25 to 36 percent. Some of the decrease in numbers stemmed from emigration, but upwards of 85 percent of the loss resulted from violence, disease, or starvation. Remmers contends that all demographic estimates remain hazardous because an accurate count was never made of (or by) the rebel Maya. Of the available data, he finds the 1861 census for Campeche and the 1862 list for Yucatán to be the most reliable. Based upon these censuses, which exclude the rebels, there were slightly more than 331,000 inhabitants in the peninsula almost fifteen years after the hostilities began—in other words, significantly fewer than prewar levels, even if generous extrapolations are made for the rebel Maya. Finally, Remmers estimates that whereas the peninsula's total population declined from the war's inception until 1855, and then began to rise, the numbers of the rebel Maya who remained in the eastern forests continued to decline at a near-calamitous rate after 1850.[36]

But such aggregate figures ultimately tell us little. Remmers and Suárez Molina also provide subregional data that help to flesh out the nature of the demographic and economic realignment brought about by the conflict. Not surprisingly, their analyses of censuses, official reports, and press accounts reveal that the impact of the Caste War was felt disproportionately in the southern and eastern frontier zones, the principal theaters of fighting. Remmers estimates that from 1846 to 1850, the population of these interior zones fell by 75 percent. According to Suárez Molina, their population dropped from 53.4 percent of the total 1845 population to 35.2 percent in 1862.[37] The sugar industry, which prior to the war had produced the lion's share of Yucatán's commercial output, was now devastated, as were other agricultural enterprises in the interior. Remmers concludes that the Caste War definitively ended the brief, one-generation reign of the southeast as the economic center of the peninsula. Despite the vast extensions of cheap fertile land available in the interior, the southeast would remain a virtual no-man's-land for decades. Although most of the Maya rebels had been driven back to the present-day borders of the state of Yucatán by 1849, the first truce was not signed until 1853 and even then provided little guarantee of security on the frontier. Economic production was largely restricted to the area safely west of a line drawn between Valladolid and Peto, a political boundary along which military cantons afforded only a modicum of protection against Indian raids.[38]

Whereas prior to the war, population tended to gather around new centers of commercial agriculture in the interior, now it congregated where safety and stability could be assured. It is not surprising, then, that following the war, more workers were available in the northwestern zone than in the frontier areas. Moreover, ladino investors would be loathe to risk their capital in the interior so soon after losing their sugar haciendas and other commercial ventures in a "race war."[39] The frontier's loss was the northwest's gain: The old colonial zone increased its share of the regional population from 46.6 percent in 1845 to 64.1 percent in 1862, and the trend continued throughout the late nineteenth century and into the twentieth.[40] Always the political center of Yucatán, Mérida and the northwest now regained their position as the region's economic hub. Remmers and Suárez Molina document that as investment in sugar and other cash crops in the southeast plummeted during the second half of the century, the northwest witnessed the dramatic rise of a relatively new agroindustry, the production and elaboration of henequen fiber.[41]

But was the henequen boom really a product of the Caste War? In the healthy debate that has developed around this question, local historians Renán Irigoyen and Fidelio Quintal Martín affirm the war as the basic cause in the rise of monoculture.[42] They grant that the production of henequen for commercial purposes had begun on a small scale several decades before the Caste War. A prototype of the modern henequen plantation had been established outside of Mérida in 1830, and in addition to the production of rope, hammocks, and sacks to meet local needs, raw fiber had been shipped to the United States as early as 1839. Yet they contend that these were only the first faltering steps of an industry that would not have developed as it did if not for the impetus provided by the devastation of war. For henequen, necessity was surely the mother of invention. With the frontier aflame and the sugar industry and other commercial enterprises in ruins, but with world demand for fiber increasing, Yucatecan entrepreneurs were compelled to turn to henequen and make the necessary provisions for its future success. On behalf of the northwestern planters, the state offered a monetary reward for the perfection of a mechanical rasping device. Once the northwest had been cleared of rebels, the hacendados successfully lobbied the government for the use of their former peones, who were then discharged from military service. Increasingly, these acasillados were joined by waves of Maya refugees from the war-torn zones of the southeastern frontier, who opted for the food and relative security of the henequen plantation rather than a renegade's life in the bush.

Thus, according to Irigoyen and Quintal Martín, early on, the turbulence of the war firmly established the zone of henequen production in the northwest as well as shaped the base of a dependent labor force that would power the ever-expanding henequen estate in subsequent decades.

Even recent critics of this interpretation freely admit that the 1847 rebellion had important consequences for the fiber industry. However, they caution against an exaggeration of the war's positive impact to the exclusion of other significant variables. Rodríguez Losa and Remmers demonstrate that too little account has been taken of the henequen industry's technological gains and rapid expansion during the first half of the nineteenth century. Even prior to 1847 it was the state's second most valuable commodity—albeit a very distant second—after sugar. Henequen had supplanted livestock as the dominant commercial product of the northwest and was challenging logwood as the state's most important export.[43] Moreover, several writers have pointed out the debilitating short-term effects that the war had on the industry, dramatically derailing its early progress. For example, in the terrible violence of the late 1840s and early 1850s, the henequen handicraft industry in the southeastern pueblos was destroyed, and production of fiber on northwestern estates was paralyzed owing to temporary rebel occupation and the press-ganging of acasillados into ladino militias.[44]

Perhaps most telling, however, is Patch's criticism of Irigoyen's and Quintal Martín's assertion that the Caste War was responsible for the delimitation of the modern henequen zone. Patch's own research on the formation of the large estate leads him to conclude that the boundaries of Yucatán's modern economic zones had essentially been defined before the Caste War. By the end of the colonial period (c. 1800), Yucatán already possessed a dichotomous agrarian structure, setting off a northwestern zone of haciendas within an eighty-kilometer radius of Mérida from a predominantly *comunero* (peasant village-based) southeastern hinterland. Since the production of henequen was extremely labor intensive, ultimately a scarcity of field hands would be the determining factor in the henequen plantation's failure to transcend greatly the old colonial zone of haciendas in the northwest, not frontier instability as Quintal Martín and

Irigoyen suggested. According to Patch, only the proprietors of the northwestern hacienda zone were in a position to combine a sufficiently stable, permanent labor force with the other necessary factors of production—land and capital—in order to increase fiber production when international demand skyrocketed in the last quarter of the nineteenth century.[45] Patch's argument must itself be modified by a consideration of other variables playing a role in the definition of the modern henequen zone. Recent studies point up the region's inadequate communications network which significantly increased the cost of transporting fiber as one moved away from Mérida. Moreover, most recent scholars join local writers who have long emphasized that unfavorable conditions of soil and rainfall also inflated costs and reduced yields because henequen grew best in the drier and rockier soil of the northwest.[46] The importance of centering the zone around Mérida, indispensable for the generation of capital, technology, and commercial facilities, has also been stressed.[47]

Remmers's final judgment regarding the Caste War's impact on the regional fiber industry seems most compelling. The war did not call forth commercial henequen production; the industry had made noteworthy progress in the generation since independence and already assumed a leadership role in the northwestern economy. But the ravages of war, coupled with ever-increasing world market demand, now put henequen in a position to dominate the entire peninsular economy and recast it in a radically new mold.

From the emphasis on diversified agricultural production geared to both domestic and foreign markets that had reigned during the first half of the century, the focus of economic activity would shift in the decades ahead to single-minded devotion to the export of henequen fiber. In Remmers's view, the Caste War played perhaps the principal role in this metamorphosis, for it toppled the existing economic edifice and dramatically scaled down the options for regional recovery. Prior to the conflagration, henequen had been forced to compete for scarce capital and labor resources with a variety of other commercial products; in the aftermath of war, these rivals no longer posed a serious challenge to the agave. The local bourgeoisie decided to commit its available resources to fiber production, first, because no viable commercial alternative to henequen existed in the thin-soiled northwest—and realistically, the northwest fostered the only stable conditions for investment and production in the turbulent decades after 1850. Second, with the possibilities for domestic consumption severely diminished, the state desperately needed an export product profitable enough to stimulate economic recovery and future growth. Once again the options were circumscribed: of Yucatán's three leading prewar exports—logwood, henequen, and livestock—only fiber held promise for future growth. The regional logwood industry had been in decline for generations; at midcentury, foreign competition and increasing replacement by synthetic dyes augured even dimmer prospects. Moreover, the war had left the livestock industry in chaos, with herds scattered or thinned by violence and military appropriation. Despite setbacks during the most violent years of the conflict, the henequen industry had not only managed to survive but—equally important—now faced expanding market possibilities. After 1850, Remmers concludes, hopes for Yucatán's economic resurgence would rest on henequen and henequen alone.[48]

Finally, Remmers argues that the bourgeoisie's reliance upon henequen as the only viable road to economic recovery had new and important consequences in the regional political arena. According to Cline, prior to 1847, Campeche- and Mérida-based factions of the Creole elite with distinct economic interests (principally a Mexico-oriented entrepôt trade in the case of the former and commercial agriculture in the case of the latter) had bitterly contested control of the peninsular economy and the state political apparatus.[49] During the 1840s this economic competition underwrote a series of complex political struggles over the issue of Yucatecan secession from the Mexican republic. Maya auxiliaries were recruited and armed to fight in these Creole factional disputes, a practice which, we have seen, most writers regard as a contributing cause of the Caste War. Although these Creole factions came together to defeat the rebel Maya during their common emergency, the alliance disintegrated as soon as the immediate threat subsided. In order to pursue traditional economic ties with Mexico proper, *campechano* commercial interests pressed for and eventually achieved independent statehood in 1858. Thereafter, contends Remmers, "any remaining vestiges of economic cleavages between elite political factions became submerged in the collective effort to promote and expand the henequen industry."[50]

This is not to suggest that intraelite squabbling ceased. Political infighting continued unabated until the beginning of Porfirio Díaz's prolonged "second term" in 1884, producing twenty-six state governors in the quarter century between 1858 and 1883. And even later, at the height of the national dictatorship, Don Porfirio despaired of entirely eliminating elite bickering ("disgusto") in remote Yucatán. However, the development of the henequen export economy represented a common enterprise, the point of reference where the interests of competing political factions coincided. Remmers argues persuasively that the stakes of this common venture were so high that internecine political conflict, however disruptive, was always superficial and never dampened entrepreneurial activity or slowed the development of the henequen industry.

Because henequen has cast such a giant shadow on the region's modern political economy, it is not surprising that so much attention has been given to assessing the Caste War's influence on the *auge henequenero* (henequen boom). Unfortunately, little research has been done on the impact that the great rebellion had on agrarian structures outside the northwest. For generations ladino pride stood in the way. In the mid-1850s with an uneasy truce prevailing on the frontier, Creole historians like Baqueiro and Ancona turned their attention away from the southeastern forests, where the Maya maintained pockets of resistance organized as independent chiefdoms, in order to chronicle the political and economic rivalries that once more preoccupied the ladino elite. As Reed aptly put it, "it was simply decided that the rebellion called the Caste War had come to an end. . . . There had been no victory, and there would be fighting for years to come. But . . . if it could not be suppressed, Yucatecan pride decreed that it should be ignored."[51]

Reed's own popular narrative of the theocratic rebel society at Chan Santa Cruz, based upon the earlier, narrowly disseminated ethnohistorical work of Villa Rojas and Cline, broke the long silence.

Almost twenty years later, the political and cultural historiography of the independent Maya states has been significantly enriched by a new generation of ethnohistorians, whose general contribution has already been acknowledged. However, only the barest outline of a postwar economic history of the frontier region has yet been traced.

In a pair of recent essays, Yucatecan historian Carlos Bojórquez Urzáiz explores a variety of themes basic to such a history—peasant maize production, land tenure, labor systems, and ladino agrarian policy toward southeastern Yucatán—and raises important questions for future research on frontier rural structures. Bojórquez Urzáiz contends that because the powerful northwestern zone gave itself up to monoculture and thereafter subsisted almost entirely on imported corn, historians have mistakenly assumed that Yucatecan history during the second half of the nineteenth century is merely the history of henequen. But based on his investigation in regional archives, Bojórquez Urzáiz demonstrates the need for an economic geography that will also account for the two large maize-producing regions located in the south-central and far eastern portions of the peninsula, which extend greatly beyond the current borders of the state of Yucatán. These preliminary essays of Bojórquez Urzáiz suffer from a failure to define precisely the limits of the frontier zones, but they correspond roughly to the political jurisdictions of the *pacíficos del sur* and the more die-hard *cruzob*.[52] The former were rebel Maya who, by accommodating the state of Yucatán with a formal truce in 1853, were permitted a relatively autonomous existence, largely in the Chenes region of what is today Campeche state. The cruzob, who pledged themselves to unremitting war with the dzules, were located northeast of the pacíficos, largely in modern-day Quintana Roo.

Bojórquez Urzáiz reminds us that although these rebel Maya failed to take Mérida, suffered severe losses, and never "won" the Caste War, at least temporarily they accomplished their fundamental objective: they put a halt to the expansion of Creole capitalist agriculture on the frontier. Moreover, for several decades they found themselves in command of virtually all of the fertile land in the peninsula. Ladino hacendados were now largely restricted to the rocky northwest, a circumstance they deeply resented. Bojórquez

Urzáiz documents that as late as 1868 they railed against having to cultivate the region's "most sterile soil . . . good only for the cultivation of henequen," while ironically "the Indians now occupy the richest lands where not long ago our industrious capitalists maintained profitable *fincas* [estates]." Of course, the full impact of the late-century fiber boom gave Creole planters a brighter perspective from which to reflect upon the war's outcome. Nevertheless, Bojórquez Urzáiz's essential point is well taken: in the remote expanses outside of the henequen zone, either by truce (in the case of the southern pacíficos) or by military stalemate (in the case of the cruzob), the war's conclusion signaled "the beginning of a process of decolonization . . . producing a reintegration of Indian culture in economic, social, political, and religious terms."[53]

Recent studies of the external and internal political milieus of these Maya states have documented that the pacíficos and cruzob would maintain their effective autonomy from ladino control at least into the early twentieth century.[54] In 1901 Chan Santa Cruz was overrun by a combined force of Yucatecan militia and Porfirian *federales,* and ladino interest in subordinating all Indians in Campeche and Yucatán was rekindled. However, prior to 1901, the cruzob waged a guerrilla war without quarter, and despite the 1853 truce, the submission of the pacíficos was far from complete. Indeed, representatives of the governments of Yucatán and Campeche frankly acknowledged that they received only the degree of obedience from these Indians that the Indians cared to give. Late in the nineteenth century, state and federal officials continued to hope that with increased contact, the development of schools, and the gradual extension of networks of communication and administration, the southernmost settlements of pacíficos would eventually be won over to the benefits of civilization. But this process had scarcely begun by the turn of the century.

Of course, prior to the conquest of Chan Santa Cruz, the ladino states of Yucatán and Campeche were quite content to allow the several pacífico chiefdoms to continue in existence as buffers against the intransigent cruzob. In particular, the large northernmost pacífico unit based around the settlements at Lochha and Xkanha (near the intersecting point of the modern states of Campeche,

Yucatán, and Quintana Roo) served as a protective hinterland for the ladino population to the northwest. As late as 1875, yucatecos and campechanos still feared that the cruzob might overrun their pacífico allies and reoccupy the south-central zone of the peninsula. Despite temporary rapprochements, diplomatic relations always remained tenuous between cruzob and pacíficos, and the latter held themselves in constant readiness to fend off incursions by the eastern rebels.[55]

The great animosity harbored by the cruzob for their neighbors grew out of the pacíficos' decision to reach an early accord with the ladinos rather than embrace the new revitalization movement centered upon a miraculous Maya-speaking cross which was founded in 1850. With military tactics ceasing to be effective against the dzules, the rebel leaders in effect transformed their social movement into a religious crusade, hoping that with added religious sanction, past triumphs might be repeated. Ethnohistorians generally view the cult of the Talking Cross as the most important factor behind the cruzob's tenacious resistance to ladino political and cultural domination—resistance which, some writers argue, continues in muted form today.[56] "The possession of the miraculous cult, formally separated as it was from institutional Catholicism . . . assume[d] importance as a psychological centrum around which the rebels rallied themselves in the fight for their very lives, a mechanism indispensable to the maintenance of unity and a decidedly revolutionary spirit through half a century and more."[57]

Interestingly, despite the sharp ideological differences that brought the leadership of these autonomous Maya states into conflict, it was not uncommon for the swidden farmers who inhabited the border areas between the pacífico and cruzob zones to shift allegiance from one side to the other when it seemed convenient. Moreover, initially the two groups were organized identically, with the local Yucatecan militia company, in which Indians served between 1839 and 1847, replacing the traditional village as the unit of identification. The substitution of military ties for community loyalties was a practical consequence of the war's turbulence: most pacíficos and cruzob were refugees from other localities who had been shaken free of their original pueblos.[58] However, mid–nineteenth-century military affiliations may not have been completely responsible for structuring these chiefdoms. According to one specialist, despite the heavy overlay of Spanish military ranks, the complex pattern of fragmentation and realignment which characterized these groups suggests forms of lowland Maya political organization that hark back to pre-Columbian times.[59]

It is against this political and cultural backdrop that Bojórquez Urzáiz's findings regarding the postwar agrarian history of these Maya frontier zones take on meaning. If the northwestern region exhibited a fundamental stability and structural continuity, with the henequen hacienda built upon the foundation of earlier forms of the great estate—a continuity facilitated by continuing peasant expropriation (descampesinación)—such was not the case in the corn-producing zones of the far east and center south. Unfortunately, with his data collection still in the early stages, Bojórquez Urzáiz contributes little to the sparse literature on the economy of Chan Santa Cruz. In this theocratic-military society made up largely of free peasants, cruzob subsistence depended upon both slash-and-burn agriculture and looting, with war booty and agricultural surplus customarily traded with mestizo merchants in Bacalar or munitions dealers in British Belize. As best as we can tell, there were no significant commercial relations between the eastern cruzob and the dispersed pacífico settlements.[60]

Bojórquez Urzáiz's notable contribution lies in his attempt to reconstruct the agrarian structures of the little-studied south-central pacífico zone. Although evidence is still sketchy, he suggests that following the 1853 truce, many pacífico settlements began to regain a measure of stability, especially those lying south of Tekax and Peto within the current borders of the state of Yucatán. Whereas the beleagured cruzob continued to live a precarious siegelike existence that frequently compelled them to relocate their sites, and the remaining free villagers of the northwestern zone faced imminent expropriation as the henequen plantation advanced, reconstituted peasant communities emerged as the dominant agrarian institution in the northern portions of the south-central zone. Moreover, they remained viable even after ladinos began to reinvest in sugar during the second half of the nineteenth century. And although historians writing on the henequen zone have emphasized the number of Maya refugees who abandoned a free life on the turbulent frontier for the more secure bondage of the northwestern plantation, Bojórquez Urzáiz suggests that migration often flowed in the other direction—at least until mobility in the northwest was severely curtailed by a series of private and state initiatives which probably took hold in the 1880s. Henequen hacendados complained during the late 1840s and 1850s that their acasillados were deserting their estates and militia companies for an opportunity to work the land freely on the far side of the southeastern frontier. The few studies we have of nineteenth-century migration support Bojórquez Urzáiz's argument. Borah and Cook and Remmers, for example, point out that throughout the century the frontier constituted an open resource area, with population low in comparison to available land, and southeastern migration representing a form of resistance for the indigenous population.[61]

The former rebels and hidalgo defectors who populated the south-central pacífico zone controlled a portion of their maize production for family consumption. Prior to 1875, sporadic cruzob raids and the constant danger of invasion from the east kept the heads of pacífico households under arms for long periods of time, frequently placing milpa chores in the hands of the women and children. Yet even during this period of chronic instability and relative autonomy from the ladino state, Bojórquez Urzáiz finds evidence of unequal commercial relations between Indian cultivators and frontier merchants who quickly came to monopolize surplus corn production. The social and ethnic background of these traders is vague and awaits further investigation. Bojórquez Urzáiz indicates that frequently they were district political chiefs (*jefes políticos*), most likely ladino intermediaries parleying increasing political influence into lucrative commercial opportunities as state power was gradually extended on the frontier. These political and economic brokers were the sole source of consumer goods in the pacífico zone and used this merchandise to buy grain which they often hoarded for later sale at inflated prices when times were hard.[62]

As the frontier stabilized and Mérida's authority gradually increased late in the century, it triggered a modest revival in ladino investment in commercial agriculture in the northern portion of the pacífico zone and in what had formerly been a no-man's-land on the western fringes of the cruzob forests.[63] However, Bojórquez Urzáiz suggests that unlike the plantations of the henequen zone, these new sugar haciendas—and a smaller number of tobacco and mixed haciendas—did not rely on a labor force of peones acasillados bound by debt. Sound political and economic arguments counseled the preservation of the southeastern peasant community, even as ladino agrarian policy sought to nullify its counterpart in the northwestern henequen zone. Most important, Creole proprietors and Maya campesinos alike had not forgotten that the Caste War was a struggle for land; indeed, the pacíficos had ceased to be rebels in 1853 only when the ladinos assured them free use of the land in the south-central zone. As they began to harvest henequen's first riches in the northwest, the last thing Yucatán's ladino rulers wanted was a renewal of hostilities in the marginal frontier zone. Moreover, maintenance of the southeastern peasant community served an important economic purpose, for it not only provided frontier haciendas with a labor force but saved proprietors the cost of feeding and reproducing that labor force. Bojórquez Urzáiz documents that, beginning in the 1870s, it was not unusual for local ladino political chiefs, often hacendados themselves or collaborating with them, to abuse the power of conscription into the local militia as a means of providing labor gangs to southeastern estates. Additional research must flesh out other mechanisms enabling ladino proprietors to draw upon free peasant labor. For example, a more detailed examination of the structure of maize production and marketing will be essential, as Bojórquez Urráiz himself admits.[64] Nevertheless, he concludes that the state never jeopardized the existence of the frontier peasant community and occasionally intervened in its behalf, exempting specific villages from onerous taxes or preventing individual hacendados from encroaching upon neighboring Maya communities.

Still, recent research by economic anthropologist R. Laura Batt on the recovery of commercial agriculture following the Caste War in the *partido* (district) of Espita (on the edge of the eastern cruzob zone) would call into question Bojórquez Urráiz's generalizations regarding the integrity of peasant communities outside the henequen zone. Her monograph reinforces statistical data presented in the more general studies of González Navarro and Suárez Molina and suggests that, beginning roughly in the 1880s, debt peonage and *descampesinación* may have been more prevalent, even in the northern areas of the pacífico zone, than Bojórquez Urzáiz allows. We will need more microstudies, such as Batt's, which carefully delimit their investigation of agrarian structures both temporally and spatially before we can speak confidently about postwar land and labor patterns outside the henequen zone.[65]

Although the Yucatecan state may have consciously promoted the social peace on the frontier, it did little to reintegrate its vast southeastern hinterland economically. Moreover, the federal government provided only vague promises to requests by progressive regional promotors for funds to improve the state's internal transportation network. Recent studies examine the growing disparity in development between Yucatán's northwestern and frontier zones that emerged during the Porfiriato (1876–1911).[66] Prior to the Caste War, in addition to sugar, cotton, and tobacco cultivation, the frontier had done a lively trade in grains and foodstuffs with the barren northwest, despite the fact that most goods were moved by cumbersome and costly muletrains. Following the war, the southeast gradually lost its traditional northwestern food markets, largely because the powerful northwestern planters who controlled the Yucatecan political economy limited infrastructural development to the henequen export sector. Rather than construct an adequate rail and road network that would lower intraregional transaction costs, Yucatán's henequen planters linked their estates by rail to the Gulf port of Progreso and, by the early 1880s, began purchasing increasing amounts of corn, beans, and even sugar from more efficient foreign and central Mexican producers.[67] Similarly, *henequenero* (henequen planter) control in Mérida limited the ability of more modest, independent producers of southeastern sugar, tobacco, and cattle to command the loan capital and favorable taxation and trade legislation necessary to further their own expansion. Ironically, following terrible famine, drought, and locust plagues in the 1880s, the marginal southeast found itself having to depend on the henequen zone for the importation of basic foodstuffs.[68] In the wake of such devastation, many southeastern villagers chose to abandon their milpa plots and become peones acasillados in the henequen zone. In addition to being a conduit of Indian labor, the southeast also served increasingly as a frontier of expansion for some of the most powerful northwestern planters. The temporary extension of the henequen hacienda beyond the limits of the modern henequen zone into an area of lower productivity and higher production costs reflected the strength of world fiber prices after 1880 as well as the disadvantaged position of sugar cane, owing partly to the state's discriminatory taxation policy and partly to the unfavorable market conditions that followed the introduction of beet sugar in the 1880s. Planters also sought new sources of fuel to fire the steam-driven rasping machines as the expansion of monoculture rapidly deforested western Yucatán.

By the turn of the century, seven-eighths of the state's population was engaged in some aspect of cultivating, processing, or marketing fiber. The southeast was now little more than a colonial appendage of the dominant henequen zone. Yet more local studies like Batt's are needed to flesh out more precisely the changing relationship between the henequen zone and its hinterland. Batt shows, for example, that western planters continued to buy a variety of foodstuffs from estates in the eastern *municipio* (municipality) of Espita throughout the Porfiriato. Employing the concept of "internal articulation," she argues that the limits of *espiteño* economic growth were set by the regional metropolis in the northwest, which, in turn, was governed by the demands of the U.S. buyers who controlled the international henequen market. Thus, in Espita, haciendas became "secondary developments," dependent on the prosperity of the henequen plantations. In addition to providing an overflow area for fiber cultivation, Espita's estates sent corn, fuel, sugar, and rum to the plantations in the west. Batt documents cases in which powerful Mérida-based planters bought agriculturally diversified eastern fincas expressly to feed their peones in the henequen zone. Only more research will enable us to gauge just how widespread such internal articulation was during Yucatán's Porfirian henequen boom.[69]

4

The Political Economy of Monoculture (c. 1880–1915)

Like so much of regional Mexico, Yucatán was thoroughly transformed by the requirements of North American industrial capitalism and governed by its fluctuating rhythms during the last quarter of the nineteenth century. The production of henequen increased furiously during the Porfiriato as exports rose from 40,000 bales of raw fiber to more than 600,000 bales. Contemporaries chronicled how, by the turn of the century, the green cornfields and idly grazing cows of the northwest's colonial-style haciendas had been replaced by endless rectilinear rows of bluish-gray spines and the brisk factorylike pace of the modern plantation. They observed that Mérida was no longer the dingy, muddy, overgrown village it had been prior to the Caste War. Now the republic's "White City," it was immaculate and modern, a fitting seat for Yucatán's newly minted henequen millionaires. Yet the writers of the day also captured another Yucatán: the isolated and miserable world of the plantation peón, who, though he underwrote urban Yucatán's rapid modernization with his labor, knew none of its wealth and amenities.[1]

Surprisingly, only recently has serious work been done on the political economy of henequen or, for that matter, on the major trends in regional life from the time Yucatán was stabilized after the Caste War until it was again disturbed by the revolutionary movements of the 1910s. When Howard Cline first took stock of regional historiography in 1945, he reported, "There is a vast bibliography on henequen, but most articles deal with its botanical features or the technical process whereby the leaves of this agave are converted to useful fiber, rather than with the social implications and its impact on Yucatecan institutions."[2]

Since the mid-1970s, local and international scholars have actively

53

redressed this imbalance. Indeed, at present no topic is more studied than the structures of the henequen export economy and no
period of regional history is under closer scrutiny than the Porfiriato
or Old Regime.[3] The first fruits of long-term research efforts have
begun to appear, most notably two monographs by historian Allen
Wells and anthropologist R. Laura Batt. Based extensively on municipal and regional archives, including tax and estate records, these
studies examine agrarian structures and social relations within the
henequen zone and on its more peripheral, agriculturally diversified
eastern fringe, respectively. Wells's and Batt's contributions, together with a proliferating article literature, constitute the beginnings of a critical mass of empirical and theoretical scholarship
which is broadly interdisciplinary and has already generated interpretative debates.[4]

Wells and other writers document that not until 1878, when the
invention of a mechanical knotting device for the McCormick binder
began to revolutionize the North American grain industry and increase demand for fiber and twine geometrically, did northwestern
proprietors feel compelled to convert their mixed haciendas from
corn, cattle, and small-scale fiber production to monoculture on a
grand scale. While such hacendados had been able to combine the
factors of production required to produce enough fiber for the mar-
itime industry's rather modest needs for rope and cordage in the
1830s and 1840s, their capacity for expansion would now be severely
tested by the galloping demands of North American capitalized agriculture. Although a dependable technology (the mechanical rasper)
had been developed during the earlier commercial period, a campaign was now launched for ever-greater amounts of land, labor, and
capital.[5]

The Planters' Progress: Appropriation of Land and Labor

As had been the case on the southeastern frontier before the Caste
War, the northwestern planters were given a free hand to expand
their land at the expense of neighboring Indian villages. Throughout

the nineteenth century and up to 1915, the percentage of free villagers living in northwestern pueblos consistently diminished as their ejidos were appropriated by henequeneros aided by a concerted legislative and judicial offensive mounted by the state and federal governments.[6] Wells's case study of the transformation of Santo Domingo Xcuyúm from mixed hacienda to henequen plantation details the mechanisms whereby monoculture virtually devoured the remaining communal sector in the northwest. At the same time, his and Ramón Chacón's careful documentary researches reveal that certain Maya pueblos in the heart of the henequen zone managed to keep their ejidos intact until the 1890s and 1900s. In this regard, Wells and Chacón qualify Robert Patch's generalization that by 1800 the northwest (within an eighty-kilometer radius of Mérida) had become a zone of haciendas in which somewhat more than 50 percent of the Indian population were peones acasillados.[7]

According to an earlier study by the Yucatecan historian Antonio Betancourt Pérez, sixty-six ejidos, representing 134,000 hectares, were alienated for henequen production between 1878 and 1912. Although the precise locations of these ejidos are not specified, it seems certain that many villages lost their communal lands outside the boundaries of the modern henequen zone. Batt demonstrates henequen's expansion into eastern municipios such as Espita, and aggregate statistical data provided by Suárez Molina and González Navarro on the dramatic rise in the number of debt peons throughout the state during the last quarter of the century suggest an even deeper (although often temporary) penetration of the old comunero hinterland by the henequen plantation. Suárez Molina's comparison of late nineteenth-century censuses reveals that the number of peones acasillados increased from 20,767 in 1880 to 80,216 in 1900, an increase of 386 percent in only two decades. Others place the number of peones as high as 125,000 by 1910.[8]

In fact, most writers suggest that by 1900 the region's dichotomous agrarian structure, which Patch posits for the late colonial period, had largely broken down.[9] In a general agrarian survey following the Mexican Revolution, Frank Tannenbaum estimated that by 1910 at least 75 percent of all rural dwellers in Yucatán were residents of large estates. According to another early study by George McBride,

96.4 percent of all family heads had no land of their own by 1910. More recently, Friedrich Katz has concluded that the expansion of the large estate in Yucatán brought "an almost total dissolution of the primitive sector . . . and an almost complete concentration of property in the hands of a small group of planters."[10] Others have joined Katz in maintaining that the advance of the large estate and the influence of henequen monoculture were so pervasive during the late nineteenth and early twentieth centuries as to discount the applicability of the traditional notion of a "free peasantry" throughout the region. For even after the plantation ceased its territorial expansion and became entrenched in the northwestern quadrant of the peninsula (about 1900), its influence extended well beyond this henequen zone, drawing campesinos into the zone to work as day laborers or as a temporary labor force. Moreover, these writers contend that even outside the henequen zone, Yucatecan haciendas with a more diversified productive base approached the archetype of the tropical southern Mexican hacienda during the Porfiriato: an extremely powerful, land-controlling institution that subordinated and proletarianized the local Indian villages to a much greater extent than its central Mexican counterpart.[11] Even in marginal Espita, for example, Batt estimates that by the turn of the century, between 70 and 80 percent of the work force of these estates producing sugar, some henequen, cattle, and corn were debt peons, with few village-based, free Maya agriculturalists still remaining in the municipio.[12]

Nevertheless, excessively broad generalizations regarding late Porfirian agrarian structures outside the henequen zone will remain hazardous until additional local studies appear. Certainly Bojórquez Urzáiz's preliminary research for a slightly earlier period on Indian corn producers in the more remote south-central and far eastern recesses of the peninsula should caution us against prematurely writing the epitaph of all free peasant communities.

By Mexican standards, the Yucatecan henequen estate was small. Although a few of the roughly one thousand late Porfirian plantations exceeded 5,000 hectares, the great majority of the large haciendas in Yucatán were approximately 2,000 to 3,000 hectares in size, and the majority of estates were between 1,000 and 2,000 hectares. Even the greatest of Yucatán's plantations, Augusto L. Peón's Yaxche

(6,000 hectares), was a veritable *pequeña propiedad* (small property) when compared to the latifundia of Mexico's north and was considerably smaller than many of the haciendas of the near north, the Bajío, and even those of the central plateau. Yucatán's largest landowning family, the Molina-Montes clan, could not have controlled more than 100,000 hectares of henequen and *monte* (woodland) on the eve of the Mexican Revolution; by comparison, the extended Terrazas-Creel family in Chihuahua owned more than 5 million hectares.[13]

Still, although these henequen plantations may have been modest by national standards, they were remarkably lucrative. Contemporary observers reported that the average return per investment during the decade 1900–1910 was no less than 50 percent and as high as 400 to 600 percent.[14] Some modern scholars have judged the planters' gains to be only slightly less extravagant. Keith Hartman estimates that in the 1880–1915 period only four years elapsed (1893–97) during which the Yucatecan planters did not realize at least an 18 percent annual profit, and he maintains that for most of those years the rate of profit was many times that figure. Wells more conservatively estimates a profit of about 9 percent, but adds that even when prices fell rapidly, as during the recession of 1893–94 and the panic of 1907–8, many planters still realized profits.[15]

Most modern students attribute the profitability of these estates in great part to the planters' systematic, often brutal exploitation of their dependent work force. As we shall see, after 1880, inexorable market demand, coupled with almost constant pressure on speculating planters to repay capital loans, so intensified plantation labor that, over the course of a generation, Yucatán was transformed into a virtual slave society. Yet as the boom heightened, the acquisition of a numerically sufficient work force would prove to be a more serious challenge to the planters than its subordination.

Sooner or later, most of Yucatán's landless campesinos went to work on the henequen plantations as temporary laborers or, more frequently, as resident peons. Wells shows that in addition to the breakup of the village ejidos, ecological disasters—drought, famine, and a succession of locust plagues—plus the twin specters of military service and forced road gangs also eroded the Maya cam-

pesino's independence. Oppressed by such natural and social constraints, and further limited in their options by stepped-up
enforcement of the old vagrancy laws, landless peasants were lured
to the great estate, where henequeneros offered an ample supply of
corn, water, and firewood, as well as legal exemptions from military
service and corvée labor.[16] Once workers came onto the estates, a
broad array of political and social control mechanisms enabled
planters to keep them working there. According to Suárez Molina,
by 1900 the system was working so well that government figures
reported less than 120 unemployed in the entire state![17]

In spite of their great recruiting success, planters discovered that
burgeoning market demand would not be satisfied by indigenous
Maya labor alone. Although the Maya continued to constitute the
overwhelming majority of their work force, throughout the Porfiriato
henequeneros sought new sources of labor, importing a diverse mix-
ture of thousands of Yaqui war prisoners, central Mexican contract
workers and political dissidents, and Korean, Chinese, Puerto
Rican, Canarian, and small numbers of European immigrants.[18]
Even the influx of these new recruits was not enough. As Patch
suggests, a *falta de brazos* (labor shortage) may well have been a
crucial factor in the henequen estate's ultimate failure to move much
beyond the old colonial zone of mixed haciendas in the northwest.[19]
In a recent theoretical essay, historian José Luis Sierra Villarreal
contends that labor scarcity was always a much more serious problem for the henequen plantation than land expansion. Planters were
often motivated as much by a desire to control the Maya villagers'
labor as they were to despoil them of their communal lands. Moreover, he hypothesizes that even as the export economy was experi-
encing its greatest expansion during the final days of the Old Regime, planters were beginning to encounter an "absolute labor
scarcity" such that future expansion, rendered moot by the disloca-
tions in production wrought by the Mexican Revolution, would have
been impossible. By 1915, Yucatán's Porfirian auge had exhausted all
of its labor reserves, including the zone of former rebel Maya resistance in Quintana Roo, and planters could no longer count on the
prospect of continued flows of imported workers, such as Yaqui
deportees and indentured foreigners.[20] Sierra Villarreal's provoca-

tive hypothesis merits empirical testing by agrarian historians and demographers.[21]

Great Debates I: Labor Conditions on Haciendas

In the surge of professional attention that has been refining our understanding of Yucatán's Porfirian monoculture over the past decade, probably no aspect has been written upon more extensively than the so-called "labor question." Still, for the better part of the seven decades that have elapsed since the celebrated North American journalist John Turner returned from Mexico and leveled his chilling indictment of Yucatecan slavery in *Barbarous Mexico* (first published as a series of articles in 1909), the complex question of working conditions on Porfirian estates was perceived more as a political issue than as an intellectual problem.[22] Apologists, invariably representing the great henequenero families and the foreign investors who did business with them, immediately repudiated Turner's portrait of oppression, and through the years have themselves painted labor conditions under the Old Regime in aristocratically benign, almost consensual terms. In their view, these were the golden years, when master and servant each participated in a secure, essentially reciprocal relationship. The Maya worker both knew and appreciated his place and with good reason: conditions of labor scarcity during the auge enhanced his worth to the *patrón* and precluded a brutal regimen. The absence of violent acts of worker resistance and a durable social peace, which was broken in 1915 only by the intrusion of an unwanted and inappropriate revolution from without, validated a well-meaning planter paternalism that protected the Maya worker from the dangers and uncertainties of life beyond the plantation.[23]

Meanwhile, critics of the labor regime, who originally included other contemporary travelers to the region and, more recently, several generations of local politicians dedicated to legitimizing the Mexican Revolution and its official party, have corroborated Turner's rather static view of violent and unceasing oppression of the faceless many by a greedy few.[24] Unfortunately, this emotionally charged climate offered little encouragement for the kind of rigorous historical investigation that might have produced a more reasoned debate.[25] Until recently, even the most basic question, precisely how relations of production and working conditions changed as market demand intensified, had not been addressed. Nor had any inquiry been made into the workers' own experience and perception of change during the auge. Ironically, both apologists and critics of Yucatecan plantation society seemed to agree, although for very different reasons, on the passive, almost inert character of the predominantly Maya work force. Critics of the system saw in the workers' docility evidence of planter brutality; supporters of the labor regime interpreted passivity as confirmation of the effectiveness of Yucatán's paternalistic ethos.[26]

In an ongoing effort to address these larger concerns pertaining to labor conditions on the estates, the current generation of regional specialists has reached a consensus on some fundamental points and raised a cluster of more circumscribed questions, on which opinions differ and more empirical research will be needed to test individual hypotheses.

While few were prepared to appropriate as gospel the "black legend" found in Turner's muckraking classic and in other contemporary accounts, modern scholars have clearly found the Turner position more plausible than that of the Old Regime's apologists. Judging conditions on Porfirian estates in terms of such diverse criteria as diet, availability of medical care and educational instruction, workload, real wages, access to cash advances and corn plots, physical coercion, and mobility, yucatecólogos have found that treatment of workers was generally bad and tended to get worse as market demand intensified throughout the period. In short, as the local economy became more engaged by, and ultimately subordinated to, the demands of international capitalism, labor conditions became "involuted," with the traditional system of peonage transformed by degrees into a neo-slave regime. In the process, Yucatán's campesinos suffered "a profound regression in terms of the quality of their lives."[27]

A variety of authors have discussed and empirically documented this involution in the labor regime. In a recent theoretical contribution, Marco Bellingeri conceptualizes the post–Caste War transformation of the former Maya comunero into a virtual plantation slave in three stages. Initially, the dispossessed villager exchanged his former colonial-style tax obligations for status as a hacienda peón acasillado, a not-very-onerous condition that Bellingeri likens to midcentury peonage on the central plateau. The peón gained security and other benefits of paternalism, including generous cash advances and the traditional milpa plot; the patrón augmented his sedentary labor force with a loyal retainer. However, with the intensification of the fiber market and the conversion to monoculture (c. 1880), the debt peon not only experienced increased physical demands on his capacity to work, he quickly lost his access to a food plot, cash, and the other softening features of paternalism. Some writers hold the loss of the traditional right of access to milpa to be crucial—the factor which primarily distinguished a debt peon from a slave.[28] Bellingeri, however, identifies a third and final moment in the transformation process: the creation, beginning in 1895, of characteristically "slave relations of production." This ultimate stage was marked by an escalation in the forms of coercion and physical abuse, further limitations on mobility, and most important, the conversion of the peón into a commodity, by assigning him a market value unrelated to his accumulated debt but determined by the fluctuations of the henequen market.[29]

Patch observes that this involution of the labor regime must also be viewed within the context of long-term institutional and political changes that gave rise to a stronger state apparatus by the late nineteenth century. During the chaotic generation following independence, or in the devastating aftermath of the Caste War, Yucatán's ruling bourgeoisie was not institutionally equipped to restrict the mobility of its work force or enforce the harsh peonage regime that would characterize the late Porfiriato.[30]

Empirical studies support Bellingeri's and Patch's general framework and add historical detail. Wells first discusses the "casual" pre-auge labor agreements that hacendados negotiated with several different categories of resident workers (peones acasillados, tenant-sharecroppers, and *luneros,* or "Monday men," more or less a hybrid of the first two types), then documents how these relatively open labor arrangements gave way to increasingly tighter control over all laborers following the onset of the boom. Gradually, renters and luneros metamorphosed into peones acasillados, mired in debt and stripped of their former degree of independence.[31] Joseph contrasts the conditions of henequen workers early in the boom with their position on the eve of the Mexican Revolution. He finds that whereas debt peons of long standing initially fared somewhat better than deportees, contract workers, and part-time workers from the villages, by the late Porfiriato the lot of most peones acasillados was probably no better than that of outsiders.[32] Interestingly, Batt paints a somewhat brighter picture for contemporary Espita. In this marginal area where monoculture never established a secure foothold, planters continued to make subsistence plots available to their peones and generally maintained a watered-down version of paternalism, which included periodic visits to the estates as well as the provision of gifts, services, and appropriate arrangements for religious celebrations.[33]

If Batt's evidence for the eastern zone points up the necessity of taking subregional variation into account in an evaluation of labor conditions, a similar caveat might be raised for the henequen zone itself. Uniform conditions did not exist within the northwest; treatment of workers varied from plantation to plantation, as did the composition of the work force. Several writers have documented that on some estates imported contract workers were used in significant numbers; others relied mainly upon their peones acasillados with an admixture of landless villagers and deportees. On certain fincas an older form of paternalism lingered, with hacendados spending extended periods of time on their estates and, in some cases, preserving the traditional regime of peonage by providing their retainers with cash advances and access to corn plots.[34]

However, as Friedrich Katz persuasively argues in his comparative regional study of labor conditions on Porfirian estates, on the whole, social relations on Yucatán's henequen plantations were among the most oppressive in the tropical southeast, a region that maintained the most onerous labor regime in the Mexican republic.[35] Katz's comprehensive review of the socioeconomic and geographical conditions that shaped the Yucatecan Porfiriato—still referred to by campesinos as the "age of slavery" (la época de esclavitud)—suggests why slavelike conditions began to appear in the region at a time when slaveholding was being legally abolished or declining irreversibly elsewhere in the Americas.[36] Beyond macrolevel conditions like sharply increased demand and the development of effective transportation links, Katz emphasizes the existence in central Mexico of a large labor surplus of landless campesinos that was not absorbed by domestic industry and constituted a ready pool for enganchadores (unscrupulous labor procurers); the lack of sufficient industry or mining in the southeast to compete with the planters for scarce labor and therefore give the worker greater mobility; federal and state governments willing to aid in the enforcement of this neoslave system; and, finally, Yucatán's geographical isolation, which facilitated control and made escape difficult. Henequen's production process was also conducive to slave labor. Because the demand for fiber was constant, it was grown year-round and required a stable, rooted work force. With the exception of a few skilled jobs in the rasping plant (for which well-paid free laborers were usually brought in from Mérida), most of the work required no specific skills or prior training. The tasks were calculated and carried out on an individual basis, making supervision relatively easy.[37]

Beyond this larger consensus on the treatment of workers, Marxist writers have tended to quibble over semantics when characterizing the mode and relations of production governing late nineteenth-century monoculture. Some students continue to view the Yucatecan Porfiriato as part of an extended transitional stage linking some sort of precapitalist mode (some speak of "feudalism," others of "slavery") to capitalism. Still other writers distinguish the predominance of "commercial capital" during the auge from that of "industrial capital" and the kind of free wage labor conditions that classically herald the arrival of the capitalist stage.[38] The great majority of recent scholars, however, have no problem asserting that the agroindustrial plantation, which was at the center of regional society during the boom, was based on a capitalist mode of production. Patch reflects this majority position in describing the henequen plantation as the institution of "triumphant capitalism in Yucatán," the culmination of a transition which began at the end of the eighteenth century. Yet if, following the Caste War—and, in certain respects, as a result of it—Yucatán was ready for capitalism, "rural society had not been transformed sufficiently to accommodate free wage labor. Consequently, the planters' recourse was to draw upon a frankly precapitalist labor system, that is to say, upon slavery and peonage."[39]

Eschewing the specialized terminology of the Marxist debate, Allen Wells agrees with Patch on the nature of these labor relations. Still, he argues that it is precisely the character of this labor system and the patronizing attitude toward workers that underwrote it that prevented the henequen hacienda—capitalist in most respects— from fully completing its transformation into the kind of "truly modernized plantation" that Wolf and Mintz identify in their classic typology.[40]

Other writers go further in attempting to account for this contradiction between the existence of a capitalist mode of production and the slavelike system of social relations embedded within it. Following recent anthropological work on the articulation of mixed modes of production, Batt argues that what is definitive is "the private appropriation and accumulation of capital through the productive process." A capitalist mode implies the domination by capital of production to such an extent that capital's encounter with labor in the productive process creates value. Wage labor is but one form— albeit the classic form for Marxists—that the relationship between capital and labor may take. She points out that in the process of penetrating underdeveloped regions, capital has adapted itself to a diversity of social formations. In order to dominate production in these areas it has sometimes utilized preexisting social forms and has sometimes created new ones. Thus, to understand the world capitalist system, one must analyze the creative manner in which capital penetrates and transforms noncapitalist social formations. In Yucatán, according to Batt, the preexisting form of labor exaction that would be dramatically transformed was debt peonage.[41]

José Luis Sierra Villarreal and Gilbert Joseph have noted the unfortunate consequences of these social relations for Yucatán's economic future. In order to maximize production for the capitalist world market, the henequen plantation utilized forms of production that blocked the path of mature capitalist development within the region. Sierra Villarreal argues that in order to satisfy market demand and ensure themselves an acceptable level of profit, about two hundred henequeneros imposed an "excessively exploitative" labor regime (*sobreexplotación*) on their workers, who constituted the vast majority of Yucatán's population. By *sobreexplotación*, Sierra Villarreal means a coercive regimen in which the worker was immobilized and his remuneration was often less than what was needed to sustain or reproduce him and his family.[42] In such a plantation society, Joseph observes, commercial relations were necessarily impeded, not to mention the kind of internal market for consumption that would support industrialization beyond an insignificant level.[43]

Regional specialists must still resolve empirically certain long-standing questions regarding the debt mechanism that curtailed the workers' mobility and, by keeping them at or below the margin of subsistence, severely limited their participation in the internal economy. First of all, debate continues as to whether workers' debts were hereditary. Most recent work on the henequen zone suggests that they were, although Batt maintains that was not the case in marginal Espita.[44] "The inheritance of debts would not have created a steady labor force since young people would have been free from debt until their parents' death, at which time they themselves would have been too old to be of use to the *hacendado*."[45] Rather, debts were created while espiteño workers were young, usually when patrones assumed the substantial costs connected with the marriages of their peones. In certain cases, hacendados provided the basic necessities for the couple to begin domestic life (house, kitchen utensils, etc.). Such a scenario seems much less probable for the late Porfirian northwest, where systematic paternalism had been phased out and, ultimately, the real debt was irrelevant if the planter was determined to keep the worker. Backed by the Porfirian political and legal establishment, the henequenero most likely had the option of making debts hereditary, in addition to falsifying records or merely declaring the indebtedness of the peón under oath.[46]

Second, the relationship between workers' debts and wages needs further clarification. Apologists for the Old Regime never tired of pointing out that the Yucatecan peón's salary was more than reasonable by national standards, and occasionally even drew international parallels to dramatize their point: "Whereas in Europe the agricultural wage doubled, in Yucatán during the second half of the nineteenth century, it increased five fold."[47] Indeed, according to figures provided by the henequeneros, the average wage did rise, from fifteen centavos per day in 1850, to about fifty to eighty centavos in 1900, and up as high as one peso in 1910.[48] Yet as recent work has shown, even if we accept the accuracy of such aggregate data on the long-term trend of nominal wages—and some have not—its significance is misleading.[49] There is consensus that throughout Mexico, rampant inflation (intensified in Yucatán by the auge) more than offset periodic salary increments. A serious decline in real wages made savings impossible and subsistence difficult. The advent of monoculture necessitated the importation of most foodstuffs and drove prices for corn, beans, and meat well above the national average, especially after 1898. Wage levels not only failed to keep pace in good times but were rolled back when fiber prices dipped, as during the 1907 panic.[50]

What seems less clear in the recent literature is the exact role which debts played in determining salary levels. Based upon press accounts and limited hacienda records, Wells maintains that like food prices, wages were pegged to fluctuations in the world market price of fiber. Following the 1907 panic, for example, henequeneros lowered wages across the board. "Salaries, therefore, were not a fixed expenditure; planters could adjust them to meet their expectations of profits." The debt peon, a fixture on the estate, had no bargaining power. He had to depend on increases in fiber quotations for his own limited wage hikes throughout the period.[51] Several Mexican social scientists go even farther: they maintain that rather than being pegged to the market price of fiber, the peón's wages were probably much more a function of his indebtedness and general condition of powerlessness. Like Wells, they draw upon contemporary press accounts but argue that those workers not yet in debt consistently claimed higher salaries than those already indebted.

Debt peons had little recourse but to accept the wage the patrón meted out, since their salaries represented little more than credits against ever-increasing debts and, moreover, the planter had a monopoly on coercion and violence.[52] An extreme exponent of this position, Sierra Villarreal, goes so far as to suggest that "far from depending on a market-generated *price,* [the salary of the] labor force *merely represented a cost* to the producer. And that cost was determined by calculating the barest level of subsistence for the members of the work force and their families."[53] Bellingeri joins Sierra Villarreal in pointing out that while debt peonage was extremely harsh in late Porfirian Yucatán, the practice of exploiting a coerced labor force "behind the facade of salary" was common throughout Mexico and had been for generations.[54] Indeed, the labor regime of the late Porfirian henequen hacienda was "built upon servile traits inherited from the colony: *fajina* [extra unpaid work for the patrón], debt, and a compressed agricultural wage."[55]

But why would planters impose such severe hardships on their debt peons in a region where labor shortage had become chronic? Better, it would seem, to promote more generous treatment, including a living wage, thereby preserving their valuable human property, the worth of which would rise steadily with the demand for fiber. Two economic arguments might have dissuaded the planters from a more magnanimous strategy. First, the thinking of most henequeneros was likely molded by the sharp fluctuations in the price of fiber that had already occurred during earlier decades of regional fiber cultivation. In certain years, prices had soared and planters had reaped fabulous profits. By the late Porfiriato, a boom mentality had taken hold: the planter realized that such dramatic price surges would characterize the industry's fortunes for only a limited time, and he was prepared to make the most of them when they occurred. This meant maximizing workload and minimizing production costs, most notably wages. Moreover, given the Yucatecan oligarchy's political connections in Mexico City and the preponderance of force that planters maintained in the region, planters might have gambled that additional Yaqui deportees and enganchados could be secured and immediately incorporated into the existing system at a low enough cost to replace "expired workers." A second consideration, related to the first, was the widespread phenomenon of planter indebtedness. Most small and medium hacendados (as well as many larger planters addicted to speculation and lavish spending) had gone deeply into debt and were consequently burdened by greatly increased production costs. Downward fluctuations in price frequently carried them to the brink of bankruptcy. While larger planters often looked to powerful kin for assistance, the most preferred method of skirting or postponing financial collapse for smaller producers was to shift the weight of their crises to their indebted, captive labor force, reducing salaries and phasing out services as they intensified work obligations.[56]

We now need additional monographs examining wage schedules on individual estates in a variety of subregions to test these generalizations regarding the relationship between workers' debts and salaries. Significantly, Laura Batt's microstudy of Espita again presents conditions at variance with those in the henequen zone. According to Batt, Espita's workers generally found the prices of basic necessities to be manageable. The peón's wage was apparently sufficient to supplement his basic diet, which he obtained from the food plot provided by his patrón.[57]

Finally, we need to know more precisely the role that the *tienda de raya* (hacienda store) played in the peón's indebtedness. Because relatively few data are currently available for the daily operations of this "company store," students of the Mexican Porfiriato have thus far failed to reach consensus on even fundamental issues regarding the tienda's impact on the peón.[58] Where Yucatán is concerned, questions far outnumber reliable answers. For example, did the hacienda store charge prices that were higher or lower than those at nearby markets? Did the hacendado gouge in order to ensure himself a supplementary profit, or did he keep prices low to draw neighboring villagers onto the estate as acasillados? And how much coercion did proprietors apply to force their own peones to shop exclusively at their tienda? On this last question, Wells suggests that peones frequented these company stores for convenience and readily available credit; Joseph and Chacón emphasize planter restrictions on their workers' movement outside the hacienda. Chacón particularly focuses on the planters' strategy of paying their peones only in *vales* (scrip) redeemable at the hacienda store. Batt contends that in eastern Espita, hacendados varied in the amount of coercion they used to influence where their workers shopped; nevertheless, many peones tended to buy at the hacienda store during the week and go to town to shop on Saturdays. The use of scrip varied from hacienda to hacienda and often changed with the economic situation, which increased or diminished the patrón's circulating capital. Moreover, the hacendado's scrip was also accepted at some shops in Espita. Significantly, these stores were usually owned by the hacendados or their close relatives. Wells also stresses commercial alliances between northwestern planters and local merchants, with the latter often leasing concessions from the former to operate company stores on the henequen estates. Yet Wells is less concerned with who took advantage of the peones; for him the important point is that the tienda de raya was instrumental in enabling planters to increase their workers' debts and further diminish their mobility. Batt and Chacón, on the other hand, seem to stress the tienda's commercial function. According to Batt, here "[the hacendado] was a merchant . . . taking back from the workers the salary he had paid them."[59]

All in all, despite the current trend in the literature on Latin American debt peonage, which plays down the notion of debt as a controlling function of labor and runs counter to the harsher judgments built into earlier novels, travelers' accounts, and historical monographs, the case of Porfirian Yucatán provides strong evidence for the older view. While opinions often differ on finer points, the draconian measures that characterized debt servitude and enabled henequen planters to tighten control over production are brought out clearly in a variety of recent contributions. There is strong agreement that, at least for the henequen zone, salaries were insufficient and working conditions were highly oppressive; laborers were often imported forcibly from without; debt was systematically manipulated to provide a legal basis for coercion; and plantation owners, backed by the local government and constabulary and, ultimately, by the national state, were able to tie workers to their estates.[60]

Just as some writers have questioned the advent of capitalism as the predominant mode of production in Yucatán, others have refused to accept the idea that the relations of production on the estates evolved from debt peonage into slavery. As we have seen, the great majority of recent work depicts a de facto slave system in late Porfirian Yucatán—servitude that was unconstitutional, though no less real for being so. Planters made an initial investment (or "advance") to secure laborers, as slaveholders did. Workers were not free to leave the estate, and fugitives were returned and punished. Laborers were bought and sold, typically with the hacienda, but the peón's value was determined by market price independent of his debt. This system contrasted with the classic system of debt peonage, in which debts were totaled when a hacienda was sold. Indeed, in analyzing the henequen plantation, these students draw much of their conceptual framework from the extensive literature of comparative slavery. Several authors explicitly compare the severity of henequen's labor system with slaveholding regimes in the Caribbean and the U.S. South, particularly on the dynamic frontiers of antebellum cotton and Caribbean sugar expansion. Extended discussions of such familiar comparative themes as defining "treatment" of workers on the plantation and assessing the impact of paternalism and cultural hegemony abound in the Yucatecan literature, and luminaries such as Genovese, Mintz, and Patterson are frequently invoked.[61] Nevertheless, certain writers have recently called for a narrower, more rigorous definition of slavery, most notably historian Allen Wells. He does not deny that the servile exploitation of Yucatán's Maya campesinos was accentuated during the Porfiriato, but he prefers to retain the rubric of debt peonage in characterizing the Maya *campesinado's* social relations on the estates.[62]

Based on extensive documentary evidence that he has culled from the state's notarial archive and other collections providing insight into contemporary commercial transactions, Wells accepts Turner's original conclusion that peones could be bought and sold, their market value determined by fluctuations in the price of fiber. (Unfortunately, explicit documentation indicating the incidence of such a trade in human beings, which would certainly have been welcome, is not provided.) Moreover, he admits that "there is a structural similarity between peonage and slavery." Indeed, no student of

Yucatecan plantation labor is more indebted to the historiography of comparative slavery than Wells, who draws heavily upon Genovesian notions of planter control and slave resistance, jousts with Elkins's concept of the "sambo," and employs the extensive literature on slave treatment. Where, then, does he take issue with the majority position?

It is Wells's reading of Orlando Patterson's recent work on the sociocultural and psychological dimensions of slavery, particularly the emphasis that Patterson gives to the slave's own perception of his bondage, that prompts Wells to demand a more restrictive definition of slavery.[63] In his view, although all workers on the henequen plantation were generally subjected to a brutal regimen, probably only the Yaqui deportees should be classified as slaves. His argument is strategic as well as substantive and arises in part from his concern that the literature on labor conditions continues to be overheated and reductionist.

Wells's examination of plantation records has convinced him that "the [Porfirian] estate was a complex organic relationship which combined a variety of labor types into a brutally effective work force." Conditions during the late Porfiriato may have been intolerable for all of these types, yet to lump them all together as "slaves" is not only misleading but prevents us from gaining insight into the responses to oppression that workers were able to make. Not all types of workers were treated identically; more important, not all types perceived their plight identically or had the same capacity to endure and respond to it. Wells challenges us, for example, to consider the relative advantages which local Maya peones enjoyed compared with the forcibly resettled Yaquis. Separated by thousands of miles from their cultural roots and loved ones, these Sonoran prisoners of war, in effect, had their death sentences commuted to lifelong servitude in Yucatán. Unlike the far more numerous Maya, "who had themselves, their customs, traditions, and language to help ward off the onslaught of the oppressive regime, or even groups of indentured foreign laborers, who had only to fulfill a finite work contract, the Yaqui were . . . alienated from all rights or claims of birth." They had a past, to be sure, but (quoting Patterson), Wells argues that "a past is not a heritage." Thus, it is Patterson's symbolic idea of "deracination," the violent and permanent alienation from one's natal ties that deprives one of any legitimate existence outside of his master, that Wells uses to distinguish the utterly powerless Yaqui slaves from their co-workers on Yucatecan estates.[64] In the process, Wells, following Patterson, sets aside the traditional notion of the slave as chattel, which "fails as a definition, since it does not really specify any distinct category of persons." After all, in most societies, including our own, everyone is or can be the object of a property relation, and historically, proprietary claims have been made upon many persons who clearly were not slaves.[65]

Some might find this new definition of slavery problematic and question whether Patterson's wedding of sociological theory to symbolic anthropology has clarified or needlessly complicated our understanding of the institution. More important, however, is Wells's effort to recover the workers' own perspective of the labor regime and his suggestion that more attention must be paid to the particular social and cultural resources that different groups of workers called upon to combat the mounting hardships of plantation life during the late Porfiriato. Other students have pointed out that as world market demand intensified and conditions on the estates deteriorated, workers experienced the shock waves in all spheres of their lives, not just in the economic realm.[66] Yet Wells's monograph represents the first attempt to examine empirically the ideological, cultural, and political aspects of the change process. Equally as important, it represents the first serious effort to portray the Maya workers as actors in history rather than merely as passive, indolent retainers and victims, the images propagated for generations in the writings of apologists and critics, respectively.

Wells argues that, even in the pacified henequen zone, the Maya cultural heritage maintained a residual strength and resilience that fueled a surprisingly high incidence of resistance to the planters' brutal regime. The Maya were no docile "sambos," meekly accepting their dependent status and extracting what meager morsels of benevolence the planter tossed in their direction. "On the whole, [Maya workers] rejected the weak paternalistic ethos which was presented to them by the white ruling class," demonstrating their dissatisfaction through spontaneous, although ultimately futile, acts

Maya wedding portrait, c. 1900.

Yaqui Indians deported from the northwestern state
of Sonora to work on the henequen plantations
during the late Porfiriato.

Workers on General Alvarado's railway, "Ferrocarriles
Constitucionalistas en Yucatán," late 1910s.

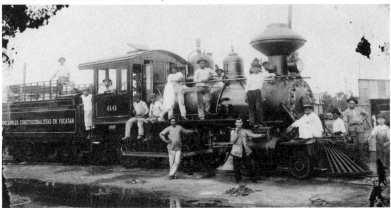

Promenade at a high society ball, Porfiriato.

Fiber stocks at a hacienda warehouse.

Peones and armed overseers haul henequen leaves on a
mule-drawn tram.

Young ladies and their headmaster, late Porfiriato.

Labor Omnia Vincit, "Work Conquers All": hacienda community assembles for religious procession.

Maya peón harvesting henequen leaves in traditional
worker's apron, Porfiriato.

Baseball comes to Yucatán; one of early nines,
Mérida, 1900s.

of local violence directed at isolated symbols of planter oppression—usually hacienda administrators and overseers, occasionally political bosses, and, in one bloody episode, the hacendado himself. In addition, Wells views frequent attempts to escape the plantation and chronic alcoholism as more common signs that "many did not accept their fate lightly."[67]

Without question, Wells provides a long-overdue corrective to the traditional caricature of a mass of passive, inert peones. Moreover, he is right to distinguish the uprooted Yaquis—and, one would assume, other exiled political prisoners whom he does not mention—from homegrown Maya campesinos, who retained a cultural heritage. It would have been helpful, however, if he had gone beyond these suggestive generalizations, providing more concrete detail on how various groups of workers were treated and the manner in which they responded. Apart from the gathering of oral life histories—a strategy which becomes more difficult with each passing year—one rich, virtually untapped source of such data is the AGE's Ramo de Justicia (Judicial Section). Wells himself reports that spot checks revealed legal actions brought by Maya villagers forcibly removed from their milpas and taken onto planters' estates. How often did Maya campesinos seek redress in the state's courts? Were they ever successful? Were other groups of workers in a position to pursue such redress within the legal system?[68]

No doubt Wells is also correct in suggesting that when they were forced to operate outside the system, the Maya campesinos' violent, circumscribed episodes of rural protest late in the Porfiriato owed something to the ethnic solidarity that grew out of a shared tradition. Wisely, he does not exaggerate the reserves of cultural or political strength that the northwestern campesinado possessed. As we shall see in the next chapter, students of the Mexican Revolution, who must account for its very late arrival in Yucatán, have pointed out how little *organized* collective protest there was in the campo. They have emphasized the planter class's ability to erode the strong tradition of Maya protest and struggle, which dated back to the conquest, through an intensification of work, various forms of repression, tight surveillance and restrictions on workers' movements outside the plantation, and the dilution of concentrations of Maya campesinos with other ethnic and linguistic groups by the creation of heterogeneous work crews.[69]

On the other hand, perhaps Wells has underestimated the cultural resources and political role of the Yaquis and other groups of deportees in these unsuccessful late Porfirian revolts. Ramón Chacón documents the fierce participation of Yaqui *jornaleros* (rural workers) in the celebrated Catmís rising of March 1911, as well as the 1913 revolt of several hundred Zapatista prisoners from Morelos.[70] Not only does Chacón find evidence of enthusiastic participation by several hundred Yaquis in the state militia in 1914–15, but he produces correspondence from Constitutionalist governor Eleuterio Avila attesting that many of the Sonorans "received good treatment," had been "completely assimilated" to regional life, and preferred to remain in Yucatán.[71] Chacón's findings suggest that more work remains to be done on the Yaqui question.

In general, we can only hope that Wells's first attempt to penetrate the ideological and cultural dimensions of Porfirian working class life will provoke further research. Many of his insights on the protective elements of culture, the limited influence of a weak paternalism, and the various forms of resistance, which are generalized for the entire henequen zone, should now be tested in local studies of specific haciendas, municipios, and partidos, employing the field methods of oral history and cultural anthropology.[72]

Great Debates II: The Impact of North American Capital

Recent studies have observed that the brutal, regressive nature of the labor regime makes more sense when it is related to the planters' pressing need for capital and their increasingly precarious position in the structure of henequen marketing during the late Porfiriato.[73]

Once the means for obtaining greater amounts of land and labor were guaranteed, the final obstacle to the expansion of monoculture was capital. It took about U.S. $130,000 to finance an average-size henequen plantation and maintain it for seven years until a return could be realized; by comparison, the traditional corn and cattle haciendas in the northwest required a mere 5,000 pesos.[74] Moreover, there was a dearth of investment capital in the region following the Caste War, owing to the devastation of Yucatán's most profitable industry, sugar. Initially, the lack of capital obliged most planters to shift piecemeal from old to new production techniques and crops, using existing *henequenales* (henequen fields) to finance the capital investment of new fields. Once international demand skyrocketed after 1880, however, Yucatecan planters felt compelled to take more active steps to overcome their capital shortage.

Scholars generally agree on the manner in which planters obtained capital and marketed their fiber prior to the turn of the century. Local banking institutions did not exist early in the Porfiriato, and rather than capitulate to the exorbitant 18 to 24 percent rates of local usurers, henequeneros became increasingly dependent upon foreign capital loaned at 9 percent, first by bankers from the North American market area they were supplying and subsequently by cordage brokers and manufacturers from the same area. In return for conceding these credits, the North Americans, working through local exporting houses, demanded to be paid back in raw fiber rather than cash, and at the market price prevailing at the moment of repayment. The yucatecos would realize in the decades ahead how burdensome this lien arrangement could be.[75]

Almost immediately, the Yucatecan henequen industry found itself compelled to adjust its basic orientation in order to satisfy the North Americans' appetite for raw fiber. Prior to 1880, henequen fiber had been used to a considerable extent in the local manufacture of ropes, cables, and other crafted articles; now the raw material would be marketed almost exclusively to the North American cordage factories, which would manufacture it into binder twine. Largely as a result of the new capital and lien arrangements, local cordage industries found themselves no longer able to obtain fiber to keep up with their North American competitors and were forced to close down by the early 1880s.[76]

Joseph and Wells contend that a collaborative bargain between foreign business interests and local exporters had to be negotiated carefully to assure North American factories a dependable supply of fiber. Foreign interests recognized that it would not do to name a U.S. representative to operate in a proud and chauvinistic region like Yucatán. Rather, they would attempt to disguise their involvement by employing one or more local "agents," each of whom would publicly project an independent image. From the 1870s on, local business leaders served as fiber purchasing agents and conduits for foreign loan capital. Thus, North American brokers and manufacturers, such as Thebaud Brothers and the National Cordage Company, operating during the first decades of the boom, enlisted the services of the large Yucatecan export houses of Eusebio Escalante, Manuel Dondé, and Arturo Pierce, among others, in their bids to corner the local market. For their own part, these "collaborators," in serving as purchasing agents and financial intermediaries for the North American banks and manufacturers, realized sizable profits, usually from commissions and kickbacks, but also by virtue of the usurious loan practice that access to foreign capital enabled them to conduct.[77]

The North Americans, always seeking to keep their options open, rarely depended upon a single export house. From the onset of its dealings with Yucatán in 1875, for example, the McCormick Harvesting Machine Company was careful to recruit a primary collaborator to purchase raw fiber and then to maintain its influence over this incumbent while cultivating other potential collaborators as well. Thus, during the late nineteenth century, bargains were struck at one time or another with a variety of *casas exportadoras* (export houses), and while McCormick and the other North American concerns might work to help one casa gain a temporary advantage over its rivals, they always made sure to have at least one reliable substitute waiting in the wings. Consequently, as Suárez Molina, and Joseph and Wells document in their recent studies, prior to 1902 a truly exclusive and powerful collaborative mechanism never characterized the Yucatecan henequen industry. North American cordage manufacturers experienced only intermittent success in controlling the hard fiber market, which fluctuated wildly throughout the quarter century following the introduction of the McCormick reaper-binder.[78]

However, with the merger in 1902 of Cyrus McCormick's Harvesting Machine Company with several rivals to form the International Harvester Company, the collaborative equation and, consequently, the balance of power within the regional industry were transformed dramatically. The very establishment of the new "International," a combination of five of the largest harvesting machine companies, with an initial capitalization of U.S. $120,000,000, eliminated the bulk of existing competition within the farm implements and twine industries and placed at the manufacturers' disposal organizational and financial resources that previously had never existed. In the years that followed, Harvester would more closely approximate a genuine "trust" than any other fiber manufacturing concern, either before or after the merger. For its part, Harvester's chosen agents in Mérida, Olegario Molina and Company, represented, even prior to its collaboration with IHC, an economic and political force in regional affairs substantially more powerful than any of its nineteenth-century predecessors.[79]

It is at this juncture, as historians have sought to capture the precise nature of Harvester's involvement in the monocrop economy and to assess the corporation's impact upon it, that consensus breaks down. Indeed, there is probably no single historiographical issue in the region's past that has generated as much controversy over the years, both in Mexico and the United States, as the debate over whether IHC established an informal empire in Yucatán on the eve of the Mexican Revolution. Moreover, unlike the extended polemic over labor conditions, which regional specialists have all but resolved, the controversy among professional scholars over corporate control of Yucatán's late Porfirian economy shows little sign of abating.

The great majority of local and foreign, popular and scholarly writers who have addressed the issues since 1902 contend that Harvester, in partnership with Molina and his dominant faction of the regional oligarchy, increasingly dominated Yucatán's political economy during the period 1902–15, virtually monopolizing local fiber production just before the Mexican Revolution.[80] In order to assure a dependable supply of raw fiber to meet the era's extraordinary demand, Harvester contracted the services of the region's most politically influential exporting firm, whose founder and boss was the new governor of the state. Olegario Molina and his faction would use their local clout, enhanced by the funneling of large amounts of Harvester capital at strategic junctures, to control production and manipulate the price of fiber—generally forcing it down—on the manufacturer's behalf. In consideration for these services, these local oligarchs would receive hefty commissions and ready access to foreign capital for their own varied entrepreneurial ventures.

Proponents of this majority view regard a secret contract between IHC and Molina and Company—which was signed in Havana, Cuba, on 27 October 1902, but was not widely publicized until 1921—as the beginning of their extended collaboration and the foundation for Harvester's informal empire.[81] Now referred to in the peninsula as the "notorious pact," it specified that Molina and Company would use "every effort within their power to depress the price of sisal [henequen] fiber," and would "pay only those prices which from time to time are dictated by the International Harvester Company." More concretely, Harvester agreed to place "as much [fiber] as may be needed at the disposal of Molina and Company for sale . . . for the express purpose of depressing prices." As for the other principals operating in the local market, it would be left to Molina to determine how he would induce his traditional rival, Escalante, to cooperate with the arrangement. Harvester, for its part, would see to it that the other leading trading firms of Peabody and Urcelay "shall not pay higher prices for sisal than those given by Molina and Company."

Advocates of this "antitrust" position maintain that over the course of the next decade, the Harvester-Molina arrangement worked as planned. Within the first year, the price fell two cents, from close to ten cents per pound to eight cents. In the years that followed, the collaborators managed to shave almost a cent a year, until, by 1911 (at the market's lowest point), raw fiber was being bought at three cents per pound, beyond which it was generally agreed all major planters would be operating in the red, and the smaller ones would be pushed to the wall. (And, these writers emphasize, as the planters felt the pinch, they, in turn, pinched their peones, whose conditions deteriorated.) Moreover, they point out that it was not until Molina's firm consummated its relationship with IHC in 1902 that it dramatically pulled away from the Pierce house (agents for Peabody), its closest competitor in the Mérida buying market. Immediately prior to the 1902 contract, Molina had done only half as much business as his rival; in subsequent years, Molina (and Harvester) would reap the lion's share of all fiber transactions.[82]

In their recent article, "Corporate Control of a Monocrop Economy: International Harvester and Yucatán's Henequen Industry during the Porfiriato," Joseph and Wells have advanced the argument a step further. They contend that IHC president Cyrus McCormick consummated a second collaborative arrangement, also in 1902, with Henry W. Peabody, president of the exporting firm that had traditionally purchased fiber for Harvester's closest rival in the manufacturing of twine, the Plymouth Cordage Company. In fact, they argue, it was no coincidence that this second agreement occurred about the same time that Harvester signed its secret pact with Molina, for the two agreements appear to have been crucially linked in IHC's strategy to control Yucatán's henequen trade. Via a series of personal letters in 1902, McCormick agreed to renew an earlier arrangement between IHC's predecessor, the McCormick Harvesting Machine Company, and Peabody that had existed from 1898 until shortly after the turn of the century. In essence, McCormick would provide capital to Peabody in exchange for market control—the right to determine Peabody's purchases and transactions in the Yucatecan fiber market. As far as they can determine, the new informal agreement seems to have terminated around the time of Peabody's death, shortly after 1910. However, by the time it did terminate, Harvester's hegemony in Yucatán had been indisputably established.

In light of this secret understanding between McCormick and Peabody, the language of the subsequent IHC-Molina contract makes more sense, especially in regard to the third parties mentioned. For how could Harvester "agree that Peabody [among others] shall not pay higher prices for sisal than those given by Molina" unless Harvester had at least some control over Peabody, if not the determining voice in the latter's transactions? We know that by 1902 IHC already had brought local buyers like Molina and Urcelay into line and that it would later use Molina's burgeoning political and economic power to eliminate more stubborn rivals like Escalante, who would not collaborate. Peabody and Company, through its local agent, Arturo

Pierce, had, prior to 1902, traditionally controlled a greater share of the henequen market than Molina and, therefore, constituted the only serious threat to the complete dominance of the industry that Harvester now sought. Adding Peabody's share of the trade to the slightly less than three-quarters of local production that Molina controlled in certain years prior to 1915, Joseph and Wells argue that "even by conservative estimates, it appears the IHC was controlling in excess of ninety percent of Yucatán's sole export commodity by the time the Revolution arrived in the region."[83]

The reality of Harvester's indirect control through collaboration with Molina and Peabody was alleged by disgruntled local hacendados and nationalistic middle-class intellectuals, as well as by IHC's threatened competitors in the U.S. cordage industry, long before the "notorious pact" was made public in 1921. Indeed, the unbroken succession of vocal charges of a Harvester-inspired conspiracy to depress prices and corner the market, which characterized the late Porfiriato in Yucatán, dates back to the final days of 1902, the very year the collaborative arrangements were consummated.[84] It was the Mexican revolutionary government's conviction that IHC exercised monopoly control over the henequen industry that led it to stern measures against the corporation during the 1915–18 period.[85]

Although this antitrust position has prevailed within Yucatán up until the present, it has not gone unchallenged. The minority view has been articulated mostly by descendants of the regional oligarchs who collaborated with IHC, as well as by some embittered intellectuals who have found the local performance of the national revolutionary regime to be wanting and have come to reassess the achievements of the Yucatecan Porfiriato. In some cases they have even longed for "the good old days." These dissenting voices have been much less concerned with refuting their opponents by presenting a countervailing analysis of henequen production and marketing than with defending the good name of Don Olegario Molina (and their own particular relations in his faction) or, more positively, trumpeting the success of regional entrepreneurship and economic development. In this latter endeavor, they have recently been joined by some North American social scientists operating in the "developmentalist" tradition who have also minimized the negative impact of

dependent capitalism and North American imperialism on the regional development process.[86]

These authors have argued that, unlike the rest of Mexico where
foreigners increasingly dominated most lines of economic activity,
yucatecos maintained their autonomy and were solely responsible
for the remarkable growth that the region enjoyed during the Porfiriato. As one local historian put it in the late 1920s: "If there is one
thing on which we can pride ourselves, it is that all the work here
was done by the sons of Yucatán and all the credit must go to our
beloved country, rather than to foreign entrepreneurs. Yucatecans
were the capitalists . . . and the laborers. Glory to Yucatán!"[87] Over
a half century later, two North American neoclassical economists
concurred that the region had been blessed with a plucky,
entrepreneurial planter class that "successfully negotiated the transformation of a traditional hacienda system into a modern . . . agri-
industrial economy—and reaped the associated rewards." Regarding the impact of Harvester's collaborative bargain with Molina in
1902, these scholars conclude that "there is little evidence to suggest
that either henequen hacendados or the people of Yucatán suffered
under the market arrangements with American buyers"; on the contrary, Yucatán emerged from the late Porfiriato as one of Mexico's
wealthiest states.[88]

Few would quarrel with certain premises of these "regionalists":
the henequen estate differed from the classical pattern of late nineteenth-century plantation agriculture in some important respects.
Land tenure and ownership of the means of production were almost
exclusively in Yucatecan hands.[89] There was no major influx of technology from abroad; indeed, Europeans and North Americans had
failed miserably in inventing the machinery required to make henequen processing economical on a commercial scale.[90] Nor was management brought in from the outside; it, too, was almost completely
Yucatecan. And finally, while capital was ultimately imported from
the United States, it was made available and distributed, as far as
the producers were concerned, on a local basis. This prompted a
leading student of the henequen plantation to conclude, "The situation in Yucatán was virtually unique in the annals of plantation
agriculture, in that the area had, by its own efforts, provided the

necessary economic basis to produce an adequate, reliable supply of its own product and fulfill a near-inexhaustible demand."[91] Even a Marxist critic of this "regionalist-developmentalist" view observed that Yucatán had the only branch of Mexican plantation agriculture that had given rise to commercial export production prior to the development of monopolistic concentration, that is to say, prior to the ascendancy of the great North American "trusts."[92]

Nevertheless, most popular and scholarly authors have dismissed the "regionalist" position as either wishful thinking or conscious mythmaking. They have argued that there is more to the question of foreign penetration of Yucatán's export economy than mere ownership of the means of production and then analyzed (with varying degrees of sophistication, specificity, and documentation) the mechanism and agents through which Harvester indirectly controlled the regional political economy. Most recently, Joseph and Wells have countered the "rosy developmentalism" of the "regionalists," indicting them for a fundamental lack of precision. It makes little sense, these critics claim, to use generalizations such as "the hacendados" or "the people of Yucatán." One must distinguish between a relatively small planter elite of approximately 300 to 400 families and a much smaller, more cohesive group of about 20 to 30 families who constituted a hegemonic oligarchical faction (or "divine caste," as they were called and came to call themselves early in the century). This ruling faction, based upon the Molina *parentesco* (clan), had homogeneous interests, a relatively closed membership, and, owing in great part to its collaboration with the Harvester trust, such control over the economic and political levers of power in the region that it was able to thwart the opportunities of rival groups in late Porfirian society. As was typically the case throughout Porfirian Mexico, the oligarchical clique was subsequently incorporated into the national superstructure. Molina himself joined Díaz's cabinet as minister of development following his tenure as state governor. And while Don Olegario's participation in Mexico City's inner circle did not alter Yucatán's marginal position in the national political structure, it did guarantee the privileges of his casta divina. Thus the success of most Yucatecan hacendados was ultimately limited by the collaborator mechanism. That most planters were still able to obtain a satisfactory profit was due to their ability to expand production while lowering production costs at the expense of the vast majority of "the people of Yucatán"—their dependent Maya labor force.[93]

Only recently has the prevailing notion of an informal empire been rigorously challenged on economic grounds. In a provocative 1977 essay, based almost entirely on published materials, North American historian Thomas Benjamin called into question the ability of foreign corporations working in concert with regional oligarchs to depress fiber prices significantly or impose a pattern of conscious control upon Yucatán's monocrop economy. Rather, he adduced other "less visible" macroeconomic variables—changing conditions in the international hard fiber market and the combined devaluating trend of two global business recessions and Mexico's 1905 monetary reform—to account for the dramatic drop in the local price of fiber during the late Porfiriato. In rejecting the collaborator mechanism, Benjamin accepted at face value the denial of both Molina and IHC that there was any relationship between them other than that of buyer and seller. He even expressed doubt regarding the authenticity of the 1902 contract; at any rate, he judged the play of larger market forces at work in Yucatán and throughout the world as more crucial in determining the price of henequen fiber.[94]

Other U.S. scholars have subsequently introduced a series of variations on Benjamin's basic themes. In certain cases, they have documented their arguments with new evidence culled from North American corporate archives. Unlike Benjamin, they do not dispute that foreign interests and Yucatecan oligarchs recognized the advantages of manipulating the price and actively collaborated on a number of occasions. Yet while documenting that such arrangements were not uncommon and were often rather complex, they argue that the end result of all this "conspiring" was rather marginal in its long-term effect on prices and control of production.[95] In their brief recent commentary on Joseph and Wells's 1982 essay, "Corporate Control of a Monocrop Economy," economist Fred Carstensen and historian Diane Roazen Parrillo have mounted the most spirited attack on the antitrust position to date. They argue that "there are neither documents in hand nor market data that show International Harvester exercised a successful monopsony in sisal." Harvester alternately collaborated and engaged in "bruising competition" with Molina and Peabody. Working with them on occasion, IHC "attempt[ed] to influence the market, both up and down, but never earned the spectacular (or even good) profits which would presumably be the primary objective of such control." Indeed, they conclude that "if there was an empire, formal or informal . . . available evidence points to Molina, not International Harvester, as the principal actor and most likely beneficiary."[96]

The debate is far from over. In their necessarily restricted commentary for the *LARR* forum, Carstensen and Roazen Parrillo serve notice that they are preparing a more detailed study of the development of the United States twine market and the parallel rise of the Yucatecan henequen industry. This work will enable them to amplify a number of points heretofore presented only in outline. Thus, while the present survey has inevitably focused on the prevailing antitrust position, we can expect a more definitive challenge of the majority view in the near future. But although the terms of the historiographical debate have been sharpened, it seems unlikely that we will ever know with certainty whether larger market forces or local power relationships exercised greater sway over Yucatán's Porfirian monocrop economy. Both were crucially important and interlinked. Above all, the controversy that continues to swirl around the role and impact of North American capital serves to remind us that history is ultimately an interpretation, a calculation of probabilities, conditioned in great part by one's theoretical orientation.

The Legacy of Monoculture

Despite the historiographical debates highlighted in this chapter, regional specialists have agreed upon the essential hallmarks of henequen's "golden age." At a time when the McCormick grain binder had created a nearly limitless market for hard fibers needed in the manufacture of binder twine, among the world's fiber-producing regions, only Yucatán had achieved the necessary economic base to satisfy demand. Far cheaper and far more accessible than any of its rivals, Yucatecan henequen virtually monopolized the world market prior to 1915. While potential competitors in Africa and Asia were still years away from establishing the stable conditions under which sisal plantations might flourish, Yucatán's henequeneros had mastered a technically advanced, highly capitalized plantation economy predicated upon a labor system that reduced production costs to a bare minimum.[97]

Thus, although the vast majority of Yucatán's producers and merchants remained outside the exclusive faction that collaborated with International Harvester, and bitterly railed against it, Yucatán's monopoly over supply, coupled with minimal labor costs, generally ensured profits attractive enough to soothe most irate members of the agrocommercial bourgeoisie. Indeed, despite intraclass tensions on the eve of the Mexican Revolution, the planter elite could still maintain its cohesiveness in the face of serious threats to its fundamental interests. It would take a large army from central Mexico to introduce the Revolution from without, after the ruling plantocracy had repeatedly demonstrated its capacity to co-opt political challenges and repress insurgencies from within. Even then, as we shall see, the landed bourgeoisie would prove a formidable opponent for the coalition of forces that endeavored to carry out a social revolution during the 1915–40 period.[98]

The small planter elite may have generally benefited from the triumph of monoculture, but historians have found few long-term benefits for regional development. Whether the collaborator mechanism successfully controlled production and depressed prices as the majority of writers maintain it did, the fact remains that from 1902 to 1915 the International Harvester Company secured a continuous supply of raw fiber from Yucatán at a low price without sinking substantial investment in the regional economy.[99] Moreover, the terms of Yucatán's dependent relationship to the world market would become progressively more unequal, since time favored the U.S. cordage manufacturers. As additional production areas opened up in the years ahead, Yucatán would be forced to come down significantly in price to remain competitive with the higher-quality strains of sisal grown by its international rivals. And whereas the monocrop region *had* to sell its fiber to the highly concentrated cordage industry, that industry could become more and more choosy about with whom it did business.[100]

Yucatecólogos point out that the region's structural dependence on a foreign-dominated market would remain even after Yucatán succeeded in industrializing its henequen and produced binder twine locally, a process that began in the 1920s and gained momentum in the 1930s and 1940s. According to International Harvester's own records, as late as 1947, IHC alone still consumed almost 60 percent of Yucatán's annual yield of fiber and cordage.[101] It is not surprising, then, that social scientists have viewed Yucatán as a classic case in which industrialization did not break the relationship of dependency and promote economic "take-off," since industrialization issued from a monocrop economy tied to a fluctuating world market, the terms of which still favored the North American buyer over the Yucatecan seller.[102] Local authors make it clear that they consider Yucatán's economic dependence on the United States—epitomized by Harvester's informal empire over the region prior to the Mexican Revolution—as more enduring and damaging than the more formal domination of the old Spanish empire or the current Mexican republic, from which, at least, yucatecos had twice been able to secede temporarily in the nineteenth century. Ironically, perhaps it is a central Mexican proverb that best captures the Yucatecan dilemma: "To divorce one's wife is simple, to divorce one's mistress, impossible."[103]

5

Imported Revolution and the Crisis of the Plantation Economy (1915–1940)

No region of Mexico experienced the turbulent Mexican Revolution in as relatively nonviolent a manner as Yucatán. On the other hand, few regional populations have found the long-term process of social change that was unleashed by the Revolution of 1910 to have been as jarring and roller-coaster-like as the yucatecos. An isolated bastion of the Old Regime as late as 1915, Yucatán became a fertile ground for radical social experimentation and agrarian reform during the 1915–24 and 1934–40 periods. Yet during the decade between these two eras of revolutionary activity, the agrocommercial elite successfully stalemated a redistribution of wealth in favor of the masses, and after 1940, many of its members skillfully adapted to the new order and maintained a privileged position in the regional power structure. The former principal source of the bourgeoisie's wealth and of the Maya campesinado's livelihood, henequen monoculture, did not fare as well. Though the plantation economy entered the revolutionary period at the height of its expansion, it emerged from it in 1940 in serious decline. Since that time, numerous critics of the institutionalized revolutionary regime and a smaller number of apologists have endlessly circled the issue of regional economic decline and heatedly debated its relationship to the revolutionary process. Only recently, however, have professional scholars begun to transcend this tradition of narrative and invective and to suggest that the political economy of decline is highly complex, turning on a set of intersecting relationships involving Yucatán, Mexico City, the United States, and the international fiber market.

Over the past decade and a half, the field of Mexican revolutionary studies has developed a high degree of methodological sophis-

94

tication and thematic complexity. Probably no branch of Mexican historiography has more effectively utilized a regional approach and social science techniques to probe central questions and test conventional interpretations. Indeed, in a 1978 survey of recent trends in the field—now virtually outdated owing to an avalanche of even more recent scholarly production—the usually understated David Bailey contended that "Mexican revolutionary studies had reached a maturity that rivaled the larger and more established fields of European and U.S. history.[1]

Given the impressive performance of the larger field, at first glance it may seem surprising that the literature on Yucatán's participation in the Mexican Revolution is still rather uneven. Certainly one would not expect to find at the regional level the range and depth of coverage that the larger field boasts. Yet one is struck by the fact that the quantity of serious work on Yucatán's revolutionary period lags significantly behind investigation of the Caste War and Porfirian eras. Only within the past five years have scholarly monographs based upon local archival collections begun to replace the political chronicles and memoirs of partisan authors. And, although these recent professional studies often showcase different methodologies and interpretations of events, frequently their thematic content overlaps. Most contributions focus on the early phase of Yucatán's revolutionary experience, particularly on the celebrated, socially active administrations of Salvador Alvarado and Felipe Carrillo Puerto (1915–24). Virtually ignored are the turbulent years that followed the assassination of socialist governor Carrillo Puerto in January 1924 and culminated in the second cycle of reform during the national presidency of Lázaro Cárdenas (1934–40).

Even the work on the earlier phase of the Revolution in Yucatán, while generally of high quality, occasionally suffers from overgeneralization and a lack of attention to subregional detail. Verifying contradictory local accounts against contemporary press reports and archival sources, yucatecólogos David Franz, Ramón Chacón, and Gilbert Joseph have now fashioned a clear political narrative of the complex chain of events that transpired between 1910 and 1924. Joined by fellow historians Moisés González Navarro and Graham Knox and sociologists Francisco Paoli and Enrique Montalvo, they

have also mapped out the social and economic contours of the revolutionary projects put forward by the Socialist Party of the Southeast, initially led by Alvarado and, subsequently, by the more militant Carrillo Puerto.[2] However, much less emphasis has been given
to determining the varying impact that these revolutionary programs, decreed in Mérida, actually had at the local level, especially
outside the dominant henequen zone. Once again, anthropologist
Laura Batt's microstudy of Espita represents a valuable precedent
for this kind of investigation.[3]

What accounts for the belated development and uneven distribution of regional revolutionary studies? No doubt, until recently,
Yucatán's geographical isolation and traditional remoteness from the
Mexican political mainstream deterred national and international
specialists from focusing on the region. Instead, they concentrated
upon the victorious caudillo-led armies of the north, the birthplace
of the Revolution, and examined the popular social movements of
central Mexico, most notably Zapatismo, the agrarian movements of
Michoacán and Veracruz, and the more widespread Cristero rebellion.[4] Not surprisingly, the first professional scholars, who
launched investigations in the mid-1970s, chose to concentrate on
the more removed and much heralded first decade of revolutionary
involvement (1915–24), when Yucatán was acknowledged to be a
social laboratory for the Mexican Revolution. Buoyed up by henequen revenues, the PSS carried out a series of bold experiments in
civil rights, land, labor, and educational reform. Conversely, revolutionary scholars initially avoided the politically delicate later phase
of the Revolution (1924–40), when Yucatán went from pacesetter to
economically depressed region. Suffering the disastrous effects of a
hastily conceived and federally imposed agrarian reform, which
speeded the decline of an already ailing henequen economy in the
late 1930s, Yucatán lost all traces of its former political and economic autonomy. The deep wounds that were opened during these
years, and the enduring legacy of bitterness that was engendered,
not only inhibited outside professional interest but also adversely
affected the local tradition of amateur historiography.

A certain amount of partisanship in the local literature on the
Revolution would have been expected. Throughout regional Mexico,

one encounters a prodigious harvest of pro-Revolution tracts written by members of the ruling political elite. These apologia invariably recount past struggles and eulogize old heroes, weaving them all into a usable past that legitimizes current rule by the official party. On the other hand, one also finds an anti-Revolution literature, of far more modest proportions, which is as old as the Revolution itself. Indeed, from 1910 until the present, a kind of "shadow history" has been written—typically by the dispossessed oligarchy, investors, and functionaries of the Old Regime or their relations—that counters the "official history" by condemning the Revolution and all its works.[5]

In Yucatán, as we might expect, the "revolutionary paladins" of the first decade, Alvarado and Carrillo Puerto, have been duly commemorated in an extensive official literature and appropriately reviled in works by a much smaller circle of class enemies.[6] Yet the normal literary pattern does not hold for the second phase of the Revolution in Yucatán. Here the "shadow history" overwhelms the legitimizing mythology of the official party (PRI). Confronted with the stark fact that over the course of a half century their region has fallen from being perhaps Mexico's richest state to one of the republic's most impoverished and troublesome areas, yucatecos of virtually every social stripe have blamed the decline on the federal government. They have judged the agrarian revolution that came from central Mexico in the 1930s to be unsuited to the region's peculiar conditions and needs and, hence, a formula for failure.[7] Middle-class intellectuals have lamented the region's loss of autonomy and cried "internal colonialism;"[8] workers have alleged corruption and inefficiency in the centralized management of the henequen industry;[9] and members of the former hacendado class have complained bitterly that, in breaking up once-productive agroindustrial units and failing to substitute a viable and integrated economic system for the old plantation economy, the Revolution led by President Cárdenas effectively scuttled the monocrop economy without conferring significant benefits upon rural workers.[10] Even some local spokesmen of the official party, while they have argued that the issue is more complicated than their critics allow and that notice must also be taken of unfavorable secular trends in the world fiber mar-

ket, have reluctantly agreed that the Mexican Revolution has relatively few lasting achievements to show for its social programs in
Yucatán.[11]

Whatever merit there may be in the yucatecos' ringing indictment
of the federal government, it seems clear that in a political climate so
pervaded by bitterness, frustration, and an almost obsessive need to
allocate blame, a rigorous historiography cannot thrive. It is not
surprising, then, that many local treatments of the later revolutionary period, in lieu of fresh research and analysis, contribute only
new rhetoric to an enduring polemic.

A Different Revolution?

By contrast, much of the recent professional work on the Revolution in Yucatán rests on solid archival foundations and illustrates
significant methodological and interpretative trends within the
larger field of Mexican revolutionary studies. If scholars agree on
anything, it is that the Revolution can no longer be viewed as a
monolithic event. Generalizations made on the basis of informants
and documentary materials in Mexico City have clouded the origins
and development of the Mexican Revolution for too long. The up-
heaval that has been called the Revolution was really a series of
regional phenomena, only some of which deserve, perhaps, to be
called revolutions. Each was governed, to a greater or lesser extent,
by a discrete set of local social, economic, political, geographical,
and cultural factors. If there were "many revolutions"—or if "revolution meant different things at different times and in different
places"—yucatecólogos generally concur that the Revolution was
later to arrive, less violent, and probably more radical in the peninsula than it was elsewhere in the republic.[12]

David Franz, and more recently Ramón Chacón, devote the better
part of their monographs to documenting these characteristic traits
of revolutionary Yucatán during the administrations of energetic
caudillos Alvarado and Carrillo Puerto. Both historians emphasize
the relatively high degree of autonomy that each governor enjoyed as
he sought to transform Yucatán into a model of what Mexico's social

revolution could achieve. Franz, in asserting that "the revolution in Yucatán seemed divorced from the Mexican Revolution," overstates Yucatán's exceptional situation; Chacón more judiciously observes that despite their relative autonomy, Yucatán's revolutionary leaders were ultimately dependent upon alliances with national presidents for their survival.[13]

In most respects, these competently researched dissertations are rather straightforward, traditional narrative histories. Chacón's monograph, while less ambitious chronologically (unlike Franz, he ends the body of his study with Alvarado's departure from the region in 1918, and treats the Carrillo Puerto regime broadly, in an extended epilogue), is built upon a firmer, richer research base. Both authors make skillful use of U.S. Department of State consular records, and Franz is particularly successful in piecing together fragments from a variety of central Mexican documentary collections, including the Archivo de Venustiano Carranza. Yet Chacón makes far better use of the local press and contemporary pamphlets and memoirs and, unlike Franz, meticulously combs local archives, most notably the AGE's voluminous *Poder Ejecutivo* (Executive Branch) section and the rich correspondence in the Archivo de la Mitra. Thus, while both studies provide useful, essentially political, narratives of the 1910–18 period, Chacón's dissertation is clearly the more definitive.

At the conceptual and theoretical level, these studies are less successful, particularly Franz's monograph. Because both authors adopt a conventional periodization, organizing their studies around national political regimes, ironically they find themselves in the awkward position of showing that revolutionary change was significantly delayed in Yucatán, yet sanctioning the hallowed date of 1910 as the beginning of the revolutionary process in Yucatán and elsewhere in the republic.[14] Chacón's problem is primarily one of emphasis, for he focuses his attention on the "1915 Revolution" of Alvarado, which became all the more necessary and "radical" owing to the "failure of moderate revolution" during the preceding five years. Franz, on the other hand, in an unsuccessful conceptual attempt to pigeonhole the Yucatecan experience into the outmoded categories that Crane Brinton designed decades ago on the basis of the French

Revolution, mistakenly concludes that revolutionary conditions existed in 1909–10—a conclusion that even his own data do not support.[15] Several other scholars, who are not invested in the traditional
periodization of the Mexican Revolution based on national political
phenomena, have tended to view the region's late Porfirian rebellions as weak, isolated, and largely unorganized episodes and
have gone on to emphasize the extended hegemony that the Porfirian
oligarchy enjoyed in Yucatán.[16]

When it is compounded by an unquestioning acceptance of dualistic modernization theory, Franz's conventional political approach
seriously mars his larger assessment of the first phase of the local
revolution. Virtually ignored in the study is the impact that
Yucatán's dependent monoculture had on the revolutionary process,
particularly the internal pattern of social relations that underwrote
monocrop dependence. Like so many of the North American scholars active in the 1950s and 1960s, whose views of the Revolution
harmonized with the official historiography written by "the Revolutionary Family," Franz draws up a "balance sheet" to assess the
performance of the Revolution in Yucatán and concludes it has been
overwhelmingly positive. He contends that, prior to the Revolution,
the henequen industry and the state's economic structure built
around it had been "modern," but the regional political and social
structure had remained "traditional." However, as a result of the
revolutionary reforms implemented between 1910 and 1924, the region "was more closely bound to the Mexican nation and molded
into a modern state." And although it did not create "a Shangrila,"
the Mexican Revolution can count among its "credits" extended liter-
acy and educational reform, gains in health care and road construction, a more equitable system of taxation, and fairer labor practices
(most notably an end to debt peonage). Franz argues that perhaps
the Revolution's greatest achievement in Yucatán was the creation of
the PSS and "the rise of a strong one-party political system [that]
reflected the modernization that had occurred . . . and brought
some balance to the political, economic, and social structure."[17]

Significantly, Franz lists only one major item on "the debit side of
the ledger": the Revolution's "failure to destroy the economic and
social power of the *henequeneros.*" Even Franz is forced to admit,

although almost as an afterthought in a concluding footnote, that failure to break the bourgeoisie's control over the political economy had severe consequences. For not only were local revolutionaries hampered in their efforts to diversify the regional economy, but the influence of the traditional elite "caused the subsequent cancellation of much of the reform achieved during the Revolution." Indeed, Franz notes that this has led many yucatecos and outside observers to speculate whether a revolution had actually occurred at all. Ultimately, almost incomprehensibly—and again in a footnote—Franz concludes that the eventual failure of the Revolution in Yucatán is not the central concern of his study; he is more concerned with the changes wrought from 1910 to 1924, however "transitory" they may have been.[18]

Ramón Chacón's analysis is not hampered by the theoretical constraints of developmentalism. His presentation is virtually atheoretical, although it is informed by a fundamental (if muted) dependency perspective. Chacón emphasizes that despite their social value, many of Alvarado's reforms were short-lived or only served as precedents for later governments. He does not minimize the power of the bourgeoisie or its ability to adapt to the new revolutionary order. All in all, Alvaradismo (or Carrillismo) did not restructure Yucatecan society. And "while the Revolution in Yucatán during the period 1915 to 1924 . . . took a different course from the national movement, since the 1920s it has been incorporated into the Revolution at the federal level which for the most part has adopted a 'conservative' stance in promoting socio-economic and political change."[19]

Whereas Franz merely adds his voice to the extensive North American literature in support of the Institutionalized Revolution and its party, the PRI—a venerable literature that Eugenia Meyer has labeled the United States' *historiografía mexicanista*—Chacón represents a transitional stage in the evolution of revolutionary historiography.[20] Without issuing a sweeping condemnation of the Mexican Revolution, he challenges the official view on specific points by focusing on a particular leader and his administration and cautiously basing his judgments on previously untapped regional archival materials.[21] Conspicuously missing from Chacón's conceptual framework is a larger understanding of *why* the Mexican Revolution ultimately assumed a conservative posture, and how the regional and national bourgeoisie were able to withstand the revolutionary drive and eventually penetrate the new institutionalized regime. Instead of analyzing the social forces and class tensions that both promoted and set parameters on the effectiveness of the revolutionary process over which Alvarado presided, Chacón occasionally verges upon an explanation of events that suggests Carlyle's "great man" thesis. To be sure, Alvarado was a powerful, talented, and highly ambitious caudillo. Yet more systematic attention to objective conditions, particularly the limiting variables of Yucatán's political economy, would have ensured a more realistic and subtle portrayal of the social experiment of this admittedly unusual and compelling chief.[22]

Other scholars of the period have gone beyond Chacón's cautious indictment of the Revolution in Yucatán. In fact, the work of sociologists Francisco Paoli and Enrique Montalvo; anthropologists Nathaniel Raymond, Marie-France Labrecque, and Laura Batt; historian Gilbert Joseph; and political scientist Margaret Goodman contributes a frontal assault on the pro-Revolutionary interpretation.[23] Working in the climate of escalating doubt and cynicism that has accompanied Mexico's mounting political and economic difficulties since the late 1960s, these "revisionists" have repudiated the once-vaunted "Mexican Revolutionary model" of progress toward national integration, political stability, and economic development.

Of course, these Yucatecan studies are part of a larger interpretative trend. Revisionist scholarship on the Mexican Revolution now encompasses a diverse and distinguished body of Mexican and international social scientists. And while it lacks a clearly marked theoretical position, with some writers critiquing the Revolutionary model from a Marxist perspective and others from a "traditionalist" stance, underlying this ideological diversity is a broad consensus regarding the fundamental nature of the epic revolution (1910–17) and its institutionalized aftermath.[24]

First of all, revisionists emphasize the essential continuity between the Old Regime and the Revolutionary Regime. Rather than viewing the epic revolution as a sharp break with a neofeudal past, as the pro-Revolutionary school holds, the new scholarship regards it more as a temporary interruption in the extended process of political centralization and capitalist development that was inaugurated during the Porfiriato, if not earlier. Viewed in this light, the traditional periodization of modern Mexican history demands reassessment. For the revisionists, far more significant than the political revolt against Díaz and his clique in 1910 is the rise of a native bourgeoisie in the 1870s. The Mexican Revolution merely permitted this incipient group to strengthen its position, achieving true hegemony following the revolutionary Thermidor. Indeed, the old Porfirians would have applauded the triumph of these latter-day *científicos*.[25] Some revisionists argue for a more chronologically and regionally specific application of the term *revolution,* since the term does not faithfully correspond to the reality lived by most Mexicans in the decades following 1910.[26]

Equally controversial, revisionist scholarship calls into question the "popular" character of the armed struggle itself. In place of the traditional notion of a series of autonomous, locally initiated campesino movements operating throughout the republic during the first decade, the revisionists contend that rather early on "hegemony [was] exercised by bourgeois groupings over most of the revolutionary coalitions."[27] Indeed, "the bitter central truth of the Mexican revolution for the revisionists is that, more often than not, the revolution constituted an aggression *against* the great majority of the Mexican people."[28]

Whether they argue from a Marxist or a traditionalist viewpoint, revisionist scholars agree that by and large the Revolution was a political movement that brought with it only incidental social reforms, which have not significantly altered glaring structural inequities in Mexican society. Following the triumph of the dominant Constitutionalist faction in 1915, the new revolutionary state evolved into a "modern leviathan," systematically incorporating opposing regional leaders and movements, subduing by violence those that refused to be co-opted. Since the goal of the leaders of this new state was capitalist development along North American lines, the social reforms that were implemented were calculated to enlist the support of the masses (or at least their acquiescence) to that end. "The

genius of the leadership, culminating with Cárdenas, lay in its success at becoming the champion both of the bourgeoisie on the one
hand and the workers and *campesinos* on the other, and then organizing the latter into corporate groups, isolated and dependent upon
a paternalistic state."[29] In the process, the revisionists maintain, the
revolutionary state gained a degree of control over its international
affairs but condemned Mexico to an intensified dependence on the
North American economy by embracing the Western capitalist
model. All in all, revisionist scholarship judges the Mexican Revolution to be part of a new stage in an old process: the development of
capitalism. The traditionalists among them add bitterly that the only
thing "revolutionary" about the Revolution was its ruthless attempt
to seal the fate of the Old Mexico, which was Catholic and rooted in
viable agrarian communities.

The revisionists have unquestionably assumed the offensive in the
historiographical debate. In fact, according to one recent survey, "we
are rapidly reaching a point where it can be said 'we are all revisionists now.' "[30] Where Yucatán is concerned, the impact of recent revisionist scholarship has been, on the one hand, to strengthen the view
that the region experienced a "different revolution"—slower to arrive, less destructive, and probably more radical in its first decade
in the peninsula than it was elsewhere in Mexico. On the other hand,
these studies contend that in a more fundamental way, the
Yucatecan case bears out the revisionist verdict on the national process: a revolution made from above and imposed from without, "a
revolution initiated, controlled and consummated by bourgeois
leadership."[31]

While revisionist scholarship has served to cast great doubt on the
popular character of the Mexican Revolution, to date the literature
has been less successful in documenting *how* the formidable structures of dependent capitalism affected regional Porfirian society, im-
peding mobilization and setting limits on the effectiveness of later
revolutionary process. In the case of Yucatán, an economy characterized by monoculture tied to an international market virtually
controlled by a single North American buyer, the equation of dependence is particularly stark. At the same time, the larger process,

wherein foreign interests penetrated the Mexican economy, collaborating with local elites and regional and national regimes (prerevolutionary and revolutionary alike), initially to maintain the Porfirian peace and ultimately to thwart the revolutionary drive, would seem to reflect the history of much of Mexico since the last quarter of the nineteenth century and rate high on the list of priorities for further empirical study.[32]

The Problem of Mobilization under the Old Regime

The new historical literature has shown that it was no accident that the Mexican Revolution took five years to reach Yucatán. Even before the outbreak of Francisco Madero's national revolt in November 1910, the peninsula's geographical isolation made it difficult for prospective local revolutionaries to obtain news of the movement's progress in the rest of the republic. More compelling, however, was the deep-seated reluctance of the region's rulers to join the revolutionary tide. In fact, as late as 1915, the southeastern portion of Mexico—and Yucatán in particular—revealed itself to be virtually free from revolutionary activity. For in Yucatán, the Porfirian system of oligarchical rule, repression and exploitation of the Mayan masses, had gained an extended lease on life.

Our survey of the recent studies of late Porfirian monoculture revealed a society in which a few hundred planters presided over substantially capitalized, technologically modern henequen estates which nevertheless drew their profitability from a brutal system of debt peonage, likened to outright slavery by Turner and other contemporary observers. This de facto slave system, though blatantly unconstitutional, existed right up until the invasion of the region by Constitutionalist general Salvador Alvarado in 1915. In addition, Yucatán's agrocommercial bourgeoisie constructed a multitiered repressive mechanism which commanded the respect and envy of their counterparts elsewhere in the republic and insulated them against any immediate threats to their power. Porfirio Díaz's defeat by Madero and the disbanding of the notorious *rurales* (the federal rural constabulary) at the national level in 1911 had little effect on

Yucatán, where the local planters generally maintained their own police forces, detectives, and bounty hunters.

Historians Friedrich Katz, Allen Wells, and Gilbert Joseph have emphasized that Yucatán's failure to join the Revolution in 1910 strongly reaffirms that severe oppression of rural masses does not, in itself, lead to spontaneous popular movements.[33] They concur that, by 1900, the amount of the worker's debt was likely irrelevant, and campesinos were probably bought and sold, their value being determined by fluctuations in the henequen market. The failure of workers to fulfill the assignment of individual tasks resulted in monetary fines and flogging. Where discipline was concerned, the planters' attitude was expressed in a crude, turn-of-the-century aphorism: "The Indians only hear with their backsides." Nevertheless, by 1910 the strong Maya tradition of peasant protest had been eroded, along with the peasant community itself. The Caste War and the henequen boom which followed revolutionized Yucatán demographically and geographically, uprooting Indian communities and rearranging traditional settlement patterns and labor systems. By the turn of the century, the great majority of free Maya pueblos had lost their land base. Those that continued to survive lacked the stability to resist that characterized the deep-rooted Zapatista pueblos of the central plateau and the free villagers of Michoacán or central Veracruz, who would form the backbone of strong peasant leagues in the 1920s.[34] Unable to hold off the expanding henequen plantations, Yucatán's campesinos were first enslaved by the plantations and then isolated on them. Hacendados made sure, for example, to separate local Maya workers from the rebel Maya prisoners taken on the Quintana Roo frontier and to discourage the build-up of great numbers of Yaqui deportees in a single area.[35]

Thus, according to these historians, a major power-shift in favor of the campesinos—the kind that General Alvarado's invasion could provide—was required merely to gain access to them for the purpose of mobilization. Wells documents that the episodes of social unrest which did exist in the *campo* prior to 1915 were not campesino rebellions or even jacqueries, but rather more diffuse incidents of social banditry and isolated episodes of protest, usually against local jefes políticos and hacienda administrators.[36] The overwhelming police power at the planters' disposal not only ensured against the success of such rebellions but, along with the plantation's regime of corporal punishment, provided the best kind of deterrent to them.

Moreover, not only did the campesinos have virtually no contact with their fellows on different estates, but also they were isolated from potential allies in the urban areas. Whenever possible, city visitors and peddlers were kept off the estates. Unlike Veracruz and Tlaxcala, where links between the urban and rural working classes developed early and membership in each sector often overlapped, Yucatán's urban and rural workers rarely interacted, let alone made common cause.[37] Whereas the campesinado remained immobilized, a small but determined urban labor movement had managed to establish itself by 1915 and would later gain recognition and patronage as the price for its co-optation by General Alvarado's populist regime.[38]

In addition to the involuted condition of the campesinado, for Yucatán as a whole the "revolutionary equation" was substantially skewed. Yucatecan society during the Porfiriato had much in common in its social organization with the colonial plantation-and-slave societies of an earlier period of Latin American history. An enormous chasm separated the two extremes on the social scale: the tiny minority of planters and the great majority of "slaves" (peones). The urban working class, though at times well organized politically, was limited in its growth by the insignificant level of industrialization in the region, due to the persistence of monocrop agriculture and the failure of an internal market. Joseph and others have estimated that prerevolutionary Yucatán possessed a very small "middle class"— small even by the Latin American standards of the time: 3 to 5 percent of the population. This middle sector consisted mostly of intellectuals, professionals, small merchants, and small rural producers, most of whom served the elite and appropriated, or at least aspired to, its social outlook. Nevertheless, an increasingly vocal minority felt pinched by a lack of opportunity in the society; for the stifling atmosphere of large-scale plantation agriculture left little room for any other major activity. Anything not connected to significant commercial production of henequen for export was relegated to secondary status.[39]

Joseph pays particular attention to the rural petty-bourgeoisie. A diverse constellation of small henequen and food producers, it found itself without political influence, vulnerable to discrimination by the existing tax structure, powerless to secure reasonable freight rates or regular rail service for its goods, and unable to acquire additional land by denouncing the untitled property of Indian villages (*terrenos baldíos*), as the larger planters did. In fact, where land was concerned, the probability was that these increasingly impoverished small henequen producers, like the even smaller *parcelarios* (rich campesinos who, in addition to growing corn and beans, harvested small plots of henequen), would become indebted to the collaborationist oligarchy of Molina and Montes and lose the land they currently had, rather than increase their holdings. Many of these smaller producers and *rancheros* (plot holders) usually lived in the pockets of the larger estates, and often eventually became their clients or tenants, or worse still, lost all and succumbed as indebted acasillados. Joseph contends that it was often from this déclassé rural petty-bourgeoisie that social bandits and rural caciques came, actors who would greatly affect the course of Yucatán's revolutionary experience in later years.[40]

We will need a more detailed mapping of the late Porfirian agrarian structure, particularly on the fringes of the henequen zone and beyond it, before we can truly reconstruct local political fabrics and speak with greater authority about patterns of social unrest and political alignment during the seemingly chaotic 1910–15 period following the revolt against Díaz's national regime. Nevertheless, recent contributions permit some larger observations.[41] Apart from the more isolated episodes of violent campesino protest that began during the late Porfiriato and came in response to specific local abuses, much of the political flurry after 1910 represented unsuccessful attempts by a variety of middle-sector formations to challenge the dominance of the traditional oligarchy. Rather fluid coalitions that brought together professionals and intellectuals, petty merchants, artisans, rural schoolteachers, and rancheros, these so-called Morenista and Pinista factions were often joined and financed by more affluent planters outside Molina's casta divina.[42] They plotted and demonstrated, came together and broke apart, formed parties and ran candidates in elections, and occasionally took up arms and mobilized peones against the state authorities when these elections were rigged or their candidates were harassed (e.g., the Valladolid rebellion, in June 1910). The catalyst for such legal and extralegal maneuvering was Francisco Madero's national presidential campaign. Indeed, but for the limited opening provided at the national level by Díaz in 1908–9, the development of even this rather moderate opposition in regional politics might have been greatly delayed.

Yet even after the overthrow of Don Porfirio's dictatorship, these Maderista-inspired políticos had little impact on local society. The evidence suggests that in a variety of cases they were themselves co-opted by the Molinista oligarchy. Meanwhile, the Molinistas had little difficulty passing themselves off as Maderistas when the circumstances warranted, and then, just as conveniently, declaring themselves Huertistas following Madero's assassination. Moreover, if Laura Batt's local study of Espita provides any indication, the casta divina successfully maintained the allegiance of its clients prior to 1915. The lesser hacendados and urban functionaries opted to support Molina's candidates against their moderate opponents and later endorsed the separatist Ortiz Argumedo revolt, which the oligarchy bankrolled in a last, short-lived effort to resist the arrival of the Mexican Revolution in 1915.[43]

Revolutionary Mobilization from Above

In 1923, Mexico's secretary of the interior, Plutarco Elías Calles, advised the young North American journalist Ernest Gruening that "if you wish to understand the Mexican Revolution, do not fail to visit Yucatán."[44] Like other high officials in the Obregón regime, Calles recognized that although Yucatán was a thousand miles away from the seat of national power and still really only accessible by sea, it had become a novel laboratory for social change. In fact, during the administration of Marxist governor Felipe Carrillo Puerto (1920–24), middle-class revolutionary cadres, recruiting urban workers, dispossessed villagers, and some resident peones, introduced what was perhaps the most radical social movement in Mexico and tested innovative reform strategies in the areas of land, labor, education, and women's rights. These social experiments, however, became possible only after General Alvarado's 8,000-man Constitutionalist Army of the Southeast had almost bloodlessly curbed much of the political and repressive power of the Old Regime and laid the foundations with more moderate reform measures during the 1915–18 period. Even in Alvarado's wake, a popular groundswell was slow to emerge. In large part, recent revisionist studies regard this limited popular mobilization to be a function of Yucatán's characteristic agrarian structure, conditioned by the region's monocrop economy. Yet they also view it as the product of Alvarado's—and President Carranza's—circumscribed bourgeois revolution "from above."

Friedrich Katz has perceptively compared the mobilization strategy of Mexico's nascent revolutionary state during the 1916–28 period to that of the Directory in the post-Jacobin era of the French Revolution. Like their French counterpart, the Carranza, Obregón, and Calles regimes attempted "to play off the left and right against each other": "When pressure from the United States, from dissident army groups, and from the hacendados became too strong, it [the Mexican Government] began mobilizing popular support and carrying out some reforms. When the popular organizations got out of hand, it called back the army and the hacendados to fight them. This policy made it necessary for the government to set up peasant [and worker] organizations but at the same time to firmly control them."[45]

Recent studies of Alvarado's caudillo rule, particularly those by Montalvo and Paoli, Joseph, González Rodríguez, González Padilla, Boils Morales, and Richmond, illustrate the successful application by the state of this "populist" strategy to Yucatán.[46] In 1915, the Constitutionalists established Mexico's first significant peasant and worker leagues (ligas de resistencia) in Yucatán. Preoccupied with costly national campaigns against the Villistas and Zapatistas, and threatened within the region by a disgruntled oligarchy backed by long-standing North American allies (International Harvester and the cordage interests), the Constitutionalists seized upon a limited mobilization of peasants and workers as a way of guaranteeing henequen revenues and gaining popular support without carrying out the kind of large-scale structural reforms (i.e., an expropriation of plantations and businesses) which they ideologically opposed. And Yucatán was eminently suited to the nationalist, bourgeois-reformist strategy of the Constitutionalists. Here was a region whose dependent economy not only provided the federal government with large receipts from henequen sales to the United States but also perpetuated a system of peonage/slavery that made it possible to win over the work force without having to give it land. It would suffice, at least temporarily, to free Yucatán's semiproletarian campesinado from its coerced labor and, simultaneously, to organize it around such bread-and-butter issues as wages and hours. In central Mexico, such a strategy of mobilization would have made little headway among the Zapatista villagers, who were fighting to regain their lands and protect a traditional way of life. In fact, prior to 1920 no serious efforts were made to mobilize campesinos outside of Yucatán, since the Carranza regime was firmly opposed to the kind of thoroughgoing reform of the agrarian structure that such a strategy was likely to entail.

Thus, the revisionist writers contend, it is not surprising that General Alvarado, a bourgeois revolutionary and Carranza's delegate in Yucatán, differed sharply from his Marxist successor, civilian governor Felipe Carrillo Puerto, in the role he assigned to the Yucatecan masses in the revolutionary process.[47] The general favored urban labor unions and rural peasant leagues as a means of giving laborers a stake in the political process. However, Alvarado's political mobilization, whether in the city or the countryside, always served an authority-legitimizing rather than an interest-articulating function. Alvarado was reluctant to let the masses actively participate, let alone rule, once they were brought into the political process. Carrillo Puerto, on the other hand, began his career as an agrarian agitator, politicizing the campesinos and encouraging them to accept responsibility for their own political destiny.[48] Significantly, Anna Macías's recent study of the Mexican women's movement reveals that although both leaders championed feminism, Alvarado's *ligas feminiles* (feminine leagues) were based exclusively upon middle- and upper-class women. By contrast, Carrillo Puerto's

PSS targeted poor campesinas in the recruitment of its *ligas feministas* (feminist leagues).[49]

Joseph emphasizes that while Alvarado had cultivated the small urban proletariat as his chief civilian ally, raising wages and improving conditions, yet denying the right to strike, Carrillo Puerto displayed little interest (and some hostility) toward the longshoremen, railroad workers, and electricians who made up Yucatán's "labor aristocracy." He realized that Yucatán was overwhelmingly an agricultural region and reasoned that it would be the campesinos in the agrarian sector who would provide his PSS with the base of power it needed to wage a socialist revolution from above. To that end, he had demonstrated from his earliest days as an agrarian leader that land was the focal point of his social vision. Whereas Alvarado had been prepared to initiate only a limited agrarian reform, under Carrillo Puerto's leadership the pace of agrarian reform accelerated to the point that Yucatán had distributed more land than any other state, save perhaps Zapata's Morelos.[50] By the time of his death in 1924, Carrillo Puerto had made sure that virtually every one of the state's major pueblos had received at least a basic ejidal grant. His regime and life were snuffed out just at the moment he seemed ready to initiate a more sweeping agrarian reform, one which would have expropriated the region's henequen plantations and turned them into collective farms owned and operated by the workers who traditionally manned them.[51]

Under Carrillo Puerto the Mexican Revolution in Yucatán became a regional or Yucatecan movement. His use of locally trained cadres of agrarian agitators and activist schoolteachers, and his network of alliances with local power brokers (caciques)—to be discussed presently—stand in some contrast to Alvarado's greater reliance upon imported intellectuals and his own military commandants, who were, in the majority of cases, *norteños* like himself. Moreover, Carrillo Puerto reinforced the regional character of his revolution in a variety of symbolic ways, most of which sought to wean the Yucatecan campesino away from the institutions and passive attitudes of the Old Regime and to develop within him a sense of ethnic pride as a prelude to class consciousness. For example, Socialist leaders were instructed to paint all church buildings red, the equilateral triangle (the logo of the PSS) replaced the cross, and "Socialist marriages and baptisms"—complete with red floral arrangements and orchestrations of "The International"—superseded the traditional Catholic versions of these sacraments. More conventionally, the speaking of Maya and the teaching of Maya culture and art forms were encouraged, and every effort was made to recall the great revolutionary tradition of protest to which the campesinos were heir.[52]

In fact, perhaps the broader area of education provides the clearest illustration of the different ideological orientations of Yucatán's two early revolutionary chiefs and their regimes. According to Mary Kay Vaughan, the leading student of educational issues during the Mexican Revolution, Alvarado, like other essentially bourgeois educators, was most concerned with transforming the servile peón into a mobile and productive worker. Carrillo Puerto, on the other hand, linked the educational process with the Marxist notion of class struggle. It was not enough to transform the campesino from a social outcast into a free worker who would accommodate himself to bourgeois society. Rather, collectively, the workers would struggle to transform the society itself, and the revolutionary school would play an instrumental role in this process. Under Carrillo Puerto the Socialists not only continued Alvarado's school-building campaign in the countryside but introduced the concept of the "rational school." Such a school would abolish all rewards and punishments, examinations, diplomas, and titles, and would emphasize knowledge that could be acquired from manual work in the field or factory. The goal, according to the PSS, was to create a "true socialist school . . . to nourish the masses," an institution that would train "men and women apt for life and liberated from all dogmas." The PSS's "rational school" provided a glimpse of the class-oriented pedagogy that would later emerge at the national level under Cárdenas, with the introduction of the *escuela socialista* (socialist school) during the 1933–38 period.[53]

There is broad consensus in the literature that although the first crucial decade of the Revolution in Yucatán established institutional precedents for social change and revealed the potential for radical reform, it did not restructure society or significantly transform the region's dependent economy. The collaborator mechanism was dismantled and, beginning with the Alvarado regime, the state increasingly expanded its control over the henequen industry, establishing an exclusive government monopoly (the Comisión Reguladora del Mercado de Henequén) that bought fiber from the Yucatecan producers and sold it directly to the North American manufacturers. Yet, except for a brief period during World War I when demand was artificially high, Yucatán was unable to alter structurally the terms of its unequal relationship vis-à-vis the U.S. corporations that consumed its exports. The two early revolutionary leaders were either not inclined (Alvarado) or unable (Carrillo Puerto) to expropriate the henequen plantations on behalf of the campesinos. They were therefore unable to transform the structure of agrarian production and the nature of Yucatecan society. Despite his unpopularity with a large segment of the planter class, Alvarado presided over a period of great hacendado enrichment during the final boom years of World War I. For all of his threats, Marxist governor Carrillo Puerto had to contend with severely depressed postwar fiber prices and never had the time prior to his fall to carry out the sweeping agrarian expropriation he had promised. Because the core unit of the region's agrarian structure remained the henequen plantation, it is difficult to argue with Moisés González Navarro's assessment that Alvarado and Carrillo Puerto were merely "the two great *precursors* of the Yucatecan agrarian revolution."[54] That revolution, yucatecólogos concur, came later, during the Cárdenas years.

Given the unfinished nature of the early revolution in the countryside, what impact, if any, did Alvaradista and Carrillista reforms have on the relations of production on estates and on rural life in general? The regional-level studies by González Navarro, Chacón, Joseph, and Paoli and Montalvo suggest that a significant impact was registered. Alvarado gave legal standing to an earlier, near-moribund decree "freeing the slaves," and Carrillo Puerto made sure that these changes were carried out in practice and that the former peón found himself embarked on the road to becoming a class-conscious, unionized agricultural worker. Labor abuses on hacien-

das would continue to be reported in later years, especially following Carrillo Puerto's death in 1924. Moreover, the process whereby
the peones acasillados were systematically mobilized would really
occur only under Cárdenas in the last years of the 1930s. Yet these
writers conclude that during Yucatán's first revolutionary decade a
definite beginning had been made. Alvarado established the precedent of "retroactive revolution," the realization in the minds of
campesinos as well as urban workers that injustices suffered years
before might now be redressed. Carrillo Puerto continued and expanded this notion, providing the rural worker with the protection
and reinforcement he had lacked under the Alvarado regime. The
fact that from 1920 to 1923 many more Maya workers took their
grievances before Socialist magistrates in Mérida and other regional
centers speaks well for the campaign by Carrillo Puerto's PSS to
instill ethnic and class pride in the campesinado.[55]

Nevertheless, our knowledge of the first decade lacks the kind of
depth that would enable us to gauge the differential impact of these
reforms in the various subregions of Yucatán. What consequences
did the peones' liberation and subsequent agrarian reform have for
local labor supply and patterns of investment and production? Did
the responses of campesinos and hacendados vary from the henequen to the maize zones? Did the new socialist education centered
on "rational schools" and a new socialist iconography really transform attitudes in the campo? Or did they only serve to confuse or
anger large numbers of traditionally devout campesinos?[56] These
are merely some of the questions that recent studies have raised,
which must now be investigated at the local level by social historians
and anthropologists.

Batt's in-depth study of the municipio of Espita is particularly
successful in exploring the local impact of revolutionary reforms on
land tenure and production.[57] By and large, Alvarado's "bourgeois
revolution" came and went, and local hacendados continued to control the *ayuntamiento* (town council) and to hold onto their estates
and businesses. In fact, several planters allied with the Molina
oligarchy actually expanded their haciendas under the Alvarado regime. Leading members of the espiteño bourgeoisie never embraced
the general's campaign to destory the collaborator mechanism and

liberate the economy for autonomous, nationalist-oriented growth, even though, as relatively small planters, they stood to benefit from his trust-busting measures. The politics of expediency demanded that they comply with Alvarado's directives and that some take positions in his administration. Still, whenever possible, they organized themselves behind the Liberal Party, which first sought to undercut the Alvarado government and later plotted to oust Carrillo Puerto's PSS. According to Batt, local hacendados feared that Alvarado's liberation of the peones would wreak havoc on their traditional system of production, aggravating the current labor shortage and reducing profit margins by depriving them of their traditional privilege of paying low wages and demanding unpaid services (fajina).

Through a series of oral history interviews with former peones, Batt found that the campesinos' response to liberation varied, depending on previous relations with the patrón and his ability to offer wages and benefits sufficient to keep them on the hacienda. She found no evidence that espiteño hacendados were able to coerce peones to stay on. Some campesinos continued to cultivate land on the estate through rental and sharecropping arrangements with their former patrones. However, most of Espita's peones (72.3 percent) "came down" (bajaron) from the haciendas between 1910 and 1921, resettling in and around the municipal seat and forcing hacendados to look to other strategies for securing labor. Alvarado's "Immigration Department," established to alleviate the labor shortage, brought more than 21,000 contract workers into the state between 1916 and 1918, some of whom found their way to Espita. Other planters privately recruited tabasqueño workers. Yet contract labor was expensive and only the largest local planters could afford it. To adjust to the reduction in resident workers, some hacendados ceased cultivating maize and focused exclusively on henequen and sugar. As a result, Espita, which had formerly supplied corn to Mérida, now produced only for local consumption. On the whole, Batt found that while profits were reduced for some proprietors, most local planters were able to withstand the impact of liberation because they now cultivated henequen, and owing to wartime demand and the elimination of the collaborator mechanism, prices had never been better. Batt's findings for marginal Espita largely confirm the data which Chacón and Joseph collected for the henequen zone, although the incidence of labor flight seems to increase as one moves farther away from the heart of the henequen zone, where social control was most pronounced.

The situation in Espita changed dramatically as the Revolution moved to the left under Carrillo Puerto. The generally negative response of local planters toward the revolutionary government hardened as the PSS consolidated its organizational network and cacique violence against Liberal Party supporters intensified. Espita's freed peones gained strength through the local PSS resistance league and applied for a communal land grant (*ejido*) under the new agrarian reform law. Formed in 1921 from land expropriated primarily from the estates of Molinista oligarchs and their espiteño allies, the ejido would provide a subsistence agricultural base for the former peones and safeguard their independence from their former patrones. (Sadly, by 1930, the failure of the government to provide financial and technical assistance had already dimmed the *ejidatarios'* future prospects.) On the other hand, agrarian reform would prove the undoing of the great estate in Espita. With the formation of the ejido, labor supply was suddenly dictated by the priorities of the campesinos rather than those of the hacendados. Moreover, the increased taxes on henequen production decreed by the Socialist government cut heavily into planters' profit margins. By 1930, all but several of the municipio's haciendas had ceased to function.

The early demise of the network of estates in Espita would appear to be atypical. In only a handful of other localities did such a large number of former peones organize themselves to form an ejido. The bulk of agrarian reform in Yucatán did not occur until the 1937 Cardenista reform. Up until that time, the majority of planters in the henequen zone had avoided expropriation largely by making the case that their agroindustrial units were indispensable to the stability of an ailing regional economy. Batt argues that such was not the case for the smaller, less productive henequen and sugar producers in the east. They became expendable when Carrillo Puerto's political goal of building mass support in the countryside outweighed economic considerations. Nevertheless, by carefully tracing the fortunes of Espita's leading families, Batt finds that although the local base of the bourgeoisie was undermined, many planters took their capital to Mérida, where they and their sons pursued business and professional careers and assumed positions in the burgeoning state bureaucracy.

Given its significant efforts in behalf of the campesinado in Espita and throughout the state, why was Carrillo Puerto's Yucatecan revolution defeated so quickly and easily during the de la Huerta rebellion in the final weeks of 1923? Carrillo Puerto's demise remains a furious controversy in local historiography. Sixty years later, the events surrounding his defeat and death continue to preoccupy the peninsula's historians and literati, whose writings fill countless volumes and articles in Yucatán and Mexico.[58] Some traditional authors have incorrectly emphasized Carrillo Puerto's reluctance to shed the campesino's blood in a direct confrontation with the insurgent federals, for, indeed, he did mobilize the ligas de resistencia for combat at the eleventh hour.[59] Other writers have put forward the fantastic notion that Carrillo Puerto was consumed by his passion for the North American journalist Alma Reed and gave up any prospects for a fight with the Delahuertistas in order to flee to the side of his lover.[60] Still others have argued, more plausibly, that his defeat and death were bought by the large henequen planters who were the targets and most bitter opponents of his agrarian reform program.[61] Still, even assuming that the hacendados were implicated in Carrillo Puerto's fall, it is difficult to explain the suddenness of the defeat that the rebels inflicted upon the Socialists, especially in light of the fact that the PSS enjoyed the support of the much-heralded resistance leagues, which supposedly were ready to provide Carrillo Puerto with "seventy thousand strong."

Gilbert Joseph presents a new interpretation of the defeat of Carrillo and the PSS. He argues that existing accounts of Carrillo's demise have omitted a sober analysis of the political alignment the Marxist caudillo had constructed to gain and maintain power within the region.[62] The Socialists' revolutionary coalition was a fragile one at best. Whereas the Alvarado regime combined civilian rule with the military power of the Army of the Southeast, Carrillo Puerto's government was based solely upon civilian authority. In the absence of federal military support, it was potentially vulnerable to attack from within and without. Moreover, Carrillo Puerto's Socialist coalition had suffered mass defections by many influential members of the bourgeoisie who had formerly been recruited by the more moderate Alvarado but now feared and opposed the Marxist chief's regime. Carrillo Puerto's PSS was led by members of the petty bourgeoisie and urban working class who had become disaffected with the Old Regime. The party drew its support in part from the small urban labor movement (never particularly enthusiastic about Carrillo Puerto, given his preference for the campesinado) but mostly from the rural masses. An effective mobilization of the countryside, however, had been impeded by a poor communications network, the military opposition of Carranza's conservative central government in the wake of Alvarado's removal from the peninsula (1919–20), and a severe economic depression (1920–22). Consequently, Carrillo Puerto had been forced to rely on existing power brokers and local rural bosses for support.

As well as Joseph can determine, most of these caciques came from a petty-bourgeois background (e.g., hacienda *mayordomo,* ranchero, artisan) and had established their power domains (*cacicazgos*) either during the first sporadic revolts surrounding the Madero rebellion (1909–11) or, more commonly, following Alvarado's occupation of Yucatán in 1915. The general had shattered the repressive mechanism of the landed bourgeoisie by eliminating the hated jefes políticos and disbanding the detachments of rurales and the private forces of individual hacendados. Rather than destroying the institutions and networks of social control themselves, Joseph contends that the Revolution merely substituted "new men" for old.[63]

This recognition of the importance of cacique politics to the Yucatecan revolutionary process suggests a demythologizing of Felipe Carrillo Puerto and his regime. Local writers of the pro-Revolutionary school have invoked notions of charismatic authority to suggest that Carrillo Puerto forged a powerful popular movement in Yucatán. Within the contours of the regional myth, which has received official sanction from the PRI, Carrillo Puerto has been viewed as a martyr, a secular saint of the proletariat, Yucatán's

Abraham Lincoln or Mahatma Gandhi, and, more recently, as the
Mexican Allende.[64] In fact, he was a shrewd and pragmatic political
leader, astute enough to realize that without sufficient guns and
ammunition, and in the absence of.a widespread grass-roots mobilization, which would take time to carry out, he would have to bestow
patronage upon local strongmen in order to keep his Socialist regime
in power.

Carrillo Puerto's demise must also be interpreted in this revisionist light, for under the pressure of the Delahuertista rising, caciques
proved to be unreliable clients, deserting their patron in many
cases. Moreover, the resistance leagues—the fabled "seventy thousand strong"—were found to be "paper tigers," organizations with
highly inflated membership lists that were nominally kept behind
the governor by the local bosses. Although such a political alignment
was well suited to maintaining control against internal threats because it possessed a virtual monopoly of force within the region, it
remained vulnerable to swift attack from without by a powerful,
well-equipped force of federal troops—precisely what occurred during the de la Huerta insurgency in December 1923.

In their prize-winning book-length essay, *El socialismo olvidado
de Yucatán,* sociologists Francisco Paoli and Enrique Montalvo
reach rather different conclusions about the character of Carrillo
Puerto's regime. While they do not enter into the kind of cult of
personality that mars traditional interpretations of Yucatecan so-
cialism, they do argue that under Carrillo Puerto the PSS created a
truly "popular" (as opposed to "populist") government. Indeed, the
party might even have engineered the transition to socialist relations
of production in Yucatán, had it been given a fighting chance. Theoretically, the authors shed light on the limits of populism in Latin
America and provide an acute dialectical analysis of the conditions
that might lead to either a socialist road or a military coup in the
aftermath of populism.[65]

Nevertheless, they are not particularly successful in applying
their theoretical framework to the case at hand. The formal political
machinery of the PSS—the local ligas de resistencia that fed into a
liga central—is examined at some length; yet, perhaps owing to a
lack of archival research, no notice is taken of the informal network

of power brokers which also played a crucial role in the revolutionary process. Surprisingly, Paoli and Montalvo never really address the central question generated by their own analysis of the party: if the PSS was truly a popular regime that was making a socialist revolution at society's base, why did it not fight more tenaciously at the end? In fact, the authors devote but one short paragraph to the problem, observing that the Delahuertistas, financed by the local bourgeoisie, seized a rare opportunity to pluck Carrillo Puerto from power, liquidate the Socialist leadership, and thereby deprive the PSS of its historic opportunity.[66] Thus, while these Marxist scholars have given us a provocative macrosociological approach to questions of the state and society in Latin America, social historians may well concur with Barry Carr's recent assessment that, at the empirical level, their work "appears somehow to have passed over those detailed layers of traditional experience that only painstaking historical analysis seems able to reveal."[67]

On another level, *El socialismo olvidado* testifies to the vitality with which a younger generation of Mexican scholars on the Left is struggling to recover and reformulate the history of the Mexican Revolution. Paoli and Montalvo seek in Yucatán's revolutionary past lessons that might provide a coherent basis for political action in the present. In the process they have attempted to rescue Felipe Carrillo Puerto and the PSS from the official mythmakers in Mexico City and Mérida and give them back to the pueblo.[68]

In the collapse of Carrillo Puerto's Yucatecan socialist revolution and in its aftermath, revisionists have found important implications for the larger problems of regionalism and mobilization in the Mexican Revolution. Labor historian Barry Carr points out that Carrillo Puerto's impressive socialist edifice, which dazzled contemporary observers as well as many modern students with its seeming ability to engage every facet of regional life, was clearly imposed from above and entailed only a limited participation by the region's masses. In its extreme fragility as well as its reliance upon hierarchically arranged informal mechanisms of authority and control, Carrillo Puerto's PSS approximated a variety of other "mass" organizations which began to proliferate during the 1920s, most notably the nationally based urban CROM and the National Agrarian Party

(PNA). According to Carr, each of these "mass parties" ultimately depended for its continued survival upon the protection of the national state, directed by the new revolutionary bourgeoisie. Increasingly preoccupied with the consolidation of its hegemony, the state needed mass support and sought it by patronizing these organizations; yet it never permitted them to obtain a large measure of political initiative.[69]

Indeed, it may well have been on these grounds that, by late 1923, Mexico City found its former clients, Carrillo Puerto and the PSS, politically expendable. Joseph speculates that Obregón and Calles resented Carrillo Puerto's pretensions to become a national leader (and rival) and were ideologically at odds with the radical social program of the PSS. Middle rancheros, these Sonoran caudillos were never as conservative on land questions as their Coahuilan hacendado predecessors, Madero and Carranza. Nevertheless, it is unlikely that they would have sanctioned the sweeping expropriation of henequen plantations that Carrillo had been planning when the insurgency broke out. Furthermore, like Carranza, Obregón was subjected to intense U.S. diplomatic pressure on behalf of the cordage interests, and he seemed reluctant to offend the North Americans in the early 1920s in the wake of the Bucareli Conferences and formal recognition of the revolutionary regime.[70]

In fact, some Yucatecan writers have charged, in a more conspiratorial vein, that Obregón effectively abandoned Carrillo Puerto during the de la Huerta revolt: first by denying him crucial ammunition and troop reinforcements, then by refusing to ransom his loyal governor from the rebels.[71] Whether or not the charge is true, recent studies have shown that during this time the incipient Sonoran dynasty deemed it essential for the promotion of national unity and the forging of a modern state to undermine the independent power of regional chiefs like Carrillo Puerto. Even had he survived the 1924 crisis, it is unlikely that his attempts to build an authentic popular movement would have drawn the continued support of the national regime. Obregón's concerted purge of influential Carrillistas from positions of power within the PSS following the Yucatecan caudillo's death and his replacement of them with more malleable clients cannot be ignored. Nor can the national regime's subsequent hostility toward the similarly independent agrarian movements of Primo Tapia in Michoacán and Adalberto Tejeda in Veracruz be minimized.[72]

The historical literature on the late twenties and thirties falls off markedly; as yet there are no contributions comparable to the thoroughly researched monographs on the Alvarado and Carrillo Puerto regimes. Contemporary observers, like Mexican labor leader Vicente Lombardo Toledano, described a society in which only the outer trappings of Carrillo Puerto's "socialist" revolution—the red shirts, the radical slogans, the formal organization of the PSS—survived his death.[73] The traditional historiography provides little insight into the failure of a socialist road in Yucatán following the assassination of Carrillo Puerto because it concentrates almost exclusively on personalities and political groups rather than on underlying social and economic relationships. The decade of 1924–34 has been analyzed largely on an ad hominem basis: hard-core hagiography of Carrillo Puerto gives way to invectives against the political leaders who succeeded him, bartering his social ideals for the gold of the hacendado elite. Having proclaimed Carrillo Puerto a martyr, local historians have regarded the next decade as an empty interval, a time when the region slumbered—or drifted back into old repressive patterns—and waited for its next redeemer, Lázaro Cárdenas.[74]

It seems clear that the decade following Carrillo Puerto's fall witnessed a decline in the membership and organization of the resistance leagues, an intensification of local violence between rival caciques, a reconsolidation of the power of the peninsular bourgeoisie, the infiltration and weakening of the PSS by that class, and a sharp fall off in ejidal distributions, especially in the henequen zone. Although some of the governors and political leaders of these years were receptive to the bribes and blandishments of the bourgeoisie, as traditional accounts hold, the preliminary results of recent investigations suggest that this was not true of the entire Socialist Party leadership, nor was it the principal explanation for the political and economic prostration that Yucatán experienced during the decade.

Instead, social scientists highlight the severe constraints that larger economic and political structures placed upon a revolutionary party tied to a dependent monoculture.[75] For, with the exception of a brief period in the mid-1920s, the price of henequen continued to plummet on the international market, and foreign competition reduced Yucatán's former monopoly to a mere third of the market by the mid-1930s.[76] Even had the revolutionary drive of the earlier period continued, a short-fall in revenues would have made an extension of the costly reform programs of Alvarado and Carrillo Puerto virtually impossible. By the mid-1930s, the reassertion of a downward secular trend in the export economy rendered obsolete Carrillo Puerto's former plans for the socialization of the henequen plantations. According to González Navarro and Joseph, the campesinos had no capital and little inclination to assume the management and upkeep of fields that had been abandoned by the planters or remained only marginally productive. Faced once again with conditions of retrenchment, they turned their full attention to eking out subsistence wages in those fields still under production. Many vehemently protested against the proposal of an agrarian reform based upon the "collective ejido," the model then gaining ascendancy in the agrarian ministry of the Cárdenas administration in Mexico City. The new model called for the expropriation and breakup of existing estates and their rearrangement into a variety of new ejidal units that would be collectively cultivated. Although they objected to this new central Mexican agrarian formula, occasionally Yucatecan campesinos did petition the Agrarian Department for access to small plots on which they might grow corn and beans to supplement their dwindling wages.

When the agrarian revolution did come to Yucatán, it came from without. Although the history of Cardenismo in Yucatán remains to be written, social scientists have begun to reconstruct the turbulent sequence of events in the mid-1930s that led up to Cárdenas's massive expropriation in August 1937, as well as to evaluate its impact. Based on a sifting of contemporary accounts and correspondence between Yucatecan governors and members of the Cárdenas administration, Joseph documents that given the increasingly centralized nature of federal-state relations in the 1920s and 1930s, federal hegemony over the land reform process was inevitable. The opportunities for independent strategy and action enjoyed by Alvarado in 1915 and Carrillo Puerto, to a lesser extent, in 1922, were nonexistent in the late 1920s and early 1930s. By 1934, the once proud and autonomous Partido Socialista del Sureste existed only in name; in actual fact, it had become the errand boy of Cárdenas's increasingly omnicompetent PNR. And, whereas the evidence shows that Obregón and Calles were opposed to substantial agrarian reform in the henequen zone, Cárdenas, a sincere *agrarista* who was also mindful of the political capital to be gained at the national level, chose Yucatán precisely for the purpose of making it, along with the Laguna cotton-producing region, a showcase for his collective ejido program.[77] The spiraling urban and rural unrest in Yucatán, which some regarded to be a bona fide *lucha de clases* (class struggle) and was itself fanned by Cardenista agents and labor organizers, merely provided the federal government with a suitable pretext to attempt a restructuring of Yucatecan society.[78]

In implementing, in August 1937, the largest single episode of agrarian reform ever carried out in Mexico, President Cárdenas sought to turn over most of the henequen fields to the campesinos. Unfortunately, it quickly became apparent that many irregularities and contradictions were embedded in the hasty distribution process.[79] Although the planters had been promised their *cascos*—the nuclei of the plantations, which included the major buildings and machinery—in some instances, these were expropriated and distributed piecemeal to neighboring ejidos. In fact, despite Cárdenas's guidelines, some hacendados suffered total loss of their estates. At the other extreme, some planter families managed to preserve much more than the stipulated 300 hectares. Typically, several members of a single family would establish legal identity and succeed in retaining a much larger block of land. By the end of 1938 it was clear that a crazy quilt of tenure arrangements had emerged as a result of Cárdenas's reform. Once reasonably productive enterprises, most plantations were now carved up in a manner that suggested the absence of rational criteria in the planning and execution of the reform. Rarely did individual ejidos receive the appropriate number of henequen plants at each stage of maturity, which they would require to maintain continuity of production. Instances were also reported in which urbanites from Mérida and Progreso had been included on the rolls of nearby ejidos, whereas many eligible campesinos in the area had been completely excluded.

Moreover, although under the terms of the new reform the campesinos had theoretically become the owners of the land they collectively cultivated, in practice the system worked to give them little participation in the management of the ejidos. Many felt alienated from the operations of these new units, pointing out that they had exchanged their former patrón—who, for all of his drawbacks, was a known quantity—for the impersonal bureaucracy of the federal government's ejidal bank. Although the bank provided technical assistance and doled out credit advances, it virtually excluded the ejidatarios from all production and marketing decisions. Not surprisingly, historians have found that by 1938 the initial trickle of memorials protesting the agrarian reform had broadened into a torrent, with the petitioners now including groups of ejidatarios as well as disgruntled former hacendados.

Joseph incorporates Yucatán's experience with Cardenismo into the broader revisionist framework. For him, the 1934–40 period, which constitutes the second phase of the Revolution in Yucatán, reveals a monocrop region caught in the throes of severe economic depression, in large part exacerbated by the region's external dependence upon the United States, and forced to accept solutions dictated by a central government that had convinced a substantial segment of that region's population that it did not understand Yucatán's peculiar problems.[80]

Undoubtedly, few states in the republic have experienced such a disappointing history of agrarian reform as Yucatán. Apologists for the revolutionary regime have sought—and still seek—to justify Cárdenas's extensive distribution, claiming that the strategy was well conceived but that it was poorly implemented by corrupt officials. Alternatively, government officials have claimed that the Yucatecan case is a special one, atypical of Mexican rural conditions. In doing so, they have taken great pains to preserve the central myths of the Revolution by writing Yucatán off as an exotic problem incapable of resolution. And, no doubt, too little attention has been given to factors beyond the regime's control, particularly the irreversible decline of the henequen industry owing to greatly increased foreign competition and the invention of synthetic fibers. Nevertheless, left- and right-wing critics alike have vehemently taken issue with official party spokesmen. The critics argue that although Yucatán's agrarian problems are unusual and the regime's failure to provide solutions is extreme, the Yucatecan case provides significant insight into the agrarian process throughout Mexico as a whole.[81]

Certainly much research remains to be done on the impact of the great land reform at both the regional and local levels.[82] Yet the final judgment that revolutionary historians are likely to reach may be, ironically, that both of these viewpoints are not only correct, they are complementary. Yucatán's checkered history of agrarian reform and frustration is indeed an idiosyncratic one, yet it brings the entire process of land reform in revolutionary Mexico sharply into focus. Significantly, the award-winning film, *México, la revolución congelada* (*Mexico, the Frozen Revolution*), chose Yucatán as its central case study in dealing with the revolutionary regime's failure to bring effective agrarian reform to Mexico. It may well be that few Mexican campesinos have experienced so many problems or disappointments as the yucatecos. On the other hand, virtually every problem typically encountered throughout the Mexican countryside—and, it should be added, in other Latin American countries that have implemented programs of agrarian reform—is to be found in contemporary Yucatán: inadequate credit and technical assistance; shrinking patrimonies; ejidal boundary disputes setting group against group and village against village; the illegal rental or sale of plots; caciquismo, *liderismo,* and the disenfranchisement of ejidatarios in agrarian affairs; chronic political unrest, factional violence, and assassination, to name only the more outstanding ones.[83]

Epilogue:
Retrospect and Prospect

As Mexican regional studies have moved to the forefront of research in Latin American history over the past decade, work on Yucatán has been particularly well represented. The current explosion in Yucatecan historiography, which rests upon a long and distinguished tradition of social science research on the region, is truly interdisciplinary, with anthropologists, sociologists, geographers, demographers, and economists making strong contributions along with historians. This recent surge of interest in the Yucatecan past has witnessed (and, in turn, benefited from) an upgrading of archives and research collections, an increased commitment by government, academic institutions, and international foundations to professional training and investigation, and the creation of new journals and forums for the dissemination of research.

Reflecting broader trends within the social sciences, the current generation of yucatecólogos has challenged traditional static periodizations of Mexican history based on national-level political phenomena (i.e., "Independence," "The Reform," "The Revolution"), which have never really suited the Yucatecan historical experience, and laid the foundation for a new interpretation of regional history based upon an analysis of the dynamic process of capitalist development in a dependent context. Recent studies have given particular attention to the changing relations of land, labor, and capital and their impact on local socioeconomic, political, and cultural processes and institutions. This has involved a younger generation of scholars in an inquiry into the evolution of regional systems of production, labor regimes, and the relations between social groups and classes. Since such problems are conditioned by the interplay of factors internal and external to the region, the framework of analysis has become more complex and frequently involves investigation at different levels of the world system. Over the course of a decade, the traditional political and institutional histories of local amateur writers have been superseded by an impressive harvest of monographs and articles on regional political economy and other social and economic themes by an ever-widening circle of domestic and international scholars.

The recent boom has seen remarkable progress in professional craftsmanship and ingenuity. Yucatecólogos have ranged far beyond standard institutional sources, the regional press, and rarer collections of *folletería*. Among a diverse constellation of materials, they have creatively mined parish registers and notarial archives; searched out land titles, litigation files, agrarian censuses, and tax lists; collected Maya oral tradition and written records; and gained access to the papers of private estates and multinational corporations. To obtain a broader field of vision, historians of Yucatán's modern past have consulted government and private collections in Mexico City and Belize, as well as in North America and Europe.

With access to archival sources much improved and researchers so methodologically equipped to use them to probe the Yucatecan past, it is not surprising that the region's historiography has come of age. Rather than marginalizing Yucatán as a special case in Mexican history, recent studies have demonstrated the heuristic value of such "exceptional regions" in approaching larger historical problems pertaining to Mexico and Latin America in general. Sometimes serving as a "limiting case" of a larger problem, sometimes as a dynamic component of a larger whole, the Yucatecan experience has illuminated broader discussions of capitalist agricultural expansion and peasant rebellion; plantation monoculture and possibilities for regional development; and revolutionary mobilization and strategies of social change, to cite some of the more relevant themes.

The steady infusion of theory and monographic research into the regional historical literature over the past five to ten years has established new interpretive trends and set the agenda for future investigation. Rather than being singled out as an apocalyptic race war, the so-called Caste War of 1847 is now viewed as the terrible outcome of an extended dialectical process of commercial agricultural expansion and free Maya response that began late in the colonial period. And while the absence of hacienda records has thus far limited monographic studies of the rise of the sugar hacienda and other commercial estates (e.g., tobacco, cotton, rice), as well as of the social relations on them prior to the Caste War, a broad consensus has developed regarding the essentially agrarian origins of the great rebellion. Based on new ethnohistorical analysis of Maya language sources, a more sophisticated understanding of the racial or "caste" nature of the war has emerged. Still, gaps continue to remain in our understanding of strategic aspects of the revolt, specifically the reasons for the rebels' loss of momentum with victory nearly within their grasp.

Finally, further study is needed of both the short- and long-term consequences of the conflict if the Caste War's full demographic, socioeconomic, political, and cultural impact is to be gauged. While a healthy debate continues to rage over the issue of whether the war caused the late nineteenth-century henequen boom, scarcely any research has been done on the rebellion's impact on agrarian structures outside of the northwest—although the ethnohistorical literature on the political and cultural dimensions of the independent rebel Maya states is now well advanced. Similarly, we must flesh out more precisely the changing relationship between the ascendant northwestern henequen zone and its increasingly peripheral hinterland in the southeast, tracing the relationship from the end of the Caste War through the late Porfirian henequen boom and into the revolutionary era.

To date, the henequen boom has received significantly more attention than any other aspect of Yucatán's modern past. And, given the extensive commitment that local researchers have made to examining the structures of the monocrop export economy, we can anticipate that this trend will continue well into the future. Yucatecólogos have systematically documented the planters' campaign of the late nineteenth-century to acquire ever-greater amounts of land, labor, and capital in order to expand production and satisfy a geometrically expanding international market. The process whereby the great estate devoured the remaining peasant villages in the northwest is now well documented, and although the communal sector seems also to have been eroded in the southeast, broad generalizations will remain hazardous until additional local studies appear.

Although recent scholars are reluctant to appropriate the "black legend" in Turner's *Barbarous Mexico* and other contemporary accounts, they have clearly found Turner's muckraking to be more plausible than the arguments of henequenero apologists. Judging conditions on Porfirian estates in terms of a diverse set of criteria, historians have found that treatment of laborers was bad and tended to get worse as the world market intensified throughout the period. The majority have concluded that as the local economy became more engaged by, and ultimately subordinated to, the demands of international capitalism, working conditions became "involuted," with the traditional system of debt peonage gradually transformed into a neoslave regime. And, while subregional variations must be taken into account in evaluating working conditions—particularly the continuation of a watered-down version of paternalism on some estates in the marginal southeast—recent scholarship suggests that, on the whole, social relations on Yucatecan plantations were among the most brutal in the tropical southeast, a region that maintained perhaps the most onerous labor regime in the republic.

Beyond this broad consensus on working conditions, yucatecólogos must still resolve a variety of empirical questions regarding the mechanism of dependent labor on late Porfirian estates. Only additional local studies will determine whether workers' debts were usually hereditary, clarify the exact relationship between debts and wage levels, and flesh out the precise role that the hacienda store played in the peón's indebtedness.

In general, the social history of the rural working class remains to be written. Conditions during the late Porfiriato may indeed have been intolerable for all types of hacienda workers, yet to lump all jornaleros together as "slaves" may not only be misleading but prevent a better understanding of the cultural and political responses that different categories of workers—for example, Maya campesinos, Yaqui deportees, and oriental indentured laborers—could make in the face of their oppression. Only recently have some historians begun to appreciate that Yucatán's rural work force was more than the inert mass of docile peones that contemporaries portrayed. Nevertheless, workers' *mentalités,* their own perceptions of the worsening labor regime, remain virtually unexplored. Unfortunately, surprisingly little effort has been made to interview the *ancianos* who lived through the época de esclavitud, and their numbers continue to dwindle.[1]

Recent studies have linked the brutal, repressive nature of the late Porfirian hacienda regime to the henequeneros' pressing need for U.S. capital and their vulnerable position in the henequen marketing structure. Yet a consensus has never been reached regarding either the terms of North American corporate involvement in Yucatán's monocrop economy or the extent of its impact. Indeed, there is perhaps no more enduring historiographical controversy in the region's past than the debate over whether the International Harvester Company established an informal empire in Yucatán. While the controversy will likely continue for some time, recent contributions have sharpened the terms of the debate, highlighting contrasting theoretical and methodological approaches as well as differences in evidence. The vast majority of local and foreign, popular and scholarly writers will continue to claim that, prior to World War I, Harvester exerted corporate control over Yucatán's henequen industry. However, a dissenting view, vigorously put forward by North American neoclassical economists and economic historians, and supported by International Harvester and the descendants of Yucatán's Porfirian oligarchy, will continue to make its own appeal. Since external market forces and local power relationships both affected the late Porfirian economy and were often intimately related, the possibility would seem to exist for a more satisfying synthesis of the contending positions.

As we have seen, the historical literature on Yucatán's participation in the Mexican Revolution is less developed than the body of work on either the Caste War or Porfirian boom eras. Only within the past five years have scholarly monographs begun to replace the standard political histories and memoirs of partisan local authors. Most recent contributions focus on the early phase of Yucatán's revolutionary experience, particularly on Alvarado's and Carrillo Puerto's activist regimes. Still virtually ignored is the period following Carrillo Puerto's assassination in 1924, which culminated during the late 1930s in the problematic expropriation of Yucatán's henequen plantations by the national regime of Lázaro Cárdenas.

Recent scholarship has clarified the complex chain of events that occurred in the region between 1910 and 1924 and has explicated the bourgeois and socialist revolutionary projects advanced by the Socialist Party of the Southeast, led initially by Alvarado and, subsequently, by the more militant Carrillo Puerto. Moreover, the political economy of Yucatán's frustrated revolution has been presented in a convincing fashion that demonstrates the interplay of local, national, and international actors and forces. Yucatán's debilitating monoculture, which subordinated the local economy to a foreign-dominated market and severely limited the possibilities for broad-based political mobilization, as well as the region's continued marginalization within the national power structure, have been identified as conditions under which social revolution proved futile.

All in all, recent studies have demonstrated the relevance of the Yucatecan case to the larger field of revolutionary history. For if, in certain respects, Yucatán seems to have experienced a "different revolution"—one later to arrive, less violent, and probably more radical in its first decade than elsewhere in the republic—embedded in the Yucatecan case are important implications for understanding the larger revolutionary process. Yucatán's new revolutionary historiography is particularly helpful in illuminating such central problems as caciquismo and informal local networks of power, the dilemmas of agrarian reform, the relationship between ideology and practice, and the larger impact of dependent capitalist structures on popular participation in the revolutionary process. In a fundamental way, recent contributions have suggested that Yucatán's revolutionary experience reinforces the emerging revisionist interpretation of the character of the larger event: a bourgeois revolution, more often than not, made from above and imposed from without upon Mexico's regions and classes.

Certainly the most urgent priority in Yucatecan revolutionary historiography is the need for comparable monographic studies of the later period of the Revolution (1924–40). Although Yucatán was one of the showcases for President Cárdenas's controversial collective ejido strategy in the late thirties, and documentation for the period is extremely rich, at present the agrarian expropriation of 1937 remains almost exclusively in the realm of partisan polemic.

Moreover, even the literature on the earlier phase of the Revolution in Yucatán, while generally of high quality, would benefit from additional local studies. It would be particularly valuable, for example, to determine the impact that specific reform initiatives, conceived in Mérida, actually had on land and labor patterns in different parts of the region, especially outside the henequen zone. More research is also needed on the nature of independent peasant and worker formations prior to the onset of General Alvarado's Constitutionalist revolution from without and above in 1915. Even for the Alvaradista and Carrillista regimes, we need additional research on political mobilization that would refine our understanding of cacique politics and the local appeal of revolutionary ideologies.

Perhaps the most exciting aspect of the rediscovery of Yucatán's past has been a new conceptualization of the physical boundaries of historical space. The new generation of historians and social scientists working on Yucatán and other parts of Mexico has demonstrated the ability of regional and local analysis to provide multilayered (even globally oriented) studies of the past of the nation's *patrias chicas*. Problems have inevitably arisen; occasionally, the new regional history has suffered from a lack of rigorous definition. Beyond a phenomenological approach, based on an almost commonsense understanding of boundaries, more attention must be given to clarifying the criteria (e.g., political, economic, geographical, and cultural) that delimit regional entities. One Mexican social scientist has even pondered whether any region, however small, can really be considered as a homogeneous entity.[2]

Nevertheless, if it is to remain vital, Yucatán's new regional history should continue to engage the past at a variety of levels, perhaps reassessing and modifying existing frameworks of analysis. For example, Laura Batt's recent microstudy of agrarian structures and class formation outside of the dominant henequen zone should shatter former notions that such peripheral areas were unimportant to the social history and political economy of Yucatán. An examination of such marginal areas raises issues that do not ordinarily arise in the study of the dominant sector of the dependent regional economy, such as the limits to capitalist expansion created by ecology, demography, and culture; the internal articulation between marginal and metropolitan areas; and the different forms that interclass and intraclass relations can take in such peripheral areas. It is to be hoped that additional historical studies will soon appear not only for southeastern Yucatán but also for areas in neighboring Campeche and Quintana Roo.[3] These areas are similarly marginal to the peninsula's northwestern hub, and their study would deepen our analysis of the impact of capital penetration and the nature of class formation in the nonmetropolitan sector. Especially overdue is an examination of the political economy of the chicle and forest industries in Quintana Roo and Campeche during the late nineteenth and twentieth centuries. Unfortunately, the municipal and state archives of Yucatán's neighbors are in poor condition (although much documentary material has been preserved in Belize), and an oral history strategy would seem essential to such a project.[4]

In general, microstudies, particularly of individual pueblos and hacienda communities, have much to contribute to the new regional historiography. Such local studies hold out the promise of integrating political, economic, and cultural levels of activity into a complex but manageable whole, as well as verifying the findings of regional-level research. As we have seen, community studies by North American and Mexican scholars have long occupied a place in the anthropological literature on modern Mexico and Yucatán. Yet owing to their inherent methodological limitations, such standard ethnographies have been of little value to regional historians. Typically, ethnographers have tended to view communities as discrete entities on the margins of regional or national political and economic structures and have made little effort to reconstruct the historical process that has shaped the ethnographic present.[5] As one recent critic of the genre put it: "Often the only acknowledgement of the relevance of historical process consists of a rapid and mechanical race through several centuries of complex change designed to whet the appetite for the real meat of the study, namely a synchronic account of the present-day structure of a given community."[6]

Still, recent work by economic anthropologists and ethnohistorians has displayed a heightened concern for the historical dimensions of communal change and has explored the interface between local and external spheres. The last decade has witnessed a proliferation of studies of mediating structures and agents, of "brokers" and middlemen, whose operations bridge micro- and macrolevels of analysis.[7] An increasing emphasis on "collaborators" and "compradors," caciques and caudillos, in recent Yucatecan historical studies reflects the current trend and promises a continuing infusion of anthropological (and other social science) methods into the historical literature.

Just as more effort must be made to integrate locality and region, the new regional historiography must also remain open to conceptual approaches inserting the region into larger interregional, national, and supranational contexts. For example, ultimately, yucatecólogos might pool their knowledge with colleagues studying other parts of southern Mexico, perhaps with a view to producing synoptic histories of the Porfirian hacienda or the epic revolution. Indeed, regional scholars might go further, transcending the nation-state as a sacrosanct unit of analysis and contemplating history on a Braudelian scale. Two Mexican revolutionary specialists recently speculated on a future study of the "Gulf of Mexico and the Caribbean in the Age of Obregón."[8] For a region that has looked outward toward the Gulf and the Atlantic since the early nineteenth century and has maintained long-standing economic and cultural links with both Cuba and the United States, such transnational projects must sooner or later find their way onto the research agenda.

Beyond a receptivity to more global formulations, Yucatecan specialists must continue to think comparatively about Mexican history. There is more at stake here than failing to see the forest for the trees: a lack of attention to broader theoretical and comparative questions embracing national processes and institutions may deny them an opportunity to showcase their rich findings. Even today, despite recent recognition, yucatecólogos (like students of other regions on the distant periphery) always run the risk that their work will be perceived to be outside the mainstream of Mexican historical concerns. Consequently, going beyond the modest comparative reflections offered in this volume, regional specialists should now work to incorporate their monographic research into larger state-of-the-art discussions of such themes as the great estate, dependent labor systems, campesino and revolutionary movements, family networks and elite establishments, and other questions of regional development.

Finally, the new surge of historical writing on Yucatán challenges us to approach old regional concerns from a fresh perspective. More attention should be given to examining central problems across temporal boundaries: for example, we might profitably trace mechanisms of social control and patterns of rural protest from the Porfiriato through the process of revolutionary institutionalization, or build greater longitude into existing studies of land tenure. Moreover, it is time to write a new political history of modern Yucatán. This new scholarship would transcend the traditional narrative and institutional format and approach politics in the light of new social history research on the consolidation and realignment of dominant parentescos and their relationship to the state from late colonial times through the revolutionary era.[9]

In a similar vein, the venerable theme of Yucatán's strained relationship with the Mexican republic might also be reappraised. Nineteenth- and early twentieth-century Mexican history makes sense only in terms of the continuing struggle between an increasingly modern, centralized state and the nation's diverse regions, fighting to protect their autonomy. Invariably, these larger struggles were related to bitter rivalries among regional factions for state-level control.[10] Thus, although it was previously written in the parochial idiom of traditional diplomatic history, Yucatán's stormy relationship with the central state is increasingly being reexamined from the perspective of political economy. Here, as elsewhere, a new synthesis of Yucatán's past is emerging, one that integrates locality, region, and nation within the overall framework of the global expansion of capitalism. And rather than being touted as "another Mexico" or "a world apart," Yucatán is increasingly assuming its place within the national and world systems.

Notes

Part 1. Writing History in Yucatán

1. The Recent Boom

1. The term *Yucatán* is subject to changing definitions. Geographically, the Yucatán peninsula today includes three Mexican states (Yucatán, Campeche, and Quintana Roo), as well as smaller parts of newly independent Belize and the Guatemalan Petén. Culturally and linguistically, the Yucatán is linked to an even more extensive portion of Mesoamerica with which it shares a common Maya heritage. Prior to the separation of Campeche (1858) and Quintana Roo (granted territorial status in 1902 and statehood in 1975), the original state of Yucatán comprised virtually the entire peninsula and, on several occasions during the nineteenth century, actually attempted to secede from the Mexican republic. While the dream of national autonomy has largely been laid to rest, many *yucatecos*, arguing common geographic, economic, cultural, and historical bonds, continue to call for the reunification of Yucatán within the Mexican federation and regard the entire peninsula as their native region. See Marvin Alisky, "The Relations of the State of Yucatán and the Federal Government of Mexico, 1823–1978," in Edward H. Moseley and Edward D. Terry, eds., *Yucatán: A World Apart* (University, Ala., 1980), 245–63; and A. J. G. Knox, "Regionalism as a Problem in Mexican National History: Yucatán, a Case Study, 1821–1940," mimeographed (University of Calgary, 1973). Events and actors in the densely populated state of Yucatán have traditionally shaped the history of the rest of the peninsula—perhaps never more so than during the late nineteenth and early twentieth centuries. The combined historical writing on Campeche and Quintana Roo is scant, and these neighboring states as well as Belize (formerly British Honduras) will receive attention in this volume only insofar as events generated in Yucatán spilled across their borders, such as occurred during the Caste War and the Mexican Revolution.

2. The move of the AGE and ANE to more spacious locales was recommended by a representative of the Archivo General de la Nación who surveyed the region's collections in 1981. The AGN has embarked on a long-

term project to locate, renovate, and catalog regional and local archives, in keeping with INAH's commitment to establish a number of vital regional centers of historical research throughout the republic. See Sergio Ortega Noriega, "Archivos históricos regionales y locales—Un proyecto de catálogo," *Boletín del Archivo General de la Nación*, 3d ser., 1 (July–Sept. 1977); and Luis González, "El oficio de historiar," *Nexos* 6 (Sept. 1983), 32–33.

3. Despite these advances, local libraries and archives remain understaffed, underfinanced, and vulnerable to the ravages of climate and insects. In large part owing to Mexico's recent economic downturn, the AGE, in particular, still lacks adequate furniture and conveniences. For a sober assessment of current problems and future priorities, see Rodolfo Ruz Menéndez, "Problemas prioritarios de la historiografía regional," *DdY*, Sept. 23, 1976, pp. 3, 7, and Miguel Civeira Taboada, "Deficiencias de Yucatán: El Archivo General del Estado," *DdY*, July 12, 1984, pp. 3, 7.

4. Luis López Rivas, "Archivo General del Estado de Yucatán," *Boletín del Archivo General de la Nación*, 3d ser., 1 (Oct.–Dec. 1977); Rodolfo Ruz Menéndez, "Los archivos del estado de Yucatán," *RUY* 22 (Mar.–Apr. 1980), 12–19; Michael J. Fallon, "El Archivo de la Secretaría del Arzobispado, Calle 58, Núm. 501, Altos, Mérida, Yucatán," *The Americas* 33 (July 1976), 149–54. A helpful earlier guide, recently reissued in the United States, is Héctor Pérez Martínez, *Yucatán: Catálogo de documentos para la historia de Yucatán y Campeche que se hallen en diversos archivos y bibliotecas de México y del extranjero* (Campeche, 1943), reprinted as *Yucatán, An Annotated Bibliography* (Salisbury, N.C., 1980).

5. Maritza Arrigunaga Coello, *Catálogo de las fotocopias de los documentos y periódicos yucatecos en la Biblioteca de la Universidad de Texas en Arlington* (Arlington, 1983). The collection includes about 60 percent of the Archivo de la Mitra and most of the *hemeroteca's* newspaper holdings. Unfortunately, of the six main sections of the AGE, only the two smallest, the colonial and congressional *ramos* (sections), have been microfilmed; the extremely rich executive, municipal, and judicial branches have not been copied. Of the ANE's 4,500 volumes, only 326 volumes, dating from 1689 to 1900, have been filmed.

The University of Alabama, in collaboration with the Universidad de Yucatán, is presently seeking major foundation support for an even more ambitious regional microfilming and accessing project. Plans include the immediate copying of all executive branch (Poder Ejecutivo) documents in the AGE (c. 2.5 million pages, spanning the 1825–1950 period), and eventually provide for the filming of holdings in the remaining Municipios, Poder Judicial, and Estado Civil ramos. The University of Alabama already holds a diverse microfilm collection (119 reels) of Yucatecan archival materials, manuscripts, pamphlets, broadsides, and periodicals that is particularly strong for the mid-nineteenth-century Caste War era. See Marie Bingham, *Catalog of the Yucatán Collection on Microfilm in the University of Alabama Libraries* (University, Ala., 1972).

A final, less publicized U.S. source of Yucatecan documents on microfilm is the complete holdings of the Archivo General de la Arquidiócesis de Yucatán, copied by the Mormons. Although this microfilmed archive contains a wealth of information on the demographic and social events of the peninsula from the sixteenth century until the 1910s (when civil records displaced those of the church), access to the collection is thus far incomplete, with an in-house finding aid prepared in 1965 serving as the only guide. The Church of Latter-Day Saints Archives has promised a detailed guide to its Yucatán collection in the near future.

6. In Yucatán, as elsewhere in the republic, some of the most exciting interdisciplinary research on regional problems is being carried out under the auspices of CIS-INAH. The Centro's bulletin, *Noticias del CIS-INAH,* carries a summary of current projects.

7. An excellent, doctoral dissertation–length master's thesis, by R. Laura Batt, has emerged from the Warman project and is discussed at length in part 2 of this book. Also see Luis Aboites, "La Revolución Mexicana en Yucatán: El caso de Espita," in Blanca González Rodríguez et al., *Yucatán: Peonaje y liberación* (Mérida, 1981), 166–77.

8. The best work emanating from the project on the *auge henequenero* (henequen boom) has been collected in González Rodríguez, *Peonaje y liberación,* and Luis Millet Cámara et al., *Hacienda y cambio social en Yucatán* (Mérida, 1984). The latter volume also contains the first fruits of the Centro Regional's new project on the Mexican Revolution. Also see Enrique Montalvo and José Luis Sierra Villarreal, "La transición al capitalismo: Apuntes de una investigación," in Centro Regional del Sureste (INAH), *Memoria del Congreso Interno, 1979* (Mexico City, 1981), 291–94. The findings of these projects are examined in part 2, chaps. 4 and 5.

9. E.g., see Alejandra García Quintanilla, "Historia de la producción en Yucatán, 1850–1915," mimeographed (Departamento de Estudios Económicos y Sociales, Universidad de Yucatán, 1983).

10. E.g., see "Editorial," *YHE* 1 (Sept.–Oct. 1977), 2, and 2 (Sept.–Oct. 1978), 2; cf. Enrique Montalvo Ortega, "Historia y política: Los usos de la historia y el Partido Socialista del Sureste," 1 (Mar.–Apr. 1978), 22–34. During its first year, the journal published, in serial form, the DEES's excellent bibliography for research on the henequen sector.

11. Thus far, however, only several of the papers have appeared in *YHE.*

12. To date only the *Memorias de la Primera Semana de la Historia* (Mérida, 1980) have been published, although a variety of individual papers from the second history week have appeared in the regional journals.

13. Beginning in the early 1970s, the Latin American Studies Program of the University of Alabama—which traditionally has maintained a strong research interest and active exchange program with Yucatán—has con-

ducted a succession of smaller, stateside seminars and conferences on Yucatecan themes, inviting the participation of yucatecólogos from Mexico and the United States. One of the principal fruits of this long-term involvement with the region is its volume of interdisciplinary contributions, *Yucatán: A World Apart* (1980). Also see Edward D. Terry et al., "Analyzing a Region: The Interaction of the University of Alabama and the Yucatán," *SECOLAS Annals* 13 (1982), 32–47.

14. For an indication of the quantity (as well as the interdisciplinary character) of the corpus of current historical writing on Yucatán, one need only search recent volumes of such representative bibliographic indexes and abstracting services as the *Handbook of Latin American Studies,* the *Hispanic American Periodical Index,* and the *Comprehensive Dissertation Index.* In 1980, the *Handbook of Latin American Studies* explicitly noted "an increase in studies of Yucatán and southern Mexico" (vol. 42, p. 189).

15. The federal government's rapid restoration of archaeological sites such as Cobah, Tulúm, and Xel-ha, all in close proximity to the resort of Cancún on the peninsula's Caribbean coast, is the most recent celebrated example. On a smaller scale, in 1971 the Yucatán state government commissioned distinguished regional artist Fernando Castro Pacheco to paint a series of murals on regional historical themes to be hung at the Governor's Palace in Mérida, in a special "salón de historia." Castro Pacheco completed the extraordinary series of twenty-five murals in 1978, and the state government commemorated the achievement in a special volume several years later. See Yucatán, *Murales de Fernando Castro Pacheco en el Palacio de Gobierno* (Mérida, 1981).

16. Harry Bernstein, "Regionalism in the National History of Mexico," *Acta Americana* 2 (Oct.–Dec. 1944), 305–14.

17. Luis González y González, *Invitación a la microhistoria* (Mexico City, 1973), 8–72, and *Nueva invitación a la microhistoria* (Mexico City, 1982), esp. chap. 7; and see Barry Carr, "Recent Regional Studies of the Mexican Revolution," *LARR* 15:1 (1980), 5.

18. E.g., see Eric Stokes, "Late Nineteenth Century Colonial Expansion and the Attack on the Theory of Economic Imperialism," *Historical Journal* 12 (June 1969), 286. Cf. James Lockhart, "The Social History of Colonial Spanish America," *LARR* 7:1 (1972), 6–45; David C. Bailey, "Revisionism and the Recent Historiography of the Mexican Revolution," *HAHR* 58 (Feb. 1978), 62–79; and Eric Van Young, "Mexican Rural History since Chevalier: The Historiography of the Colonial Hacienda," *LARR* 18:3 (1983), 34, 45–46 n. 47, who distinguishes parochial "local history of the traditional, antiquarian stamp" from "microhistory," which reflects "broader regional or national themes in local realities."

19. John Womack, Jr., *Zapata and the Mexican Revolution* (New York, 1969).

20. Antonio Mediz Bolio, "Prólogo" to Salvador Alvarado, *Actuación revo-*

lucionaria del General Salvador Alvarado en Yucatán (Mexico City, 1965), 14.

21. For a provocative discussion of this theme, two older studies are still of great value. See Jorge Ignacio Rubio Mañé, *El separatismo de Yucatán* (Mérida, 1935), and Mary Wilhelmine Williams, "The Secessionist Diplomacy of Yucatán," *HAHR* 9 (May 1929), 132–43. Among other things, yucatecos eat different food, wear different clothes, and great numbers continue to speak a vastly different Indian language (Maya) in the countryside from those of their central and northern Mexican counterparts, who are the partial product of the Nahua tradition. There are none of Mexico's impressive sierras (and indeed, only a few rolling hills) nor any lakes or rivers in Yucatán. The state might best be characterized as a flat sheet of limestone rock, verging at various points in the northwest upon a desert environment. Poor soil and lack of water discourage most agricultural production but favor cultivation of the obstinate, hardy henequen plant, an agave from which agricultural twines and rope are made. For a succinct, incisive analysis of the impact of geography on the regional economy, see Robert Patch, "Agrarian Change in Eighteenth-Century Yucatán," *HAHR* 65 (Feb. 1985), 21–49. For a delightful glimpse of how geography can influence a region's cultural tradition, see Hermann Bellinghausen, "Trova yucateca: La península cantable," *Nexos* 6 (Aug. 1983), 51.

22. Yucatán was connected by rail with the Mexican "mainland" in 1950; the paved highway was not completed until 1961.

23. E.g., see Héctor Aguilar Camín, *La frontera nómada: Sonora y la Revolución Mexicana* (Mexico City, 1977), and G. M. Joseph, *Revolution from Without: Yucatán, Mexico, and the United States, 1880–1924* (Cambridge, 1982), xiii–xiv and passim. Cf. Moseley and Terry, *Yucatán: A World Apart*, which, despite its title emphasizing the uniqueness of Yucatecan society, also approaches the region as a "cultural and social laboratory, a microcosm of Latin American and Mexican society" (ix). John Womack's forthcoming study of the making of the Mexican working class, with its focus on revolutionary Veracruz, will further underscore the importance of examining exceptional regions.

24. For a discussion of these categories, see Joseph L. Love, "An Approach to Regionalism," in Richard Graham and Peter H. Smith, eds., *New Approaches to Latin American History* (Austin, 1974), 137–55.

2. Principal Currents in the Early Development of Yucatecan Historiography

1. Up until about a generation ago, the old trilogy of war, politics, and diplomacy—particularly as it pertained to modern Yucatán's strained rela-

tionship with the Mexican central state—constituted the major preoccupation of Yucatecan historians, to the almost total exclusion of social, economic, and even cultural themes. The high points of this venerable Creole historiographical tradition include: Serapio Baqueiro, *Ensayo histórico sobre las revoluciones de Yucatán desde el año 1840 hasta 1864*, 3 vols. (Mérida, 1878–87); Eligio Ancona, *Historia de Yucatán desde la época más remota hasta nuestros días*, 5 vols. (Mérida and Barcelona, 1889–1905); Juan Francisco Molina Solís, *Historia de Yucatán desde la independencia de España hasta la época actual*, 2 vols. (Mérida, 1921–27); Alvaro Gamboa Ricalde, *Yucatán desde 1910*, 3 vols. (Veracruz and Mexico City, 1943–55); Eduardo Urzáiz R., *Del Imperio a la Revolución, 1865–1910* (Mérida, 1946); Yucatán, *Enciclopedia Yucatanense*, 8 vols. (Mérida, 1944–47, with additional volumes currently in preparation; articles primarily treat regional political history and geography but also include coverage of economic, social, and cultural themes); Antonio Bustillos Carrillo, *Yucatán al servicio de la patria y la Revolución* (Mexico City, 1959); Ramón Berzunza Pinto, *Guerra social en Yucatán* (Mérida, 1965); Edmundo Bolio Ontiveros, *Yucatán en la dictadura y en la Revolución* (Mexico City, 1967); Carlos Loret de Mola, *Yucatán en la patria*, 2 vols. (Mexico City, 1969); Bernardino Mena Brito, *Reestructuración histórica de Yucatán*, 3 vols. (Mexico City, 1969); Jaime Orosa Díaz, *Apuntes elementales de la historia de Yucatán* (Mérida, 1976). The last several decades have witnessed the appearance of a number of valuable socioeconomic and cultural studies as more local historians have come to appreciate that political phenomena, while important, often reflect deeper structural changes in regional life. Representative of this historiographical current among local amateur writers are Antonio Betancourt Pérez, *Revoluciones y crisis en la economía de Yucatán* (Mérida, 1953) and *Historia de Yucatán* (Mérida, 1970); Rodolfo Ruz Menéndez, *Por los viejos caminos del Mayab: Ensayos históricos y literarios* (Mérida, 1973) and *Ensayos Yucatanenses* (Mérida, 1976); Renán Irigoyen, *Ensayos henequeneros* (Mérida, 1975); Fidelio Quintal Martín, *Yucatán. Carácter de la guerra campesina en 1847: Una síntesis interpretativa* (Mérida, 1976); and Víctor M. Suárez Molina, *La evolución económica de Yucatán*, 2 vols. (Mérida, 1977). For an excellent bibliographical essay on the Creole historiographical tradition prior to 1945, see Howard F. Cline, "Remarks on a Selected Bibliography of the Caste War and Allied Topics," appendix to Alfonso Villa Rojas, *The Maya of East Central Quintana Roo* (Washington, D.C., 1945), 165–78.

2. The following discussion of the "Carnegie Generation" draws upon Grant D. Jones's insightful introduction to his edited volume *Anthropology and History in Yucatán* (Austin, 1977), x–xxiii, and Marie-France Labrecque, "From Peasantry to Proletariat: The Rural Proletariat in the Henequenera Region of Yucatán, Mexico" (Ph.D. diss., City University of New York, 1982), 2–23.

3. Labrecque, "From Peasantry to Proletariat," 14.

4. John L. Stephens, *Incidents of Travel in Central America, Chiapas, and Yucatán,* 2 vols. (New York, 1841), and *Incidents of Travel in Yucatán,* 2 vols. (New York, 1963; originally published in 1843).

5. For the early years of Yucatecan archaeology and its impact on Maya studies, see R. L. Brunhouse, *Sylvanus G. Morley and the World of the Ancient Maya* (Norman, Okla., 1971); cf. Labrecque, "From Peasantry to Proletariat," 14–15, 24, and Alfredo Barrera Vásquez, "Four Centuries of Archaeology in Yucatán: A Bibliographical Essay," in Moseley and Terry, *Yucatán: A World Apart,* 306–19. The more recent long-term commitments to archaeological excavation and restoration by Tulane University's Middle American Research Institute, the University of Alabama, and, of course, INAH, have similarly stimulated complementary anthropological and historical research.

6. E.g., see Ralph L. Roys, *The Indian Background of Colonial Yucatán* (Washington, D.C., 1943), and *The Political Geography of the Yucatán Maya* (Washington, D.C., 1957); Roys and France V. Scholes, *The Maya Chontal Indians of Acalán-Tixchel: A Contribution to the History and Ethnography of the Yucatán Peninsula* (Washington, D.C., 1948); Robert S. Chamberlain, *The Conquest and Colonization of Yucatán, 1517–1550* (Washington, D.C., 1948); Robert Redfield and Alfonso Villa Rojas, *Chan Kom: A Maya Village* (Washington, D.C., 1943); Villa Rojas, *The Maya of East Central Quintana Roo.*

7. E.g., see Roys, *The Book of Chilám Balám of Chumayel* (Washington, D.C., 1933) and *The Titles of Ebtún* (Washington, D.C., 1939); France V. Scholes et al., eds., *Documentos para la historia de Yucatán,* 3 vols. (Mérida, 1936–38).

8. Carnegie Institution of Washington, *Reports of the Division of Historical Research* (Yearbooks 29–49) (Washington, D.C., 1930–50) and *Reports of the Department of Archaeology* (Yearbooks 50–57) (Washington, D.C., 1950–58); and see Howard F. Cline, "Introduction: Reflections on Ethnohistory," in Cline, ed., *Guide to Ethnohistorical Sources* (Austin, 1972), 11.

9. Jones, "Introduction," xii, and D. E. Dumond, "Independent Maya of the Late Nineteenth Century: Chiefdoms and Power Politics," in Jones, *Anthropology and History,* 130.

10. Victoria Reifler Bricker, "The Caste War of Yucatán: The History of a Myth and the Myth of History," in Jones, *Anthropology and History,* 251, and Irwin Press, *Tradition and Adaptation: Life in a Modern Yucatán Maya Village* (Westport, Conn., 1975), 27–28; cf. Robert Redfield, *The Little Community* (Chicago, 1958), 111.

11. Arnold Strickon, "Hacienda and Plantation in Yucatán: An Historical-Ecological Consideration of the Folk-Urban Continuum in Yucatán," *América Indígena* 25 (Jan. 1965), 37; cf. Robert Redfield, *The Folk Culture of Yucatán* (Chicago, 1941), 341.

12. Redfield, *Folk Culture of Yucatán*, 341, and "Culture Change in Yucatán," *American Anthropologist* 36 (Jan.–Mar. 1934), 61.

13. Redfield, *Folk Culture of Yucatán*, 11, 369, and passim, and "The Folk Society," *American Journal of Sociology* 52 (Jan. 1947), 295–98.

14. Redfield, *Folk Culture of Yucatán*, 339–40.

15. Ibid., 359; cf. Strickon, "Hacienda and Plantation," 39.

16. Redfield, *A Village That Chose Progress: Chan Kom Revisited* (Chicago, 1950).

17. E.g., see Howard F. Cline, "The Sugar Episode in Yucatán, 1825–1850," *Inter-American Economic Affairs* 1 (Spring 1948), 79–100; "The Henequen Episode in Yucatán," *Inter-American Economic Affairs* 2 (Autumn 1948), 30–51; and *Related Studies in Early Nineteenth Century Yucatecan Social History*, 3 pts., Microfilm Collection of Manuscripts on Middle American Cultural Anthropology, no. 32 (University of Chicago Library, 1950); cf. Jones, "Introduction," xiii. And see Cline's tactful but apt criticism of Redfield's manner of collecting and utilizing historical data in "Remarks on a Selected Bibliography of the Caste War," 177.

18. Victor Goldkind, "Social Stratification in the Peasant Community: Redfield's Chan Kom Reinterpreted," *American Anthropologist* 67 (Aug. 1965), 863–84, and "Class Conflict and Cacique in Chan Kom," *Southwestern Journal of Anthropology* 22 (Winter 1966), 325–45; cf. Oscar Lewis, *Life in a Mexican Village: Tepoztlán Restudied* (Urbana, Ill., 1951), 432.

19. A recent, more explicitly materialist analysis of caciquismo in Chan Kom is Rhoda Halperin, "Redistribution in Chan Kom: A Case for Mexican Political Economy," in Halperin and James Dow, eds., *Peasant Livelihood: Studies in Economic Anthropology* (New York, 1973), 79–85. For the historical origins of revolutionary caciquismo in Yucatán, see Gilbert M. Joseph, "Caciquismo and the Revolution: Carrillo Puerto in Yucatán," in D. A. Brading, ed., *Caudillo and Peasant in the Mexican Revolution* (Cambridge, 1980), 193–221.

20. Strickon, "Hacienda and Plantation," 36–39. Sidney Mintz first called attention to Redfield's neglect of the henequen plantation and its rural proletariat in his rather cautious critique, "The Folk-Urban Continuum and the Rural Proletarian Community," *American Journal of Sociology* 59 (Sept. 1953), 136–43; cf. Labrecque, "From Peasantry to Proletariat," 15–23. Other early skirmishes with (and defenses of) Redfield's Yucatecan folk-urban construct are discussed in D. E. Dumond, "Competition, Cooperation, and the Folk Society," *Southwestern Journal of Anthropology* 26 (Autumn 1970), 261–86. The historical development and contemporary operation of the henequen plantation first received comprehensive treatment in Roland E. P. Chardon's *Geographic Aspects of Plantation Agriculture in Yucatán* (Washington, D.C., 1961)—still valuable as a basic orientation.

21. Strickon, "Hacienda and Plantation," 37, 39.

22. Ibid., 37, 60–61.

23. While Strickon's dynamic analysis approximates the "historical-structural" approach of the more sophisticated "dependency theorists" and world systems proponents, his essay actually predated even André Gunder Frank's first strident articulation of "the development of underdevelopment" (1966), appearing four years before Cardoso's and Faletto's classic statement of the dependency theme (1969) and almost a full decade before the first of Wallerstein's volumes on the world system (1974). (See Bibliography for full citations.) Clearly the recent historical studies by anthropologist R. Laura Batt, and historians Robert Patch, Lawrence Remmers, Allen Wells, and Gilbert Joseph—all discussed in part 2—follow in the conceptual tradition blazed by Strickon. Representative of the work of a new generation of economic anthropologists investigating more contemporary (i.e., postrevolutionary) problems of political economy are Nathaniel C. Raymond, "The Impact of Land Reform in the Monocrop Region of Yucatán, Mexico" (Ph.D. diss., Brandeis University, 1971) and "Land Reform and the Structure of Production in Yucatán," *Ethnology* 7 (Oct. 1968), 461–70; Malcolm K. Shuman, "The Town Where Luck Fell: The Economics of Life in a Henequen Zone Pueblo," (Ph.D. diss., Tulane University, 1974); Rodney C. Kirk, "San Antonio, Yucatán: From Henequen Hacienda to Plantation" (Ph.D. diss., Michigan State University, 1975); Alice Littlefield, *La industria de las hamacas en Yucatán, México* (Mexico City, 1976) and "The Expansion of Capitalist Relations of Production in Mexican Crafts," *Journal of Peasant Studies* 6 (July 1979), 471–87; Rosemary Lee, "The Tourist Industry in Yucatán: A Case Study in the Interaction between Class Structure and Economic Development" (Ph.D. diss., University of California, Irvine, 1977); Halperin, "Redistribution in Chan Kom" (1977); Margarita Rosales González, "La actividad comercial de Oxkutzkab entre 1900 y 1950," *RUY* 25 (Apr.–June 1983), 159–72; and Labrecque, "From Peasantry to Proletariat" (1982), which contains a succinct review (pp. 9–24) of recent contributions by economic anthropologists on Yucatán's henequen zone.

24. Nelson Reed, *The Caste War of Yucatán* (Stanford, Calif.), 1964.

25. Ibid., x (quotation), 3–49, 159–228. Recent additions to Caste War historiography are discussed in part 2, chap. 3. For a professional anthropologist's recent assessment of the value of Reed's work, see Dumond, "Independent Maya," 131; cf. the hypercritical view of Yucatecan historian J. Ignacio Rubio Mañé, in "La guerra de castas según un escritor anglo-americano," *RUY* 2 (Jan.–Feb. 1969), 9–20.

26. E.g., see Karen Spalding, "The Colonial Indian: Past and Future Research Perspectives," *LARR* 7:1 (1972), 47–76; Jones, "Introduction," xi–xii; Cline, "Introduction: Reflections on Ethnohistory," 3–16; Robert Carmack, "Ethnography and Ethnohistory: Their Application in Middle American Studies," *Ethnohistory* 18 (Spring 1971), 127–45.

27. Spalding, "The Colonial Indian," 47; Cline, "Introduction: Reflections on Ethnohistory," 6; Van Young, "Mexican Rural History," 30.

28. Jones, *Anthropology and History in Yucatán.*
29. E.g., see Dumond, "Competition, Cooperation and Folk Society" (1970); Grant D. Jones, "La estructura política de los mayas de Chan Santa Cruz: El papel del respaldo inglés," *América Indígena* 31 (Apr.–June, 1971), 415–21, "Maya Intergroup Relations in Nineteenth Century Belize and Southern Yucatán," *Journal of Belizean Affairs* 1 (June 1973), 3–13, "Revolution and Continuity in Santa Cruz Maya Society," *American Ethnologist* 1 (Nov. 1974), 659–83, and "Mayas, Yucatecans and Englishmen in the Nineteenth Century Fiesta System of Northern Belize," *Belizean Studies,* 10:3–4 (1982), 25–42; Miguel A. Bartolomé and Alicia M. Barabas, *La resistencia maya: Relaciones interétnicas en el oriente de la península de Yucatán* (Mexico City, 1977); Barabas, "Profetismo, milenarismo y mesianismo en las insurrecciones mayas de Yucatán," in INAH, *Cuadernos de los Centros Regionales,* no. 5 (Mexico City, 1974); Bartolomé, "La insurrección de Canek: Un movimiento mesiánico en el Yucatán colonial," in Centro Regional del Sureste, INAH, *Cuadernos de los Centros Regionales* (Mexico City, 1978); Marie Lapointe, "La prolongation de la guerre des castes au Yucatán (1850–1901)" (Ph.D. diss., Institut des Hautes Etudes de l'Amérique Latine de Paris, 1978), and *Los mayas rebeldes de Yucatán* (Zamora, Michoacán, 1983); Victoria Reifler Bricker, "Algunas consecuencias religiosas y sociales del nativismo maya del siglo XIX," *América Indígena* 33 (Apr.–June 1973), 327–48, and *The Indian Christ, the Indian King: The Historical Substrate of Maya Myth and Ritual* (Austin, 1981); Nancy M. Farriss, "Indians of Colonial Yucatán: Three Perspectives," in Murdo J. MacLeod and Robert Wasserstrom, eds., *Indians and Spaniards in Southern Mesoamerica* (Lincoln, Nebr., 1983).
30. Jones, "Levels of Settlement Alliance among the San Pedro Maya of Western Belize and Eastern Petén, 1857–1936," 139–89; Dumond, "Independent Maya," 103–38; and O. Nigel Bolland, "The Maya and the Colonization of Belize in the Nineteenth Century," 64–99, make especially good use of British documents. Bricker, "The History of a Myth," 251–58, and Allen F. Burns, "The Caste War in the 1970s: Present-Day Accounts from Village Quintana Roo," 259–73, creatively employ Maya oral history and written sources. On demographic change, see James W. Ryder, "Internal Migration in Yucatán: Interpretation of Historical Demography and Current Patterns," 191–231. Also see Sherburne F. Cook and Woodrow Borah, "The Population of Yucatán, 1517–1960" in vol. 2 of their *Essays in Population History: Mexico and the Caribbean* (Berkeley and Los Angeles, 1974), 1–170; and Salvador Rodríguez Losa, "Población y 'guerra de castas,'" *RUY* 20 (Nov.–Dec. 1978), 123–35.
31. Jones, "Introduction," xiiiff.; cf. Roys, *The Titles of Ebtún.*
32. Jones, "Introduction," xiv; Anne C. Collins, "The *Maestros Cantores* in Yucatán," in Jones, *Anthropology and History,* 233–47; Paul Sullivan, *A Maya Apocalypse: Contemporary Maya Prophecy in Ethnographic and His-*

torical Context, forthcoming; and, of course, Reed, Caste War, 41, 134, and passim. Since most members of this new generation of ethnohistorians have preoccupied themselves with the society and culture of the rebel frontier Maya and their modern descendants in Quintana Roo and Belize, much research remains to be done on the cultural forms and world view of the more outwardly assimilated Maya of northwestern Yucatán. Nancy M. Farriss's new Colonial Maya Society: The Collective Enterprise of Survival (Princeton, N.J., 1984)—received as this study went to press—makes an important contribution on this theme for the colonial era; also see Carlos Bojórquez Urzáiz's recent series of essays in DdY: e.g., "Milenarismo y crisis política: La Casa de Josué en Campeche," June 13, 1982, p. 7, and "Agitadores subalternos: Duendes, brujos y vampiros en Yucatán," Mar. 5, 1984, p. 7.

33. E.g., see Bricker, Indian Christ; Bartolomé and Barabas, La resistencia maya; and Burns, "The Caste War in the 1970s."

34. E.g., see Cook and Borah, "The Population of Yucatán," 178, and Ryder, "Internal Migration in Yucatán" (case study of Pencuyut). While less demographic research has been done regarding mobility within and migration out of the northwestern henequen zone following the onset of the late nineteenth-century export boom, recent qualitative studies by Bojórquez Urzáiz, Katz, Wells, Chacón, and Joseph (all reviewed in part 2) suggest that mobility in general, and fugitivism as a form of resistance, were severely curtailed during the Porfiriato. For the Mayas' demonstrated preference for mobility during pre-Columbian and colonial times, see Nancy M. Farriss, "Nucleation versus Dispersal: The Dynamics of Population Movement in Colonial Yucatán," HAHR 58 (May 1978), 187–216, and Robert Patch, "A Colonial Regime: Maya and Spaniard in Yucatán" (Ph.D. diss., Princeton University, 1979), chap. 6.

Part 2. From Caste War to Class War

1. Claude E. Guyant to Department of State, June 10, 1916, Dept. of State Consular Post Records, Correspondence: Progreso, 1916, vol. 1, 125.3, RG 84, National Archives, Washington, D.C.

3. The Early Expansion of Commercial Agriculture and Its Consequences

1. E.g., see Jean Meyer, Problemas campesinos y revueltas agrarias (1821–1910) (Mexico City, 1973), 66–67; Quintal Martín, Carácter de la

guerra campesina en 1847 (1976); Víctor Suárez Molina, "La guerra de castas y el problema de la tierra," *RUY* 19 (Jan.–Feb. 1977), 49–55; Eric Villanueva Mukul, "Las causas de la guerra campesina de 1847," *YHE* 1 (Mar.–Apr. 1978), 42–49; Robert Patch, "El fin del régimen colonial en Yucatán y los orígenes de la guerra de castas: El problema de la tierra, 1812–1846," *BECA* 10 (May–June 1983), 17–26.

2. Ancona, *Historia de Yucatán,* 4:6–15 and passim; Baqueiro, *Ensayo histórico,* 1:448 and passim; Molina Solís, *Historia de Yucatán,* 1:148, 304–5; cf. Cline, "Remarks on a Selected Bibliography of the Caste War," 165–69; Bricker, *Indian Christ,* 92–93.

3. Antonio Canto López, *La guerra de castas en Yucatán* (Mérida, 1976); Leopoldo Peniche Vallado, "Una tesis histórica rigurosa y racional acerca de la llamada guerra de castas," *RUY* 19 (Jan.–Feb. 1977), 56–70; Berzunza Pinto, *Guerra social;* Edward D. Terry, "Revolution and Social Struggle: Three Plays by Leopoldo Peniche Vallado" (Paper presented at the 1983 meeting of the South Eastern Council of Latin American Studies, San Juan). This interpretation has subsequently been put forward by some foreign writers. E.g., see Labrecque, "From Peasantry to Proletariat," 115.

4. Robert Patch, *La formación de estancias y haciendas durante la colonia* (Mérida, 1976; also found in *BECA* 4 [July–Aug. 1976]); "A Colonial Regime" (1978); "El mercado urbano y la economía campesina en Yucatán durante el siglo XVIII," *RUY* 20 (May–Aug. 1978), 83–96; "Apuntes acerca de los orígenes y las características de la hacienda henequenera," *YHE* 2 (Sept.–Oct. 1978), 3–15; "Agrarian Change in Eighteenth-Century Yucatán;" and "El fin del régimen." The literature on colonial agrarian and economic structures is sparse, but there are some other important milestones. See Marta Espejo-Ponce de Hunt, "Colonial Yucatán: Town and Region in the Seventeenth Century" (Ph.D. diss., University of California, Los Angeles, 1974); Hunt, "The Process of the Development of Yucatán, 1600–1700," in Ida Altman and James Lockhart, eds., *Provinces of Early Mexico: Variants of Spanish American Regional Evolution* (Los Angeles, 1976), 33–63; Manuela Cristina García Bernal, *La sociedad de Yucatán, 1700–1750* (Seville, 1972); Pablo Emilio Pérez-Mallaina Bueno, *Comercio y autonomía en la Intendencia de Yucatán (1797–1814)* (Seville, 1978); Farriss, "Nucleation versus Dispersal;" and Farriss, "Propiedades territoriales en Yucatán en la época colonial: Algunas observaciones acerca de la pobreza española y la autonomía indígena," *RUY* 25 (Apr.–June 1983), 37–86.

5. Patch, *La formación,* 17–42. Patch's thesis delimiting a northwestern colonial zone of haciendas surrounded by a large southeastern hinterland of "free villages" was originally based upon data taken from the *visitas pastorales* housed in Mérida's Archivo de la Mitra Emeritense, and more recently corroborated by research in tithe and notarial records, late-colonial censuses, and a listing of *cofradía* estates. See Patch, "Agrarian Change in

Eighteenth-Century Yucatán." A more theoretical conceptualization of Yucatán's dichotomous agrarian structure is found in Marco Bellingeri, "Proyecto de investigación: La hacienda y la sociedad yucateca en el siglo XIX," *YHE* 1 (Nov.–Dec. 1977), 5–6. Recent archival research by Nancy Farriss and Yucatecan historians Carlos Bojórquez Urzáiz and Sergio Quezada supports Patch's suggestion that simultaneously with the rise of corn and cattle haciendas in the northwest, the first modest tobacco, sugar, rice, and cotton estates were being established in the more fertile soils of southern and eastern Yucatán. For this as yet little-studied dimension of the formation of the Yucatecan hacienda, see Farriss, "Propiedades territoriales," 42; Bojórquez Urzáiz, "Yucatán: Plantaciones colonialistas y sistema de trabajo a fines del siglo XVIII," *YHE* 6 (Sept.–Oct. 1982), 28–34; and Quezada, "El origen de la producción y el capital comercial en la provincia de Yucatán, a mediados del siglo XVIII," *BECA* 5 (Jan.–Feb. 1978), 12–29; cf. Patch, "Agrarian Change in Eighteenth-Century Yucatán."

6. Patch, *La formación,* 8–9, 22–26, and "El mercado urbano," 86–94. Nevertheless, Patch, Farriss, and other colonial historians have shown that Yucatán's eighteenth-century economy was still the most backward and "parasitic" in Mexico. Owing to the region's lack of mines and exportable crops, the Crown permitted an extension of the encomienda until 1785. Despite the rise of the hacienda, Indian tribute figures prominently both as a source of goods for internal consumption and for the small export trade right up until the eve of independence. See, e.g., Bellingeri, "Proyecto de investigación," 5–7.

7. Patch, "Apuntes," 14–15; cf. Villanueva Mukul, "Las causas de la guerra campesina," 43. See, e.g., Bojórquez Urzáiz, "Yucatán: Plantaciones colonialistas," 32, who documents the existence of *plantaciones clandestinas,* late colonial commercial ventures that sought to circumvent imperial restrictions on the production of tobacco. Cf. Patch, "Agrarian Change in Eighteenth-Century Yucatán," who discusses colonial regulation of the sugar and *aguardiente* industry.

8. Patch, "El fin del régimen."

9. Indeed, as we have seen (n. 5), some new research suggests that cash crop production began well in advance of independence. For more detail on the neglected logwood and tobacco industries, see Gilbert M. Joseph, "British Loggers and Spanish Governors: The Logwood Trade and Its Settlements in the Yucatán Peninsula," *Caribbean Studies* 14 (July 1974), 7–37; and Víctor Suárez Molina, "El tabaco en Yucatán en el siglo XIX," *RUY* 16 (May–Aug. 1974), 16–25.

10. Lawrence J. Remmers, "Henequen, the Caste War and the Economy of Yucatán, 1846–1883: The Roots of Dependence in a Mexican Region" (Ph.D. diss., University of California, Los Angeles, 1981), pt. 1, pp. 65–297. Howard Cline, "The Sugar Episode" (1948); "The Aurora Yucateca and the Spirit of

Enterprise in Yucatán, 1821–1847," *HAHR* 27 (Feb. 1947), 30–60; and "The Henequen Episode" (1948).

11. Remmers, "Henequen, the Caste War," especially 1–5, 83–100.

12. Ibid., 274–79; cf. 829–35.

13. Ibid., chap. 4 ("Portrait of the Pre-Caste War Economy"). Yucatecan writers have also drawn attention to the dynamic subregional character of the prewar economy. See Víctor Suárez Molina, "Espíritu y características de las regiones yucatecas en la primera mitad del siglo XIX," *RUY* 20 (Mar.–Apr. 1978), 69–83, and Manuel López Amabilis, "Yucatán en la estadística antes de la guerra de castas," *RUY* 5 (Jan.–Feb. 1963), 115–29.

14. Remmers, "Henequen, the Caste War," pt. 1, especially pp. 97–100, 121–31; Moisés González Navarro, *Raza y tierra: La guerra de castas y el henequén* (Mexico City, 1970), 54–63; Suárez Molina, "La guerra de castas;" Villanueva Mukul, "Las causas de la guerra campesina;" Patch, "El fin del régimen."

15. With the exception of Remmers and Suárez Molina, little attention has been given to social relations on estates producing tropical cash crops other than sugar—a gap in the literature that should be filled. No doubt, the papers of many sugar and other estates were destroyed in the Caste War. In reconstructing conditions on haciendas, Strickon, Reed, and particularly Cline, in his series of publications on sugar and the origins of the Caste War (see chap. 2, n. 17), made especially good use of the classic accounts of John L. Stephens, *Incidents of Travel in Central America* and *Incidents of Travel in Yucatán,* and José M. Regil and Alonso M. Peón, "Estadística de Yucatán," *Boletín de la Sociedad Mexicana de Geografía y Estadística* 1:3 (1853), 237–339. More recent studies, while they are based on a larger body of printed materials, have not challenged their line of interpretation, a summary of which follows.

16. The basic typology is set forth in Sidney W. Mintz and Eric Wolf, "Haciendas and Plantations in Middle America and the Antilles," *Social and Economic Studies* 6:3 (1957), 380–412. For a rigorous application of the typology to the Yucatecan great estate, see Robert Patch, "Apuntes," 13–15, and R. Laura Batt, "Capitalist Class Formation in Dependent Economies: The Case of Espita, Yucatán" (master's thesis, University of Kentucky, 1981), 104–9.

17. Bellingeri, "Proyecto de investigación," 5–9, while not dismissing the advance of capitalist agriculture as a cause of the war, chooses to highlight the local oligarchy's stubborn attempt following independence to reintroduce colonial era tributary relations in the form of "new" civil and ecclesiastical exactions upon Maya peasant production. This theme is also developed by González Navarro, *Raza y tierra,* 1, 63–79, and Bricker, *Indian Christ,* 89–95.

18. Suárez Molina, "La guerra de castas," 49–54, and "Espíritu y carac-

terísticas de las regiones yucatecas," 74–76. Suárez Molina also documents the more modest expansion of commercial tobacco production on the frontier. In his brief theoretical essay, "Las causas de la guerra campesina," the Yucatecan Marxist sociologist Eric Villanueva Mukul similarly argues that the causes of the war were neither "racial" nor "feudal" in character but were directly related to the development of capitalist agriculture in the peninsula. Villanueva contends that by 1847, Yucatán was a capitalist society with precapitalist traits ("profundos rasgos feudales y esclavistas") owing to the capitalist hacendados' need to tie a cheap, dependent labor force to their expanding sugar estates in a time of labor shortage.

19. Bricker, *Indian Christ*, 5, 87–118, and "The History of a Myth," 251–58.

20. Bricker, *Indian Christ*, 5.

21. Ibid., 93–99. The role played by Indian caciques in the origins of the Caste War, as well as in its later millenarian phase is a central theme in the comparative research project of Todd A. Diacon. See "The Brazilian Contestado Movement and the Caste War of Yucatán: The Social Origins of Millenarian Movements (Ph.D. diss., University of Wisconsin, forthcoming).

22. E.g., see Baqueiro, *Ensayo histórico*, 2:5–29.

23. Ibid., 38–39.

24. Bricker, *Indian Christ*, 102. The oral tradition was originally presented in Edward H. Thompson, *People of the Serpent: Life and Adventure among the Mayas* (Boston, 1932), 70–71.

25. Carlos Bojórquez Urzáiz, "El Yucatán de 1847 hasta 1851: Breves apuntes sobre el trabajo y la subsistencia," *BECA* 5 (Nov.–Dec. 1977), 19, and "Regionalización de la política agraria de Yucatán en la segunda mitad del siglo XIX," *RUY* 21 (May–Aug. 1979), 33. Yet elsewhere, Bojórquez Urzáiz reports that it was not uncommon for such hidalgos to desert if they could, exchanging their status as peones for the chance to cultivate their own land beyond the frontier ("Estructura agraria y maíz a partir de la 'guerra de castas,'" *RUY* 20 [Nov.–Dec. 1978], 21–24).

26. Philip C. Thompson, personal communications, Mérida, 1974–75; cf. Bricker, *Indian Christ*, 102; cf. Patch, *La formación*, 39–40, and "Agrarian Change in Eighteenth-Century Yucatán."

27. Patch, *La formación*, 39–40; Leticia Reina, *Las rebeliones campesinas en México* (Mexico City, 1980), 365–66; cf. Remmers, "Henequen, the Caste War," 44–45; also see Edward H. Moseley, "From Conquest to Independence: Yucatán under Spanish Rule, 1521–1821," in Moseley and Terry, *Yucatán: A World Apart*, 113.

28. On the indigenous agrarian rebellions of the period, see Meyer, *Problemas campesinos*; Moisés González Navarro, "Las guerras de castas," *RUY* 21 (Sept.–Oct. 1979), 25–53; Miguel Mejía Fernández, *Política agraria en*

México en el siglo XIX (Mexico City, 1979), especially 74–83; Gastón García Cantú, *El socialismo en México, siglo XIX* (Mexico City, 1969); and Reina, *Las rebeliones campesinas.*

29. Moisés González Navarro, *Raza y tierra,* 1–2.

30. Iván Menéndez, "Aproximación a la historia de Yucatán," *RUY* 22 (May–Aug. 1980), 71–72.

31. Cline, "Remarks on a Selected Bibliography of the Caste War," 165.

32. E.g., see Alejandra García Quintanilla, "La formación de la estructura económica de Yucatán: 1850–1940," *YHE* 2 (Nov. 1978–Apr. 1979), 49–50.

33. For years, Howard Cline's "The War of the Castes and Its Consequences," in his *Related Studies* (1950), remained the best general treatment of the war's short- and long-term effects on the region. Recently, however, it has been superseded by Remmers's lengthy dissertation, "Henequen, the Caste War and the Economy of Yucatán, 1846–1883," which, in pts. 2 and 3 (pp. 299–835), examines the war's impact on the northwest and, to a lesser extent, on the frontier region.

34. Rodríguez Losa, "Población y 'guerra de castas.'" Contemporary census data were notoriously inaccurate with undercounting prevalent in districts in the face of tax assessments and militia quotas. Cf. the widely differing estimates of casualties found in Reed, *Caste War,* 127–28, and González Navarro, *Raza y tierra,* 173.

35. Suárez Molina, *La evolución económica,* 1:47–48.

36. Remmers, "Henequen, the Caste War," 309–27.

37. Ibid., 6; Suárez Molina, *La evolución económica,* 1:49–50.

38. Remmers, "Henequen, the Caste War," 327–97.

39. When the Caste War had erupted, many prominent Creole families (and many soon to be prominent, like the Escalantes and the Molinas) fled the southeast for the northwest, there to invest in cattle, commerce, and, increasingly, the henequen trade. See Renán Irigoyen, "Don Us Escalante, precursor de la industria henequenera," *Revista de Estudios Yucatecos* 1 (Feb. 1949), 17–32; for the Molinas, see José María Valdés Acosta, *A través de los siglos,* 3 vols. (Mérida, 1923–26), 2:1–19, and Allen Wells, "Family Elites in a Boom-and-Bust Economy: The Molinas and Peóns of Porfirian Yucatán," *HAHR* 62 (May 1982), 232–42.

40. Suárez Molina, *La evolución económica,* 1:49–50; Remmers, "Henequen, the Caste War," 319–20, 643–44.

41. Suárez Molina, *La evolución económica,* 1:118–19; Remmers, "Henequen, the Caste War," 371–74, 418–704.

42. Renán Irigoyen, *¿Fué el auge del henequén producto de la guerra de castas?* (Mérida, 1947) and Quintal Martín, *Carácter de la guerra campesina,* 37.

43. Salvador Rodríguez Losa, "El henequén: Hoy, ayer y mañana," mimeographed (Mérida, n.d.); Remmers, "Henequen, the Caste War," 4, 386–

87. Rodríguez Losa lists henequen as the state's leading prewar export; Remmers places it second, behind logwood.

44. E.g., Chardon, *Geographic Aspects*, 27–28. However, Remmers, "Henequen, the Caste War," 381, maintains that in temporarily paralyzing Yucatecan fiber production, the war actually benefited the regional industry, since it starved world demand and drove up prices. Then, when the Crimean War cut off shipments of Russian hemp to Europe in the 1850s and 1860s, the revived Yucatecan industry found itself in a most enviable position.

45. Robert Patch, *La formación*, 40–42, and "Apuntes," 6–10.

46. Remmers, "Henequen, the Caste War," 430–32; Allen Wells, "Economic Growth and Regional Disparity in Porfirian Yucatán: The Case of the Southeastern Railway Company," *South Eastern Latin Americanist*, 22 (Sept. 1978), 3; Joseph, *Revolution from Without*, 316–17, n. 43.

47. Chardon, *Geographic Aspects*, 138–42, 164; cf. Remmers's critique of Chardon, in "Henequen, the Caste War," 430–32.

48. Remmers, "Henequen, the Caste War," 371–416.

49. Cline's doctoral research and the microfilm publications that grew out of it, although now almost thirty-five years old, remain the most authoritative studies of the regionally based intraelite rivalries that figured among the causes of the Caste War and were affected by its consequences; see especially "Regionalism and Society in Yucatán, 1825–1847: A Study of 'Progressivism' and the Origins of the Caste War," and "The War of the Castes and Its Consequences," both in the microfilm collection *Related Studies*.

50. Remmers, "Henequen, the Caste War," 29, and pt. 3, passim.

51. Reed, *Caste War*, 155–56; also see Cline, "War of the Castes and the Independent Indian States of Yucatán," in *Related Studies*.

52. Bojórquez Urzáiz, "Estructura agraria y maíz" (1978) and "Regionalización de la política agraria" (1979). Also see the initial findings of Belizean historian Angel Cal, who is investigating commercial sugar production and labor force in the ladino-dominated refugee society of late nineteenth-century northern Belize: "The Yucatec Maya of Belize, 1847–1900: A Preliminary Overview," mimeographed (Belize College of Arts, Science, and Technology, 1984). Even Remmers's massive economic history of the Caste War and its consequences is weighted much more heavily toward the consolidation of henequen monoculture in the northwest. Once he demonstrates the magnitude of the war's devastation on the interior economy, Remmers turns his attention almost exclusively to the henequen zone. For a more recent appreciation of the importance of carefully defining Yucatán's subregions, see Carmen Morales Valderrama, "Delimitación y características de la región sur de Yucatán," *YHE* 5 (Sept.–Oct. 1981), 54–66, and Margarita Rosales González, "Etapas en el desarrollo regional del Puuc, Yucatán," *YHE* 3 (Mar.–Apr. 1980), 41–53.

53. Bojórquez Urzáiz, "Estructura agraria y maíz," 32, 20.

54. E.g., Lapointe, *Los mayas rebeldes;* Dumond, "Independent Maya," especially 111–26; cf. Reed, *Caste War,* 159–249.

55. Dumond, "Independent Maya," 111–28; Bojórquez Urzáiz, "Estructura agraria y maíz," 27.

56. Dumond, "Independent Maya," 127; Lapointe, *Los mayas rebeldes;* Charlotte Zimmerman, "The Cult of the Holy Cross: An Analysis of Cosmology and Catholicism in Quintana Roo," *History of Religions,* 3:1 (1963), 50–71; Bricker, "The History of a Myth;" Burns, "The Caste War in the 1970s;" Bartolomé and Barabas, *La resistencia maya;* Barabas, "Profetismo, milenarismo y mesianismo;" Diacon, "The Brazilian Contestado Movement and the Caste War of Yucatán;" Lorena Careaga, "Historia contemporánea de Chan Santa Cruz," *YHE* 4 (Sept.–Oct. 1980), 66–75; Eric Villanueva Mukul, "La lucha de la comunidad de Chemax," *YHE* 8 (July–Aug. 1978), 35–51; Rosendo Solís, "Vida cotidiana y salud en X-Can," *YHE* 2 (Sept.–Oct. 1978), 16–22; Sullivan, *A Maya Apocalypse.* But cf. Jones, "La estructura política de los mayas," which emphasizes the cruzob's unrestricted access to gunpowder through British merchants in Belize as the crucial factor in cruzob resistance.

57. Dumond, "Independent Maya," 127. According to Bricker, who has emerged in the wake of Reed as the leading student of the cult, the cruzob made a classic effort to revitalize their culture. They attempted to cast off ladino domination, culturally as well as politically, by reinterpreting the symbols of the European Catholicism which had been imposed on them in order to make them more relevant to the Maya experience. Crosses dressed in native costume were substituted for images of white saints; Maya priests now officiated at masses and sacraments instead of ladino *sacerdotes;* ultimately the Second Coming of Christ—in the form of Juan de la Cruz, an Indian—was proclaimed. In these ways, the oppressive caste system was stood on its head and a more satisfying culture was fashioned in which "the Indian was master and the ladino became slave." Bricker, *Indian Christ,* 115, and "The History of a Myth," 251–58. For the classic typology of "revitalization movements," upon which Bricker draws, see Anthony F. C. Wallace, "Revitalization Movements," *American Anthropologist* 58 (1956), 264–81. For a provocative debate on the identity of Juan de la Cruz and his role in the establishment of the Talking Cross cult, compare Bricker's account with Zimmerman, "The Cult of the Holy Cross," 63–71, and Jones, "Revolution and Continuity," 667–69.

58. Dumond, "Independent Maya," 106–28; Bricker, *Indian Christ,* 113–15.

59. Jones, "Levels of Settlement Alliance," 172–75, and "Revolution and Continuity."

60. Bojórquez Urzáiz, "Regionalización de la política agraria," 33, and "Estructura agraria y maíz," 31; cf. Dumond, "Independent Maya," 110–26;

Jones, "La estructura política de los mayas;" and Charles John Emond, *The History of Orange Walk* (Belize City, 1983), 15–17.

61. Bojórquez Urzáiz, "Estructura agraria y maíz," 21–24; Borah and Cook, "Population of Yucatán," 178; Remmers, "Henequen, the Caste War," 122, 319–20; cf. Ryder, "Internal Migration in Yucatán," 191, who also regards migration as a means of resisting the dominant society. Planter and state mechanisms of control in the northwest which curtailed Maya mobility during the Porfiriato are most comprehensively discussed in Allen Wells, "Violence and Social Control: Yucatán's Henequen Plantations," in Thomas Benjamin and William McNellie, eds., *Other Mexicos: Essays on Regional History, 1876–1911* (Albuquerque, 1984), 213–41.

62. Bojórquez Urzáiz, "Estructura agraria y maíz," 31–34; cf. Bojórquez Urzáiz, "Crisis maicera de la comunidad campesina yucateca en la segunda mitad del siglo XIX," *BECA* 6 (Mar.–Apr. 1979), 49–50.

63. Suárez Molina, *La evolución económica,* 1:169–71; Batt, "Capitalist Class Formation," 59–67. Remmers, "Henequen, the Caste War," 371–75, documents that although the state of Yucatán regained self-sufficiency in sugar production, investment remained modest and the southeastern frontier no longer monopolized production. Rather, it was the protected narrow belt of land around and to the south of Campeche, on the west coast of the peninsula, that now replicated on a smaller scale the diversified pattern of commerical agriculture (sugar, cotton, tobacco, rice) previously found in the Yucatecan interior. Also see Cal, "The Yucatec Maya," for ladino investment in sugar and (briefly) cotton in northern Belize.

64. Bojórquez Urzáiz, "Regionalización de la política agraria," 38–45; "Estructura agraria y maíz," 31; "Crisis maicera," 50. A comparison with Robert Patch's preliminary research on peasant maize production and sale in both the northwestern and southern Puuc regions during the late colonial period, as well as with Margarita Rosales González's examination of more recent maize trading in the Puuc (1900–50), might reveal some structural continuities and suggest lines for future research. See Patch, "El mercado urbano," 91–94; Rosales González, "La actividad comercial," 163–71.

65. Suárez Molina, *La evolución económica,* 1:161; González Navarro, *Raza y tierra,* 199–200; and Batt, "Capitalist Class Formation," 64–130. More recently, another economic anthropologist, Margarita Rosales González, has found widespread evidence of debt peonage around the turn of the century in the Puuc region near Oxkutzcab ("La actividad comercial" [1983], 160–63, 166–67, 171).

66. Remmers, "Henequen, the Caste War," pt. 3; Batt, "Capitalist Class Formation," chap. 3; Wells, "Economic Growth and Regional Disparity;" Joseph, *Revolution from Without,* 26–32; Suárez Molina, *La evolución económica,* 2:28, 49–50; Keith Hartman, "The Henequen Empire in Yucatán: 1870–1910" (master's thesis, University of Iowa, 1966), 76; Rosales González, "La actividad comercial," 159–61, 168–71.

67. Throughout Porfirian Mexico, railroads invariably serviced the lucrative export sector at the expense of domestic production and diversified economic development. See John H. Coatsworth, *Growth against Development: The Economic Impact of Railroads in Porfirian Mexico* (DeKalb, Ill., 1981).

68. Bellingeri, "Proyecto de investigación," 12, presents aggregate figures revealing that Yucatán's per capita production of basic foodstuffs plummeted from one of Mexico's highest in 1877 to the republic's lowest in 1910, when the state led the nation in per capita production of agricultural products for export.

69. Batt, "Capitalist Class Formation," 114. The concept of "internal articulation" has been effectively used by Angel Palerm, *Modos de producción y formaciones socioeconómicas* (Mexico City, 1976), to analyze the relationship between northern mining camps and central Mexican corn and cattle haciendas during the colonial period.

4. The Political Economy of Monoculture

1. E.g., see Frederick J. T. Frost and Channing Arnold, *The American Egypt* (New York, 1909), and Henry Baerlein, *Mexico: The Land of Unrest* (Philadelphia, 1914). For an anthropological analysis of Mérida's transformation, see Asael T. Hansen and Juan R. Bastarrachea M., *Mérida: Su transformación de capital colonial a naciente metrópoli en 1935* (Mexico City, 1984).

2. Cline, "Remarks on a Selected Bibliography of the Caste War," 177.

3. Prior to the recent boom, apart from the enduring polemic generated by critics and apologists of the rural labor regime (discussed below), students of the period had recourse only to the better political narratives, such as Eduardo Urzáiz's *Del Imperio a la Revolución* (1946); Albino Acereto's "Historia política desde el descubrimiento europeo hasta 1920," in Yucatán, *Enciclopedia Yucatanense*, 3:5–388 (1947); and Edmundo Bolio's *Yucatán en la dictadura y en la Revolución* (1965), plus Moisés González Navarro's highly professional but general socioeconomic survey, *Raza y tierra* (1970). Synthesizing agrarian and social questions from colonial times up until the present, González Navarro devotes but a single chapter to the Porfirian political economy.

4. Allen Wells, *Yucatán's Gilded Age: Haciendas, Henequen, and International Harvester, 1860–1915* (Albuquerque, forthcoming); Batt, "Capitalist Class Formation." For references to the best work on the henequen boom by a new generation of local social scientists, see chap. 1, nn. 8–9.

5. Wells, *Yucatán's Gilded Age*, chap. 5; Joseph, *Revolution from Without*, 26–32; Gilbert M. Joseph and Allen Wells, "Corporate Control of a Monocrop Economy: International Harvester and Yucatán's Henequen Industry

during the Porfiriato," *LARR* 17:1 (1982), 73–79; Ramón D. Chacón, "Yucatán and the Mexican Revolution: The Pre-Constitutional Years, 1910–1918" (Ph.D. diss., Stanford University, 1982), chap. 1; Hartman, "Henequen Empire;" Blanca González Rodríguez, "Henequén y población en Yucatán: Dzemul a manera de ejemplo" (Tesis de Licenciatura en Antropología Social, Universidad de Yucatán, 1979), esp. chap. 3; García Quintanilla, "Historia de la producción."

6. For a thorough discussion of Porfirian land legislation and Indian policy, see Carol Lee Carbine, "The Indian Policy of Porfirio Díaz in the State of Yucatán, 1876–1910" (Ph.D. diss., Loyola University of Chicago, 1977).

7. Wells, *Yucatán's Gilded Age,* chap. 5; Chacón, "Yucatán and the Mexican Revolution," 51–54. For further evidence of the alienation of specific ejidos within the henequen zone, see Roland E. Chardon, "Hacienda and Ejido in Yucatán: The Example of Santa Ana Cucá," *Annals of the Association of American Geographers* 53 (1963), 181–82, and *Geographic Aspects,* 33–34, 81–127, 169–93; also see Robert Platt, "Chichi: An Hacienda in Yucatán," in *Latin America: Countrysides and United Regions* (New York, 1942), 63–67.

8. Betancourt Pérez, *Revoluciones y crisis,* 52; Batt, "Capitalist Class Formation," 54–130; Suárez Molina, *La evolución económica,* 1:160; González Navarro, *Raza y tierra,* 199–200; John K. Turner, *Barbarous Mexico* (Chicago, 1910), 15; Friedrich Katz, "El sistema de plantación y la esclavitud," *Ciencias Políticas y Sociales* 8 (Jan.–Mar. 1962), 114.

9. For a theoretical statement, see Bellingeri, "Proyecto de investigación," 9.

10. Frank Tannenbaum, *The Mexican Agrarian Revolution* (Washington, D.C., 1930), 33; George M. McBride, *The Land Systems of Mexico* (New York, 1923), 154; Katz, "El sistema," 130.

11. Joseph, *Revolution from Without,* 27–29; Francisco Benet, "Sociology Uncertain: The Ideology of the Rural-Urban Continuum," *Comparative Studies in Society and History* 6 (Oct. 1963), 1–12; Strickon, "Hacienda and Plantation," 56; Alan Knight, "Peasant and Caudillo in Revolutionary Mexico, 1910–1917," in Brading, *Caudillo and Peasant,* 26, Friedrich Katz, "Labor Conditions on Haciendas in Porfirian Mexico: Some Trends and Tendencies," *HAHR* 54 (Feb. 1974), 14–23.

12. Batt, "Capitalist Class Formation," 78.

13. Joseph, *Revolution from Without,* 36–37; Chacón, "Yucatán and the Mexican Revolution," 55; and Chardon, *Geographic Aspects,* 35 and chap. 4, provide well-documented general discussions of the comparative size of the henequen plantation; cf. Batt, "Capitalist Class Formation," 79–81, for extensive data on the size of haciendas in the municipio of Espita.

14. E.g., see Frost and Arnold, *The American Egypt,* 366–67, and see the discussion in Joseph, *Revolution from Without,* 36–37, 318, n. 12.

15. Hartman, "Henequen Empire," 84–85, 221; cf. Chacón, "Yucatán and the Mexican Revolution," 36; Wells, *Yucatán's Gilded Age,* chap. 5.

16. Wells, "Violence and Social Control," 221–24.

17. Suárez Molina, *La evolución económica,* 1:71. It would be helpful, however, if future studies could tell us more precisely the percentages of the estate's labor force made up respectively of "part-timers" (villagers working for a finite period of time) and "full-timers" (resident peones).

18. For the succession of "colonization" schemes proposed and implemented during the period, see Wells, *Yucatán's Gilded Age,* chap. 6; Moisés González Navarro, *La colonización en México* (Mexico City, 1960), 33, 83–84; Lapointe, "La prolongation," 187–92. According to Betancourt Pérez, *Revoluciones y crisis,* 73, and Chardon, *Geographic Aspects,* 33, the Yaquis and all the contract workers put together never amounted to more than 10 to 15 percent of the total work force on the estates. On the lucrative politics of Yaqui deportation, in which President Díaz and Vice-President Corral were implicated with leading members of the Sonoran and Yucatecan oligarchies, see Evelyn Hu-Dehart, "Development and Rural Rebellion: Pacification of the Yaquis in the Late *Porfiriato,*" *HAHR* 54 (Feb. 1974), 72–93; Jesús Luna, *La carrera pública de Don Ramón Corral* (Mexico City, 1975), 37–55, 107–11; and Gerald Barber, "Horizon of Thorns: Yucatán at the Turn of the Century" (master's thesis, University of the Americas, 1974), chap. 4.

19. Patch, "La formación," 36, 40–42.

20. José Luis Sierra Villarreal, "Hacia una economía política de la hacienda henequenera" (pt. 2), *YHE* 4 (July–Aug. 1980), 21–22.

21. For example, Manuel Martín, "Acerca del capitalismo en Yucatán (siglo XIX)," *YHE* 1 (Nov.–Dec. 1977), 22–23, suggests that the drastic reduction in the region's current and potential work force during the bloodiest years of the Caste War was probably a greater factor in henequen's labor crisis a half century later than most writers have acknowledged.

22. For a thorough discussion of Turner and the contemporary impact of *Barbarous Mexico,* see Chacón, "Yucatán and the Mexican Revolution," 64–75; also see "Apéndice: Comentarios contemporáneos sobre *México bárbaro,*" *Problemas Agrícolas e Industriales de México* 7:2 (1955), 159–84. The same issue of the journal also includes a Spanish translation of Turner's classic.

23. E.g., see Alberto García Cantón, *Memorias de un ex-hacendado* (Mérida, 1965); International Harvester Company, *The Binder Twine Industry* (Chicago, 1912); and Gustavo Molina Font, *La tragedia de Yucatán* (Mexico City, 1941).

24. E.g., see Frost and Arnold, *American Egypt;* Baerlein, *Mexico: The Land of Unrest;* Friedrich Katz, ed., *La servidumbre agraria en México en la época porfiriana* (Mexico City, 1976).

25. For example, in 1970, González Navarro, *Raza y tierra,* chap. 6, indi-

cated the need for a comprehensive, analytical review of Porfirian labor conditions, but ultimately relied heavily upon Turner's sensationalized account.

26. For an insightful critique of the traditional debate on the labor question, see Wells, "Violence and Social Control," 214–16.

27. Sierra Villarreal, "Hacia una economía política" (pt. 2), 16–17.

28. Katz, "Labor Conditions," 18; Joseph, *Revolution from Without*, 73.

29. Bellingeri, "Proyecto de investigación," 9–11. Cf. the other general treatments of this process of involution in Martín, "Acerca del capitalismo;" Marie F. Labrecque, "La herencia maya del proletariado rural de Yucatán," *YHE* 5 (Jan.–Feb. 1982), 25–30; A. J. Graham Knox, "Henequen Haciendas, Maya Peones, and the Mexican Revolution Promises of 1910: Reform and Reaction in Yucatán, 1910–1940," *Caribbean Studies* 17 (Apr.–July 1977), 63–65; and González Rodríguez et al., *Yucatán: Peonaje y liberación,* passim.

30. Patch, "Apuntes," 11. Patch's provocative essay, like Remmers's monograph on the origins of henequen monoculture, hints at the need for a new study of nineteenth-century Yucatecan political history that would correlate institutional trends in state formation with the growth of commercial agriculture.

31. Wells, "Violence and Social Control," 217–26. Wells draws upon Tomás Aznar Barbachano, *Las mejoras materiales,* 2 vols. (Campeche, 1859), 1:7, for these labor categories. Some pre-auge tenant-sharecroppers, who managed to avoid debt, lived in neighboring towns; most resided on the estate like peones and *luneros.* According to Wells, prior to the boom, luneros and tenant-sharecroppers received milpa while the peón was prohibited from planting corn. In exchange for his plot, the lunero was obliged to work one day a week for the patrón—hence the term *Monday man.* For the late-colonial origins of the lunero, see Patch, "Agrarian Change in Eighteenth-Century Yucatán." Remmers, "Henequen, the Caste War," 471–82, reports findings on labor conditions from 1847–83 that support Wells's characterization of the pre-auge regime. Also see Wells, *Yucatán's Gilded Age,* chap. 6.

32. Joseph, *Revolution from Without,* 71–75; also see Katz, "Labor Conditions," 17–19; and Chacón, "Yucatán and the Mexican Revolution," 76–77.

33. Batt, "Capitalist Class Formation," 110. Developing the point that paternalism was rapidly phased out in the northwest, Wells, *Yucatán's Gilded Age,* chap. 5, points out the high incidence of *permuta,* or estate-swapping, between and within large henequenero families. Such trading, he argues, underscores the absentee planter's attenuated connection with the estate and its work force.

34. Joseph, *Revolution from Without,* 79; Katz, "Labor Conditions," 18; Chardon, *Geographic Aspects,* 103–16; Siegfried Askinasy, *El problema agrario de Yucatán* (Mexico City, 1936), 30–31; Wells, *Yucatán's Gilded Age,* chap. 6.

35. Katz, "Labor Conditions," 14–23.

36. E.g., see Esther Iglesias L., "Historias de vida de campesinos hene-queneros," *YHE* 2 (May–June 1978), 3–15, which provides excerpts from oral history interviews with former peones, who discuss with candor and some poignancy their former experience with "slavery." Significantly, an-thropologists believe that the Spanish word *esclavitud* passed directly into the Maya language from that period. See, e.g., Labrecque, "From Peasantry to Proletariat," 137.

37. Katz, "Labor Conditions," 23, and "El sistema," 131; also see Joseph, *Revolution from Without*, 79–80, and Wells, *Yucatán's Gilded Age*, chap. 6.

38. García Quintanilla, "La formación de la estructura económica," 49.

39. Patch, "Apuntes," 15; Martín, "Acerca del capitalismo," 21–22, would date the onset of capitalism as "the predominant mode of production" in Yucatán even earlier, with the arrival of the sugar boom, ca. 1825–30.

40. Wells, *Yucatán's Gilded Age*, "Introduction;" and see chap. 3, n. 16.

41. Batt, "Capitalist Class Formation," 112–13.

42. Sierra Villarreal, "Hacia una economía política" (pt. 2), 17.

43. Joseph, *Revolution from Without*, 86, 327 n. 40; cf. José Luis Sierra Villarreal, "Hacia una economía política de la hacienda henequenera" (pt. 1), *YHE* 3 (Jan.–Feb. 1980), 62.

44. Wells, "Violence and Social Control," passim, and Martín, "Acerca del capitalismo," 23–24, suggest they were hereditary; Batt, "Capitalist Class Formation," 99–100, disagrees. Martín also discusses an earlier round of the debate, providing references to positions first staked out in the 1930s and 1940s.

45. Batt, "Capitalist Class Formation," 99.

46. Joseph, *Revolution from Without*, 74; Katz, "Labor Conditions," 18.

47. Gonzalo Cámara Zavala, "Historia de la industria henequenera hasta 1919," in Yucatán, *Enciclopedia Yucatanense*, 3:703.

48. E.g., see ibid., and Hartman, "Henequen Empire," 118; cf. the slightly lower range of figures in Katz, "El sistema," 120–21.

49. E.g., see Fidelio Quintal Martín, *Carácter de la guerra campesina de 1847*, 38, and *Yucatán: Un período de historia contemporánea, 1910–1924* (Mérida, 1974), 8.

50. Katz, "Labor Conditions," 1; Wells, "Violence and Social Control," 229–31; Joseph, *Revolution from Without*, 74.

51. Wells, "Violence and Social Control," 231. Wells's argument that wages fluctuated with the price of fiber seems borne out by Chacón's documentary research on the last years of the Old Regime. See Chacón, "Yucatán and the Mexican Revolution," 177.

52. E.g., Martín, "Acerca del capitalismo," 19–20; and García Quintanilla, "La formación de la estructura económica," 58.

53. Sierra Villarreal, "Hacia una economía política" (pt. 2), 21.

54. Bellingeri, "Proyecto de investigación," 5.

55. Sierra Villarreal, "Hacia una economía política" (pt. 2), 18; also see Bojórquez Urzáiz, "Yucatán: Plantaciones colonialistas;" Quezada, "El origen de la producción."

56. Joseph, *Revolution from Without*, 78–79.

57. Batt, "Capitalist Class Formation," 102–3.

58. Wells, "Violence and Social Control," 221; Katz, "Labor Conditions," 19–20.

59. Wells, "Violence and Social Control," 221; Joseph, *Revolution from Without*, 84–85; Chacón, "Yucatán and the Mexican Revolution," 120–21, 194–95; Batt, "Capitalist Class Formation," 124, 102–3.

60. For a discussion of the revisionist trend in interpreting debt peonage, see Arnold J. Bauer, "Rural Workers in Spanish America: Problems of Peonage and Oppression," *HAHR* 59 (Feb. 1979), 34–63. Bauer explicitly refers to late nineteenth-century Yucatán and Mexico's tropical southeastern lowlands as extreme cases that justify the more traditional view (p. 36). Recent work on neighboring Guatemala around the turn of the century suggests some interesting parallels. See David McCreery, "Debt Servitude in Rural Guatemala, 1876–1936," *HAHR* 63 (Nov. 1983), 735–59.

61. González Navarro, *Raza y tierra*, chap. 6; Batt, "Capitalist Class Formation," 106–7; Joseph, *Revolution from Without*, 81–84; Lee, "The Tourist Industry," 128; Bellingeri, "Proyecto de investigación," 11–12; Labrecque, "From Peasantry to Proletariat," 137–38; Chacón, "Yucatán and the Mexican Revolution," chap. 1; Francisco J. Paoli and Enrique Montalvo, *El socialismo olvidado de Yucatán* (Mexico City, 1977), 38–39.

62. Wells, *Yucatán's Gilded Age*, chap. 6; also see Sierra Villarreal, "Hacia una economía política" (pt. 2), 20–22.

63. Patterson, *Slavery and Social Death: A Comparative Study* (Cambridge, Mass., 1982).

64. Ibid., 5–10. Wells bases his interpretation of the plight of the Yaqui on Turner's account.

65. Patterson, *Slavery and Social Death*, 21.

66. E.g., see Sierra Villarreal, "Hacia una economía política" (pt. 2), 17.

67. Wells also develops these themes in "Violence and Social Control," 232–36.

68. Wells and Gilbert Joseph are currently investigating legal and extralegal responses to the plantation regime by peones and villagers during the final years of the Porfiriato.

69. E.g., see Joseph, *Revolution from Without*, 71, 83–85, and Labrecque, "La herencia maya," 29–30.

70. Chacón, "Yucatán and the Mexican Revolution," 99–100, 146–47.

71. Ibid., 179–80; cf. Knox, "Henequen Haciendas, Maya Peones," 67.

72. For example, in the eastern municipio of Espita, a marginal henequen area, Batt, "Capitalist Class Formation," chap. 3, seems to suggest a connec-

tion between the institutionalization of some important paternalistic benefits and maintenance of the social peace.

73. Katz, "Labor Conditions," 19, and "El sistema," 107–14; Joseph, *Revolution from Without*, chaps. 1–3; Wells, *Yucatán's Gilded Age*, chaps. 2–3, 6; Joseph and Wells, "Corporate Control."

74. Patch, "Apuntes," 12. Prior to 1905, the peso was at par with the U.S. dollar; after 1905, the peso was fixed at 2:1 with the dollar.

75. E.g., see Katz, "El sistema," 104–7; Irigoyen, "Don Us Escalante," 17–32; Remmers, "Henequen, the Caste War," pt. 3; Joseph and Wells, "Corporate Control," 73–75; Raquel Barceló Quintal, "La oligarquía henequenera. Un estudio de caso: La familia Escalante" (Tesis de Licenciatura en Antropología Social, Universidad de Yucatán, 1982); Barceló Quintal, "El desarrollo de la banca y el henequén, *YHE* 5 (Jan.–Feb. 1982), 3–24; and José Luis Sierra Villarreal, "Oro amarillo, oro verde y oro negro: Tres colores y . . . ¿una misma dependencia?" *YHE* 5 (July–Aug. 1981), 23–54.

76. Remmers, "Henequen, the Caste War," chap. 7; Víctor Suárez Molina, "La industria cordelera en Yucatán en el siglo XIX," *DdY*, Feb. 20, 1972, pp. 3, 11; Labrecque, "From Peasantry to Proletariat," 110–34; Cámara Zavala, "Historia de la industria henequenera," 692; Esther Iglesias, "Yucatán, monocultivo, oro verde y decadencia henequenera: La región y dependencia del mercado norteamericano" (Paper presented at the "Primer encuentro sobre impactos regionales de las relaciones económicas México-Estados Unidos," Guanajuato, 1981); Joseph, *Revolution from Without*, 30.

77. In their attempt to analyze late Porfirian Yucatán's stark condition of economic dependence, particularly the intermediary role which ruling local elites played in furthering penetration of the monocrop economy by North American capital, Joseph and Wells utilize functional dimensions of the "collaborator model," developed by Ronald Robinson, John Gallagher, and other "imperial historians" of Africa and Asia. See Joseph and Wells, "Corporate Control," 72–86, 93–94, nn. 6–8, and "Collaboration and Informal Empire in Yucatán: The Case for Political Economy," *LARR* 18:3 (1983), 204–18. Diane Roazen Parrillo borrows their conceptual framework in her recent study, "U.S. Business Interests and the Sisal Industry of Yucatán, Mexico, 1876–1924" (Ph.D. diss., University of Chicago, 1984).

78. Suárez Molina, *La evolución económica*, 1:41–66; Joseph and Wells, "Corporate Control," 74–75. Also see Cámara Zavala, "Historia de la industria henequenera," 691–708, and Barceló Quintal, "La oligarquía henequenera," chap. 4.

79. On the formation of IHC and Olegario Molina's early political and economic career, see Joseph and Wells, "Corporate Control," 75–80; Wells, "Family Elites," 232–37; Roazen Parrillo, "U.S. Business Interests," chap. 2; Francisco A. Casasús, "Ensayo biográfico del Licenciado Olegario Molina Solís," *RUY* 14 (May–June 1972), 68–95.

80. Thomas Benjamin, "International Harvester and the Henequen Marketing System of Yucatán, 1898–1915: A New Perspective," *Inter-American Economic Affairs* 31 (Winter 1977), 3–19, provides a comprehensive discussion of the historiographical debate and extensive bibliographical references for the major positions prior to the surge in scholarly production beginning in the 1970s. Recent contributions asserting Harvester's increasing control over the monocrop economy include the aforementioned works by Katz, Joseph and Wells, Suárez Molina, Paoli and Montalvo, Chacón, Labrecque, Knox, Barber, Barceló Quintal, and Iglesias L., as well as Ross Williams, "Yucatán Henequen: A Study in Microeconomics" (master's thesis, University of the Americas, 1972); David A. Franz, "Bullets and Bolshevists: A History of the Mexican Revolution in Yucatán, 1910–1924" (Ph.D. diss., University of New Mexico, 1973); Renán Irigoyen, "Origen y trayectoria del henequén," *RUY* 15 (Mar.–Apr. 1973), 114–28; Kendrick A. Clements, "'A Kindness to Carranza': William Jennings Bryan, International Harvester, and Intervention in Yucatán," *Nebraska History* 57 (Winter 1976), 479–90; Sierra Villarreal, "Oro amarillo;" García Quintanilla, "La formación de la estructura económica;" Jorge Montalvo, "Apuntes sobre el capitalismo y el henequén en Yucatán," *YHE* 1 (Sept.–Oct. 1977), 36–43; Raquel Barceló Quintal, "El ferrocarril y la oligarquía henequenera," *YHE* 5 (July–Aug. 1981), 23–54; and Iván Franco C., "Casta divina y monopolio," in González Rodríguez et al., *Yucatán: Peonaje y liberación*, 45–57.

81. The contract was published in *Revista de Yucatán* (Mérida), Nov. 27, 1921, p. 1, and has been reproduced in a variety of secondary accounts, e.g., Mena Brito, *Reestructuración histórica*, 2:205. An English version and analysis is found (on microfilm) in United States, National Archives, *Record Group 59, Records of the Department of State Relating to the Internal Affairs of Mexico, 1910–1929* (Washington, D.C., 1959), 812.61326/372, 375 (Dec. 1921); and in Hartman, "Henequen Empire," 195–98.

82. E.g., see Joseph and Wells, "Corporate Control," 80–90.

83. Ibid., 84–86; also see Chacón, "Yucatán and the Mexican Revolution," 29–30, 33, 131. Fred V. Carstensen and Diane Roazen Parrillo, "International Harvester, Molina y Compañía, and the Henequen Market: A Comment," *LARR* 18:3 (1983), 197–203, agree that, prior to 1903, Peabody was financially supported by the McCormick Harvesting Machine Company but, pending further evidence, doubt that "McCormick controlled or even had detailed knowledge of Peabody's activities." Previously, in a paper presented at the 1978 American Historical Association meeting, entitled "American Enterprise, American Government, and the Sisal Industry of Yucatán, Mexico, 1876–1924," Roazen Parrillo had no doubts regarding Peabody's complicity and cited a "statement by Dr. Fred V. Carstensen . . . research consultant for the International Harvester Co." and "evidence found in the McCormick files, Madison Historical Society," to substantiate her case. For a

further discussion of the various claims and evidence involved, see Joseph and Wells, "Collaboration and Informal Empire."

84. Benjamin, "International Harvester and the Henequen Marketing System," 3–4, 6–8; Joseph and Wells, "Corporate Control," 72, 86, 96–97, nn. 40, 57; Joseph, *Revolution from Without*, 53–60.

85. Joseph, *Revolution from Without*, 133–149; Benjamin, "International Harvester and the Henequen Marketing System," 4–8, 17–19.

86. E.g., Casasús, "Ensayo biográfico;" Liga de Acción Social, *Biografía del Señor Licenciado Don Olegario Molina Solís* (Mérida, 1925); Molina Font, *La tragedia de Yucatán*, especially 58, 82; Manuel Irabién Rosado, *Historia de los ferrocarriles* (Mérida, 1928); Benjamin, "International Harvester and the Henequen Marketing System," 4–5; Jeffery Brannon and Eric N. Baklanoff, "Corporate Control of a Monocrop Economy: A Comment," *LARR* 18:3 (1983), 193–96, and "Forward and Backward Linkages in a Plantation Economy: Immigrant Entrepreneurship and Industrial Development in Yucatán, Mexico," Working Paper Series, College of Commerce and Business Administration, University of Alabama, 1983.

87. Irabién Rosado, *Historia de los ferrocarriles*, 13. Irabién's primary focus was railroad development, but Mexican and foreign writers have applied his sentiments uniformly to the evolution of the henequen industry as well. E.g., Molina Font, "La tragedia," 58. Indeed, as Chacón, "Yucatán and the Mexican Revolution," 9–10, 221–24, has shown, direct foreign investment in the state during the Porfiriato was insignificant, amounting to less than $2 million.

88. Brannon and Baklanoff, "Corporate Control: A Comment."

89. However, Joseph and Wells, "Corporate Control," 89–90, reveal that on a variety of occasions IHC received offers from powerful Yucatecan henequeros to purchase some of Yucatán's largest and most profitable plantations. According to the authors, this "suggests that the extent of the oligarchy's dealings with the cordage trust were even more widespread than is commonly held, and it qualifies the rather exaggerated regional assertion that Yucatecans jealously guarded their plantations from foreign ownership to the extent of categorically eschewing all forms of direct foreign investment." President McCormick of Harvester rejected these offers, Joseph and Wells contend, because the corporation was content to control production indirectly, through the market.

90. Alejandra García Quintanilla, "Historia y etapas de la producción de una mercancía: Henequén, 1850–1915," *YHE* 5 (July–Aug. 1981), 3–22; Baklanoff and Brannon, "Forward and Backward Linkages."

91. Chardon, *Geographic Aspects*, 160.

92. Katz, "El sistema," 133n.

93. Joseph and Wells, "Collaboration and Informal Empire." For more on this distinction between "elite" and "oligarchy," which emphasizes the pro-

gressive concentration of land, productive capacity, and political power in the hands of fewer and fewer families, see Joseph and Wells, "Corporate Control," 77–80; Wells, *Yucatán's Gilded Age,* chap. 3; Hartman, "Henequen Empire," 35; Irigoyen, "Origen y trayectoria," 125. Wells, "Family Elites" and *Yucatán's Gilded Age,* chap. 3, distinguishes two distinct types of planter families which intermarried to form a dynamic, closely knit oligarchy: (1) traditional large hacendado families like the aristocratic Peóns, whose power and prestige dated back to the colony; and (2) nouveau-riche families, like the Molinas, whose principal source of wealth was the burgeoning import-export trade rather than land, and who parleyed their brokerage for foreign corporations into local control of the henequen trade, then bought plantations.

94. Benjamin, "International Harvester and the Henequen Marketing System."

95. Baklanoff and Brannon, "Corporate Control: A Comment;" Carstensen and Roazen Parrillo, "International Harvester, Molina y Compañía;" Roazen Parrillo, "U.S. Business Interests."

96. Carstensen and Roazen Parrillo, "International Harvester, Molina y Compania." For a fuller statement of their position, as well as Joseph and Wells's response, see the freewheeling "Commentary and Debate" in *LARR* 18:3 (1983), 193–218.

97. E.g., see González Navarro, *Raza y tierra,* chap. 7; Joseph, *Revolution from Without,* chap. 1; Wells, *Yucatán's Gilded Age,* chap. 2; Roazen Parrillo, "U.S. Business Interests," chaps. 1–3; Remmers, "Henequen, the Caste War," pt. 3.

98. Wells, "Family Elites," 252–53; Chacón, "Yucatán and the Mexican Revolution;" Joseph, *Revolution from Without.*

99. Joseph and Wells, "Corporate Control," 73, 90–92. Joseph and Wells contend that Harvester's preference for market control through local collaborators reflected modern economic imperialism in its earlier stages. Prior to 1914, the predominant strategy of North American "supply-oriented" investors in Mexico and elsewhere called for substantial direct stakes in agriculture, oil, and mining enclaves, which frequently entailed the construction of "company towns" and an expensive network of horizontal and vertical linkages in the host country. By contrast, the very informal nature of IHC's control relationship absolved the corporation from putting anything back into Yucatán in the form of social investment and obviated the development of all economic infrastructure beyond that needed to get fiber quickly to market. Today it has become almost standard practice for modern corporations to penetrate the economies of Third World societies indirectly, channeling capital through powerful local intermediaries, and thereby avoiding "sunken" investments in infrastructure and technology. Cf. Mira Wilkins, *The Emergence of Multinational Enterprise: American Business Abroad*

from the Colonial Era to 1914 (Cambridge, Mass., 1979), 115–24; and for an excellent discussion of regional variation in the development of the Porfirian export economy, which focuses on the relationship between foreign investors and local elites, see Mark Wasserman, *Capitalists, Caciques, and Revolution: The Native Elite and Foreign Enterprise in Chihuahua, Mexico, 1854–1911* (Chapel Hill, 1984), esp. 148–64.

100. Roazen Parrillo, "U.S. Business Interests," pts. 3 and 4; Joseph and Wells, "Corporate Control," 90–92.

101. Joseph and Wells, "Corporate Control," 92; Carstensen and Roazen Parrillo, "International Harvester, Molina y Compañía;" Eric N. Baklanoff, "The Diversification Quest: A Monocrop Export Economy in Transition," in Moseley and Terry, *Yucatán: A World Apart,* 202–44; "History of the International Harvester Company," H. L. Boyle Files, International Harvester Company Archives, Chicago, n.d. (1947).

102. E.g., see Joseph and Wells, "Corporate Control," 92–93; Joseph, *Revolution from Without,* 288–304; Roazen Parrillo, "U.S. Business Interests," pt. 4; but cf. Baklanoff and Brannon, "Forward and Backward Linkages," for a somewhat more hopeful interpretation.

103. Joseph and Wells, "Corporate Control," 93.

5. Imported Revolution and the Crisis of the Plantation Economy

1. Bailey, "Revisionism," 62.

2. Franz, "Bullets and Bolshevists" (1973); Chacón, "Yucatán and the Mexican Revolution" (1982); Joseph, *Revolution from Without* (1982); González Navarro, *Raza y tierra* (1970); Knox, "Henequen Haciendas, Maya Peones" (1977); Paoli and Montalvo, *El socialismo olvidado* (1977). Of great value to these professional scholars has been the earlier work of Yucatecan economic historian Renán Irigoyen. E.g., see "El impulso a la economía de Yucatán durante el gobierno de Alvarado," *RUY* 7 (Mar.–Apr. 1965), 45–71.

3. Batt, "Capitalist Class Formation" (1981), chap. 4.

4. For a review of recent trends in the regional historiography of the Mexican Revolution, see Gilbert M. Joseph, "Mexico's 'Popular Revolution': Mobilization and Myth in Yucatán, 1910–1940," *Latin American Perspectives* 6 (Summer 1979), 46–50; Carr, "Recent Regional Studies;" John Womack, Jr., "The Mexican Economy during the Revolution, 1910–1920: Historiography and Analysis," *Marxist Perspectives* 4 (Winter 1978), 80–123; and W. Dirk Raat, *The Mexican Revolution: An Annotated Guide to Recent Scholarship* (Boston, 1982).

5. Bailey, "Revisionism;" Michael C. Meyer, "Perspectives on Mexican Revolutionary Historiography," *New Mexico Historical Review* 44 (Apr. 1969), 167–80; Montalvo Ortega, "Historia y política."

6. Enduring pro-Revolutionary treatments include: Edmundo Bolio Ontiveros, *De la cuna al paredón: Anecdotario de la vida, muerte y gloria de Felipe Carrillo Puerto* (Mérida, 1929); José Castillo Torre, *A la luz del relámpago: Ensayo de biografía subjetiva de Felipe Carrillo Puerto* (Mexico City, 1934); Acrelio Carrillo Puerto, *La familia Carrillo Puerto de Motul* (Mérida, 1959); Bustillos Carrillo, *Yucatán al servicio de la patria y la Revolución* (1959); Bolio Ontiveros, *Yucatán en la dictadura y en la Revolución* (1967); Renán Irigoyen, *Salvador Alvarado: Extraordinario estadista de la Revolución* (Mérida, 1973); Renán Irigoyen, *Felipe Carrillo Puerto: Primer gobernante socialista en México* (Mérida, 1974); Alberto Cámara Patrón and Vicente Ayora Sarlat, "Vida y obra de Felipe Carrillo Puerto," in *Memoria de los actos realizados en el quincuagésimo aniversario de la Universidad de Yucatán* (Mérida, 1973), 97–127; and Antonio Betancourt Pérez, *El asesinato de Carrillo Puerto* (Mérida, 1974). Alvarado has also been eulogized in his native Sonora, most recently in Juan Antonio Ruibal Corella, *Los tiempos de Salvador Alvarado* (Hermosillo, 1982). For anti-Revolutionary works see, e.g., Anastasio Manzanilla D., *El bolchevismo criminal de Yucatán* (Mexico City, 1921); Adolfo Ferrer, *El archivo de Felipe Carrillo Puerto: El callismo; la corrupción del régimen obregonista* (New York, 1924); and Bernardino Mena Brito, *Bolchevismo y democracia en México: Pugna entre dos partidos políticos en Yucatán durante de la Revolución Constitucionalista* (Mexico City, 1933).

7. A partial bibliography of negative evaluations of Yucatán's agrarian reform appears in Gilbert M. Joseph, "Apuntes hacia una nueva historia regional: Yucatán y la Revolución Mexicana, 1915–1940," *RUY* 19 (Jan.–Feb. 1977), 21–22.

8. E.g., Manuel M. Escoffié, *Yucatán en la cruz* (Mérida, 1957); Mena Brito, *Reestructuración histórica*, vol. 3.

9. Joseph, *Revolution from Without*, 370, n. 11, provides a series of citations in the local press.

10. E.g., Molina Font, *La tragedia*, which also contains an articulate critique by Luis Cabrera; Manuel Zapata Casares, *Vía-Crucis del henequén: Colección de escritos sobre el gran problema de Yucatán* (Mérida, 1961).

11. See the discussion and references in Joseph, *Revolution from Without*, xiv, 295–97, 370 n. 16, and Thomas G. Sanders, "Henequen: The Structure of Agrarian Frustration," *American University Field Staff Reports*, North American Series, 5 (July 1979).

12. Quotation from Bailey, "Revisionism," 73; see, e.g., Gilbert M. Joseph, "Revolution from Without: The Mexican Revolution in Yucatán, 1910–1940," in Moseley and Terry, *Yucatán: A World Apart*," 144–145; Chacón, "Yucatán and the Mexican Revolution," 1–20; Knox, "Henequen Haciendas, Maya Peones."

13. Franz, "Bullets and Bolshevists," 284; Chacón, "Yucatán and the Mexican Revolution," 18.

14. Knox, "Henequen Haciendas, Maya Peones," adopts a similar organizational structure.

15. Chacón, "Yucatán and the Mexican Revolution," 19; Franz, "Bullets and Bolshevists," 5–43, 284–85.

16. Wells, *Yucatán's Gilded Age*, chap. 6; Joseph, *Revolution from Without,* chap. 3; Batt, "Capitalist Class Formation," chap. 4; Paoli and Montalvo, *El socialismo olvidado,* 36–47.

17. Franz, "Bullets and Bolshevists," 280, 287–88.

18. Ibid., 281, 289–90 n. 15.

19. Chacón, "Yucatán and the Mexican Revolution," 489.

20. Eugenia Meyer, *Conciencia histórica norteamericana sobre la Revolución de 1910* (Mexico City, 1970), 200; cf. Bailey, "Revisionism," 68–70. The work of Frank Tannenbaum, most notably *The Mexican Agrarian Revolution* (1930) and *Peace by Revolution: Mexico after 1910* (New York, 1933), was particularly influential in establishing this pro-Revolutionary tradition among North American academics.

21. Cf. Bailey, "Revisionism," 76, 79.

22. E.g., see Chacón's "Yucatán and the Mexican Revolution," 13–14. The same critique would also apply to Knox, "Henequen Haciendas, Maya Peones," and to James C. Carey, *The Mexican Revolution in Yucatán, 1915–1924* (Boulder, Col., 1985), which was received as this book went to press. Cf. Guillermo Boils Morales, "La reformas progresistas durante el gobierno de Salvador Alvarado en Yucatán," *YHE* 1 (Mar.–Apr. 1978), 15, who discusses the historiographical problem of weighing Alvarado's capacity for forceful leadership against the conjuncture of political and social conditions in which he operated.

23. In addition to the works of these authors previously cited, see Montalvo Ortega, "Caudillismo y estado en la Revolución Mexicana: El gobierno de Alvarado en Yucatán," *Nova Americana* 1 (1979), 13–36; Paoli Bolio, "Carrillo Puerto y el PSS," *RUY* 16 (Jan.–Feb. 1974), 75–91, *Salvador Alvarado y la Revolución en Yucatán* (Mérida, 1981), and "Yucatán, embrión del estado mexicano: Gobierno de Salvador Alvarado, 1915–1918" (Ph.D. diss., Universidad Ibero-Americana, 1982); Joseph, "The Fragile Revolution: Cacique Politics and Revolutionary Process in Yucatán," *LARR* 15: 1 (1980), 39–64; and Margaret A. Goodman, "The Effectiveness of the Mexican Revolution as an Agent of Change in the State of Yucatán, Mexico" (Ph.D. diss., Columbia University, 1970).

24. See Bailey, "Revisionism," and the historiographical surveys cited in n. 4. The most significant and sustained Marxist critique appears in the works of Arnaldo Córdova, most notably *La ideología de la Revolución*

Mexicana: La formación del nuevo régimen (Mexico City, 1973). The most influential traditionalist critique has been delivered by the French historian, Jean Meyer. E.g., see *The Cristero Rebellion: The Mexican People between Church and State, 1926–1929*, tr. Richard Southern (Cambridge, 1976) and *La Revolución Mejicana* (Barcelona, 1973).

25. E.g., Albert L. Michaels and Marvin Bernstein, "The Modernization of the Old Order: Organization and Periodization of Twentieth Century Mexican History," in James W. Wilkie, Michael C. Meyer, and Edna Monzón de Wilkie, eds., *Contemporary Mexico: Papers of the IV International Congress of Mexican History* (Berkeley, 1976), 687–710.

26. E.g., see Eugenia Meyer, "La periodización de la historia contemporánea de México," in Wilkie, Meyer, and Wilkie, *Contemporary Mexico*, 730–46.

27. Carr, "Recent Regional Studies," 7.

28. Joseph, "Mexico's 'Popular Revolution,'" 48.

29. Bailey, "Revisionism," 77–78.

30. Carr, "Recent Regional Studies," 7.

31. Knight, "Peasant and Caudillo," 19.

32. E.g., see Friedrich Katz, *The Secret War in Mexico: Europe, the United States and the Mexican Revolution* (Chicago, 1981); Lorenzo Meyer, *Mexico and the United States in the Oil Controversy, 1917–1942* (Austin, 1977); Wasserman, *Capitalists, Caciques, and Revolution;* and Roazen Parrillo, "U.S. Business Interests." Cf. Alex M. Saragoza, "The Formation of a Mexican Elite: The Industrialization of Monterrey, Nuevo León, 1880–1920" (Ph.D. diss., University of California, San Diego, 1978), for a regional case where domestic entrepreneurs had some success in keeping foreign interests at a distance. And see Womack's thoughtful analysis of the new literature on Mexico's political economy ("The Mexican Economy during the Revolution").

33. Katz, "Labor Conditions," 14–23; Wells, *Yucatán's Gilded Age*, chap. 6; Joseph, *Revolution from Without*, chap. 3.

34. Cf. Womack, *Zapata;* Paul Friedrich, *Agrarian Revolt in a Mexican Village*, 2d ed. (Chicago, 1977), 58–142; Heather Fowler Salamini, *Agrarian Radicalism in Veracruz, 1920–38* (Lincoln, Nebr., 1978), chap. 1.

35. In Iglesias L., "Historias de vida," 9–10, former peones recall their isolation and the hard work regimen which made it impossible for them to participate in the early skirmishes of the revolutionary era.

36. Wells, *Yucatán's Gilded Age*, chap. 6.

37. Joseph, *Revolution from Without*, 85–86; cf. Salamini, *Agrarian Radicalism*, chaps. 1–2; Raymond Th. Buve, "Peasant Movements, Caudillos and Land Reform during the Revolution (1910–1917) in Tlaxcala, Mexico," *Boletín de Estudios Latinoamericanos y del Caribe* 18 (June 1975), 112–52.

38. Montalvo Ortega, "Caudillismo y estado," 21–22; and see the account

of a contemporary labor organizer, Carlos Loveira, *El socialismo en Yucatán* (Havana, 1923).

39. Joseph, *Revolution from Without*, 86–89, cf. Franz, "Bullets and Bolshevists," 12–23; Wells, *Yucatán's Gilded Age*, "Epilogue."

40. Joseph, *Revolution from Without*, 87 and chaps. 4, 7, and 9, passim. Joseph first developed an appreciation for these little-noticed smaller fiber producers, rancheros, and *parcelarios* from the property census which was commissioned by General Alvarado's revolutionary government and published serially in the *Diario Official* during 1916–17.

41. Antonio Betancourt Pérez, *La problemática social: ¿Primera chispa de la Revolución Mexicana?* (Mérida, 1983); Gilbert M. Joseph and Allen Wells, "The Crisis of an Oligarchical Regime: Elite Politics, Rural Rebellion, and Patterns of Social Control in Yucatán, 1910–1913" (Paper presented at the meeting of the Latin American Studies Association, Albuquerque, 1985); José Luis Sierra Villarreal, "Prensa y lucha política en Yucatán, 1895–1915," mimeographed (Centro Regional del Sureste, INAH, 1984); Chacón, "Yucatán and the Mexican Revolution," chaps. 1–3. Also see Franz, "Bullets and Bolshevists," chaps. 1–3; Knox, "Henequen Haciendas, Maya Peones," 66–69; Joseph, *Revolution from Without*, 82–89. Still useful are the older political histories by Ramón Berzunza Pinto, "Las vísperas yucatecas de la Revolución," *Historia Mexicana* 6 (July–Sept. 1956), 75–88, and Bolio, *Yucatán en la dictadura*, and the contemporary account of Carlos R. Menéndez, *La primera chispa de la Revolución Mexicana* (Mérida, 1919).

42. The Morenistas were supporters of Delio Moreno Cantón, a distinguished lawyer and nephew of former governor, planter, and regional hero General Francisco Cantón. The Pinistas backed Tabascan-born José María Pino Suárez, a journalist and poet, who would later become Francisco Madero's vice-president.

43. Batt, "Capitalist Class Formation," 117–23, 131–39.

44. Ernest H. Gruening, *Un viaje al estado de Yucatán: Felipe Carrillo Puerto, su obra socialista* (Guanajuato, 1924), 5.

45. Friedrich Katz, "Peasants in the Mexican Revolution of 1910," in Joseph Spielberg and Scott Whiteford, eds., *Forging Nations: A Comparative View of Rural Ferment and Revolt* (East Lansing, Mich., 1976), 76.

46. Montalvo, "Caudillismo y estado;" Paoli and Montalvo, *El socialismo olvidado*, chaps. 1–2; Joseph, *Revolution from Without*, chaps. 4–5; Blanca González Rodríguez, "Cuatro proyectos de cambio en Yucatán," in Millet Cámara et al., *Hacienda y cambio social*, 75–102; Beatriz González Padilla, "La dirigencia política en Yucatán, 1909–1925," in Millet Cámara et al, *Hacienda y cambio social*, 103–66; Boils, "Las reformas progresistas;" and Douglas W. Richmond, "Yucatán durante la época carrancista" (Paper presented at the "Segunda Semana de la Historia de Yucatán," Mérida, 1980). While the focus is not theoretical, Chacón's "Yucatán and the Mexican Revo-

lution," chaps. 4–6, and "Salvador Alvarado and the Catholic Church: Church and State in Yucatán, 1914–1918," *Journal of Church and State,* forthcoming, also document the Constitutionalists' brand of caudillo populism.

47. Although there is a basic consensus in recent studies that Alvarado was a bourgeois reformer and Carrillo Puerto a Marxist revolutionary, Alvarado fancied himself a socialist and Carrillo Puerto often professed a vague and idiosyncratic Marxism. Characterizations of both chiefs as Bolsheviks abound in the contemporary literature (see n. 6). Some recent contributors have also portrayed Alvarado as a "utopian socialist." E.g., see Diego Valadés, "Ideas políticas y sociales de Salvador Alvarado," *Estudios de Historia Moderna y Contemporánea de México* 5 (1976), 109–18; and Antonio Pompa y Pompa, "Prólogo" to Salvador Alvarado, *Antología ideológica* (Mexico City, 1976), 7–17. A thorough discussion of their respective ideologies appears in Paoli and Montalvo, *El socialismo olvidado;* and Joseph, *Revolution from Without,* especially 101–2, 199–202.

48. For an explicit comparison of the Alvarado and Carrillo Puerto regimes, consult the monographs by Paoli and Montalvo, Joseph, and Franz, as well as González Rodríguez, "Cuatro proyectos."

49. Anna Macías, *Against All Odds: The Feminist Movement in Mexico to 1940* (Westport, Conn., 1982), chaps. 3–4; cf. Joseph, *Revolution From Without,* 217–19.

50. Based on an examination of agrarian files in the AGE, Joseph, *Revolution from Without,* chap. 5; Chacón, "Yucatán and the Mexican Revolution," chap. 6; and Knox, "Henequen Haciendas, Maya Peones," 68–73, have now documented that although Alvarado favored a moderate agrarian program, weighted heavily toward wage increases with little emphasis upon the division of existing estates, he did preside over a minimal program of ejidal distribution prior to a "stop order" by his superior, Carranza, in 1916. Moreover, largely to feed a hungry population during the 1915–16 seasons and to relieve mounting social tensions, Alvarado persuaded a number of hacendados to rent or temporarily cede parcels of milpa land to groups and entire communities of campesinos. At no point, however, did the general touch lands cultivated in henequen. The reason for Mexico City's opposition to even minimal land reform by Alvarado in Yucatán has been the subject of some discussion. Pressures applied on Carranza by the U.S. government on behalf of the cordage interests, Carranza's jealous defense of the prerogatives of the central government in the face of a challenge from a powerful regional subordinate, and Carranza's own ideological opposition to land reform have all been advanced, individually and in combination. For a discussion of the evidence supporting each argument, with appropriate citations, see Joseph, *Revolution from Without,* 125–33.

51. Carrillo Puerto's land policy remains perhaps the least understood of

his programs. Some writers have argued that Carrillo Puerto wanted to do away entirely with henequen monoculture and the great estate in order to restore the Maya campesino to his former way of life centered around the peasant village and maize-and-beans autarky. E.g., see González Navarro, *Raza y tierra*, 248. Others have contended that despite his reputation as a Marxist, where the land was concerned, Carrillo Puerto leaned more toward the bourgeois revolutionary tradition of Alvarado than the conservative peasant tradition of Zapata. They maintain that like Alvarado, Carrillo never intended to expropriate the henequen fields and, had he not been assassinated, would ultimately have sought to meet the campesinos' needs with better wages and working conditions. See e.g., Franz, "Bullets and Bolshevists," 243–45. The most recent interpretations of Carrillo Puerto's agrarian strategy argue that although he was a proponent of the ejido from his early days as a Zapatista, by the time he became Yucatán's governor he was a committed socialist and never lost sight of his goals to collectivize the operation of the ejido and, ultimately, to socialize the entire notion of property relationships in Yucatán. Carrillo Puerto sought to implement this strategy in two successive, although potentially overlapping phases. The first phase, virtually concluded before his death, centered on his promise to distribute ejidos to the state's pueblos. The selective inclusion of some *henequenales* in this first phase—expropriated from the largest and most intransigent planters—has generally gone unnoticed. Carrillo Puerto began to launch the second phase, which would have culminated in the socialization (but not the break-up) of plantation units, just two weeks before his regime was toppled. For a discussion of the debate and recent findings on Carrillo Puerto's agrarian program, see Joseph, *Revolution from Without*, chap. 8.

52. Joseph, *Revolution from Without*, chap. 7, especially 213–27. Carrillo Puerto's politicoreligious syncretism and the hagiographic cult that grew up in the campo following his execution in 1924 have drawn the attention of German scholar Manuel Sarkisyanz (University of Heidelberg), whose study, *Felipe Carrillo Puerto: Säkulare hagiographie aus dem revolutionären Mexiko*, is forthcoming. And see Santiago Domínguez Aké, *Aniversario del fusilamiento de Felipe Carrillo Puerto en Muxupib, Yucatán (Bilingüe: Español-Maya)* (Mérida, 1982), for a graphic illustration of this hagiographic cult today.

53. Mary Kay Vaughan, *The State, Education, and Social Class in Mexico, 1880–1928* (DeKalb, Ill., 1982), 98–115; also see Ramón D. Chacón, "Rural Educational Reform in Yucatán: From the Porfiriato to the Era of Salvador Alvarado, 1910–1918," *The Americas*, forthcoming. Earlier noteworthy contributions by local historians on Alvarado's and Carrillo's educational programs include Luis Álvarez Barret, "Orígenes y evolución de las escuelas rurales en Yucatán," *RUY* 13 (Nov.–Dec. 1971), 26–51; Antonio Betancourt Pérez, "La verdad sobre el origen de las escuelas rurales en Yucatán," *RUY*

13 (July–Aug. 1971), 34–76; and Fernando Gamboa Berzunza, "Visión pedagógica de Felipe Carrillo Puerto," *RUY* 3 (Jan.–Feb. 1961), 35–41.

54. González Navarro, *Raza y tierra,* 250.

55. On "retroactive revolution," see Chacón, "Yucatán and the Mexican Revolution," chap. 6; and Joseph, *Revolution from Without,* 108–10, 213–14.

56. Paoli and Montalvo, *El socialismo olvidado,* 171–72, and Joseph, *Revolution from Without,* 222, suggest that Carrillo Puerto's anticlerical approach to education likely encountered stiff resistance in the countryside. But cf. Iglesias L., "Historias de vida," 12–13, which provides enthusiastic endorsements for Carrillo Puerto's rural schools by former peones who claim their education enabled them to overcome alienation and passivity. For an oral history-based inquiry into the impact of socialist education on campesinos in Michoacán that might serve as a model for future work in Yucatán, see Marjorie Becker, "The Schoolhouse Rebellion: Revolution and Counterrevolution in the Mexican Countryside, 1934–1940" (Ph.D. diss., Yale University, forthcoming).

57. Batt, "Capitalist Class Formation," 131–63. Also see Aboites, "La Revolución Mexicana," and José Luis Domínguez, "Situación política en el partido de Sotuta (1911–1916)," in González Rodríguez et al., *Yucatán: Peonaje y liberación,* 178–205. Much awaited are the complete published findings of the Centro Regional del Sureste's current project on the PSS, its bases of support, and its impact throughout the region.

58. E.g., see the acrimonious debate between Betancourt Pérez, *El asesinato* and Roque Armando Sosa Ferreyro, *El crimen del miedo: Cómo y por qué fue asesinado Felipe Carrillo Puerto* (Mexico City, 1969). In the area of literature, see the award-winning play by Jaime Orosa Díaz, *Se vende un hombre* (Mérida, 1974; originally published 1959), and Antonio Magaña Esquivel, *La tierra enrojecida* (Mexico City, 1951).

59. E.g., Betancourt Pérez, *El asesinato;* Alma Reed, "Felipe Carrillo Puerto," *Boletín de la Universidad Nacional del Sureste,* época 2, 4 (June 1924), 20–21. This view has found its way into the popular oral tradition. See Domínguez Aké, *Aniversario del fusilamiento,* 6.

60. E.g., Sosa Ferreyro, *El crimen,* 42, 114ff.; cf. Antonio Betancourt Pérez, "¿Angel, o demonio?: Carrillo Puerto y 'Peregrina,'" *Juzgue* 2 (May 1973), 19.

61. E.g., Betancourt Pérez, *El asesinato;* Irigoyen, *Felipe Carrillo Puerto,* 41; [Rius], "Felipe Carrillo Puerto: El Salvador Allende Mexicano," *Los Agachados* 5 (June 1974), 20; Paoli and Montalvo, *El socialismo olvidado,* 175. Many of the proponents of this interpretation suggest as a corollary that the North American corporations whose control of the henequen market Carrillo Puerto sought to break were also parties to the murder contract which the planters took out on Carrillo Puerto.

62. Joseph, *Revolution from Without*, chaps. 7 and 9, and "The Fragile Revolution."

63. Joseph's incomplete, disparate data on the social background and political careers of these caciques were pieced together during the course of year-by-year archival and press research for 1910–24. Documentary evidence was corroborated in certain instances by interviewing at the local level. Joseph's research on these local bosses has afforded but a glimpse of their participation in the revolutionary process. In Yucatán and throughout Mexico as a whole, we need to know more about the means by which these "new men" recruited and maintained their followers and were, in turn, incorporated into larger regional coalitions.

64. E.g., see Jaime Orosa Díaz, "Carrillo Puerto en la historia y en la literatura," *Orbe* 31 (Aug. 1951), 75–77; Renán Irigoyen, "Carrillo Puerto, mártir de la cultura," *RUY* 16 (May–Aug. 1959), 20–23; [Rius], "Felipe Carrillo Puerto;" Carleton Beals, *Mexican Maze* (Philadelphia, 1931), 11–12.

65. See particularly the introductory chapter of *El socialismo olvidado*, "Lo populista y lo popular," 7–31.

66. Ibid., 175.

67. Carr, "Recent Regional Studies," 10.

68. Cf. Montalvo, "Historia y política;" Labrecque, "La herencia maya;" Joseph, *Revolution from Without*, 281–87. Although they are professional scholars, Paoli and Montalvo express the hope that Mexico's regional and local history will not remain the exclusive preserve of academicians. With other Marxist scholars, they advocate the design of historical projects that will tap the experience and creative energies of Mexican working people. Interestingly, the appearance of their study of Carrillo Puerto and the PSS in 1977 coincided with the organization of a series of regional labor history workshops by the Centro de Estudios Históricos del Movimiento Obrero Mexicano and the publication of transcripts of interviews with former associates of Carrillo Puerto in CEHSMO's journal, *Historia Obrera*.

69. Carr, "Recent Regional Studies," 10.

70. Joseph, *Revolution from Without*, 273–75.

71. Betancourt Pérez, *El asesinato*, 124–30; Irigoyen, *Felipe Carrillo Puerto*, 36–37.

72. Cf. Salamini, *Agrarian Radicalism*, 125–35; Friedrich, *Agrarian Revolt*, 124–30; and the essays in Brading, *Caudillo and Peasant*, which examine how the state undermined independent regional movements in the 1920s and 1930s. At present, historian Daniela Spenser (Centro de Investigaciones y Estudios Superiores en Antropología Social) is working on a comparative study of southeastern Mexican socialist parties (Yucatán, Chiapas, Tabasco) in the 1920s that will further clarify their relationships with an increasingly powerful bourgeois central state.

73. Vicente Lombardo Toledano, *El llanto del sureste* (Mexico City, 1934).
74. E.g., Bustillos Carrillo, *Yucatán*; Fernando Benítez, *Ki: El drama de un pueblo y de una planta,* 2d ed. (Mexico City, 1962).
75. González Navarro, *Raza y tierra,* 246–81; Joseph, *Revolution from Without,* 288–304; Jeffery Brannon and Eric N. Baklanoff, *Agrarian Reform and Public Enterprise in Mexico: The Political Economy of Yucatán's Henequen Industry* (University, Ala., forthcoming), chap. 3; Knox, "Henequen Haciendas, Maya Peones," 77–82; Iglesias L., "Yucatán, monocultivo."
76. In addition to the works referred to in the preceding note, see Eric Villanueva Mukul, *Así tomamos las tierras* (Mérida, 1984), a brief case study of agrarian struggle in the pueblo of Dzidzantún, based on interviews with former *agraristas*; Esther Iglesias L., *Estado y alianza de clases en la reforma agraria cardenista: El campesinado henequenero* (Mexico City, forthcoming); and Marie Lapointe, "Indigenisme et réforme agraire au Yucatán, 1937–1940" (Paper presented at the 44th International Congress of Americanists, Manchester, Engl., 1982).
77. For incisive analyses of the agrarian and political considerations behind the Cardenista land reform, see Lyle C. Brown, "Cárdenas: Creating a Campesino Power Base for Presidential Policy," in George Wolfskill and Douglas W. Richmond, eds., *Essays on the Mexican Revolution: Revisionist Views of the Leaders* (Austin, 1979), 101–36; and Nora Hamilton, *The Limits of State Autonomy: Post-Revolutionary Mexico* (Princeton, 1982), especially 162–83.
78. Two contemporary accounts of the chaos and violence in the mid-1930s are Fernando López Cárdenas, *Revolucionarios contra la Revolución* (Mexico City, 1938), and Askinasy, *El problema agrario.*
79. The following analysis draws upon the new scholarship cited in nn. 75–76, as well as on Raymond, "The Impact of Land Reform;" Kirk, "San Antonio, Yucatán;" and Sanders, "Henequen: The Structure of Agrarian Frustration."
80. Joseph, *Revolution from Without,* 294–98.
81. See nn. 10–11; cf. Mario Menéndez Rodríguez, *Yucatán o el genocidio* (Mexico City, 1964); Enrique Manero, *La anarquía henequenera de Yucatán* (Mexico City, 1966).
82. E.g., Canadian anthropologist Marie Lapointe is currently undertaking a study of the economic and cultural impact of Cardenista land reform on Maya campesinos in both the henequen zone and more peripheral maize-producing zone. Some of her preliminary findings appear in "Indigenisme et réforme agraire." A recent Mexican study on a similar theme is Oscar M. Pintado Cervera, *Estructura productiva y pérdida de la indianidad en Yucatán en el proceso henequenero (dos ensayos)* (Mexico City, 1982).
83. Eric Villanueva Mukul, *Crisis henequenera y movimientos campesinos (1966–1983),* forthcoming; Iván Menéndez, *Lucha social y sistema*

político en Yucatán (Mexico City, 1982). Cf. the problems experienced by campesinos in other collective ejido regimes, described by David Ronfeldt, *Atencingo: The Politics of Agrarian Struggle in a Mexican Ejido* (Stanford, 1973); Salomon Eckstein, *El ejido colectivo en México* (Mexico City, 1966); Eckstein and Iván Restrepo, *La agricultura colectiva de La Laguna* (Mexico City, 1975); and Rodolfo Stavenhagen, "Collective Agriculture and Capitalism in Mexico: A Way Out or a Dead End?" *Latin American Perspectives* 2 (Summer 1975), 146–63.

Epilogue

1. But see Villanueva Mukul, *Así tomamos las tierras,* and Iglesias L., "Historias de vida," which anticipates a full-length oral history by Iglesias L., focusing on the social relations of henequen production before and after the Mexican Revolution. For a successful methodological precedent for such a study, which focuses on the agrarian history of a municipio in Jalisco, see Ann L. Craig, *The First Agraristas: An Oral History of a Mexican Reform Movement* (Berkeley, 1983).

2. Lydia Espinosa, "Historia regional: El rincón de la fatalidad," *Nexos* 1 (July 1978), 11–13; cf. Carr, "Recent Regional Studies," 11; Van Young, "Mexican Rural History," 26, 33–34; and Barbara Weinstein, "Brazilian Regionalism," *LARR* 17:2 (1982), 272.

3. Margarita Rosales González's recent preliminary articles on the Puuc subregion hold out the promise of a monograph similar to Batt's.

4. Herman Konrad, an ethnohistorian at the University of Calgary, is undertaking a study of the production of chicle following the Caste War. Also awaited is "A Maya Apocalypse," Paul Sullivan's forthcoming study of changing agricultural conditions and cultural forms among the Xcacal Guardia rebel group and their twentieth-century descendants in Quintana Roo.

5. See chap. 2 for a discussion of Redfield, Villa Rojas, and earlier ethnographic studies of Yucatán. Two more recent examples of this tradition are Richard Thompson, *The Winds of Tomorrow: Social Change in a Maya Town* (Chicago, 1974), and Press, *Tradition and Adaption* (1975).

6. Carr, "Recent Regional Studies," 5–6. Cf. the incisive critiques of the ethnographic tradition found in William B. Taylor, "Time and Community Studies: Four Books on Rural Societies in Contemporary Mexico," *Peasant Studies* 4 (Apr. 1975), 13–17, and "Revolution and Tradition in Rural Mexico," *Peasant Studies* 5 (Oct. 1976), 31–37; and Gerrit Huizer, *The Revolutionary Potential of Peasants* (Lexington, Mass., 1972), 21–63.

7. E.g., see Eric Wolf, "Aspects of Group Relations in a Complex Society: Mexico," in Teodor Shanin, ed., *Peasants and Peasant Societies: Selected*

Readings (Harmondsworth, 1971), 50–68; Paul Friedrich, *Agrarian Revolt;* and Barbara L. Margolies, *Princes of the Earth: Subcultural Diversity in a Mexican Municipality* (Washington, D.C., 1975); cf. Taylor, "Revolution and Tradition," 33–34, and the theoretical discussion in Carol A. Smith, "Local History in Global Context: Social and Economic Transitions in Western Guatemala," *Comparative Studies in Society and History* 26 (Apr. 1984), 193–228.

8. Carr, "Recent Regional Studies," 11, 14 n. 33; cf. González y González, "El officio de historiar," 34.

9. Particularly lacking is a "new political history" of the Yucatecan Porfiriato. Two recent Brazilian studies provide a model for examining the links between a regional political elite and the dominant economic class. See Linda Lewin, *Politics and Parentela in Paraiba: A Case Study of Family-based Oligarchy in Brazil's Old Republic* (Princeton, forthcoming), and Barbara Weinstein, *The Amazon Rubber Boom, 1850–1920* (Stanford, 1983); cf. Stuart F. Voss, Diana Balmori, and Miles Wortman, *Notable Family Networks in Modern Latin America* (Chicago, 1984).

10. Cf., e.g., Romana Falcón, *Revolución y caciquismo: San Luis Potosí, 1910–1938* (Mexico City, 1984); Stuart F. Voss, *On the Periphery of Nineteenth-Century Mexico: Sonora and Sinaloa, 1810–1877* (Tucson, 1982); Ian Jacobs, *Ranchero Revolt: The Mexican Revolution in Guerrero* (Austin, 1982); Salamini, *Agrarian Radicalism;* William K. Meyers, "Interest Group Conflict and Revolutionary Politics: A Social History of La Comarca Lagunera, Mexico, 1888–1911" (Ph.D. diss., University of Chicago, 1979); also see Benjamin and McNellie, eds., *Other Mexicos,* passim.

Bibliography

Aboites, Luis. "La Revolución Mexicana en Yucatán: El caso de Espita." In González Rodríguez et al., *Yucatán: Peonaje y liberación*, 166–77.

Acereto, Albino. "Historia política desde el descubrimiento europeo hasta 1920." In Yucatán, *Enciclopedia Yucatanense* 3 (1947): 5–388.

Aguilar Camín, Héctor. *La frontera nómada: Sonora y la Revolución Mexicana*. Mexico City, 1977.

Alisky, Marvin. "The Relations of the State of Yucatán and the Federal Government of Mexico, 1823–1978." In Moseley and Terry, *Yucatán: A World Apart*, 245–63.

Altman, Ida, and Lockhart, James, eds. *Provinces of Early Mexico: Variants of Spanish American Regional Evolution*. Los Angeles, 1976.

Alvarado, Salvador. *Actuación revolucionaria del General Salvador Alvarado en Yucatán*. Mexico City, 1965.

———. *Antología ideológica*. Mexico City, 1976.

Alvarez Barret, Luis. "Orígenes y evolución de las escuelas rurales en Yucatán." *RUY* 13 (November–December 1971): 26–51.

Ancona, Eligio. *Historia de Yucatán desde la época más remota hasta nuestros días*. 5 vols. Mérida and Barcelona, 1889–1905.

"Apéndice: Comentarios contemporáneos sobre *México bárbaro*." *Problemas Agrícolas e Industriales de México* 7, no. 2 (1955): 159–84.

Arrigunaga Coello, Maritza. *Catálogo de las fotocopias de los documentos y periódicos yucatecos en la Biblioteca de la Universidad de Texas en Arlington*. Arlington, 1983.

Askinasy, Siegfried. *El problema agrario de Yucatán*. Mexico City, 1936.

Aznar Barbachano, Tomás. *Las mejoras materiales*. 2 vols. Campeche, 1859.

Baerlein, Henry. *Mexico: The Land of Unrest*. Philadelphia, 1914.

Bailey, David C. "Revisionism and the Recent Historiography of the Mexican Revolution." *HAHR* 58 (February 1978): 62–79.

Baklanoff, Eric N. "The Diversification Quest: A Monocrop Export Economy in Transition." In Moseley and Terry, *Yucatán: A World Apart*, 202–44.

Baklanoff, Eric N., and Brannon, Jeffery. "Corporate Control of a Monocrop Economy: A Comment." *LARR* 18, no. 3 (1983): 193–96.

———. "Forward and Backward Linkages in a Plantation Economy: Immigrant Entrepreneurship and Industrial Development in Yucatán, Mexico."

179

Working Paper Series. College of Commerce and Business Administration, University of Alabama, 1983. Mimeographed.

———. *The Political Economy of Agrarian Reform and State Enterprise: The Henequen Industry of Yucatán.* University, Ala. Forthcoming.

Baqueiro, Serapio. *Ensayo histórico sobre las revoluciones de Yucatán desde el año 1840 hasta 1864.* 3 vols. Mérida, 1878–87.

Barabas, Alicia M. "Profetismo, milenarismo y mesianismo en las insurrecciones mayas de Yucatán." In INAH, *Cuadernos de los Centros Regionales,* no. 5, Mexico City, 1974.

Barber, Gerald. "Horizon of Thorns: Yucatán at the Turn of the Century." Master's thesis, University of the Americas, Cholula, Mexico, 1974.

Barceló Quintal, Raquel. "El desarrollo de la banca y el henequén." *YHE* 5 (January–February 1982): 3–24.

———. "El ferrocarril y la oligarquía henequenera." *YHE* 5 (July–August 1981): 23–54.

———. "La oligarquía henequenera. Un estudio de caso: La familia Escalante." Tesis de Licenciatura en Antropología Social, Universidad de Yucatán, 1982.

Barrera Vásquez, Alfredo. "Four Centuries of Archaeology in Yucatán: A Bibliographical Essay." In Moseley and Terry, *Yucatán: A World Apart,* 306–19.

Bartolomé, Miguel A. "La insurrección de Canek: Un movimiento mesiánico en el Yucatán colonial." In Centro Regional del Sureste, INAH, *Cuadernos de los Centros Regionales.* Mexico City, 1978.

Bartolomé, Miguel A., and Barabas, Alicia M. *La resistencia maya: Relaciones interétnicas en el oriente de la península de Yucatán.* Mexico City, 1977.

Batt, R. Laura. "Capitalist Class Formation in Dependent Economies: The Case of Espita, Yucatán." Master's thesis, University of Kentucky, 1981.

Bauer, Arnold J. "Rural Workers in Spanish America: Problems of Peonage and Oppression." *HAHR* 59 (February 1979): 34–63.

Beals, Carleton. *Mexican Maze.* Philadelphia, 1931.

Becker, Marjorie. "The Schoolhouse Rebellion: Revolution and Counterrevolution in the Mexican Countryside, 1934–1940." Ph.D. diss. Yale University. Forthcoming.

Bellingeri, Marco. "Proyecto de investigación: La hacienda y la sociedad yucateca en el siglo XIX." *YHE* 1 (November–December 1977): 3–13.

Bellinghausen, Hermann. "Trova yucateca: La península cantable." *Nexos* 6 (August 1983): 51.

Benet, Francisco. "Sociology Uncertain: The Ideology of the Rural-Urban Continuum." *Comparative Studies in Society and History* 6 (October 1963): 1–12.

Benítez, Fernando. *Ki: El drama de un pueblo y de una planta.* 2d ed. Mexico City, 1962.

Benjamin, Thomas. "International Harvester and the Henequen Marketing System of Yucatán, 1898–1915: A New Perspective." *Inter-American Economic Affairs* 31 (Winter 1977): 3–19.

Benjamin, Thomas, and McNellie, William, eds. *Other Mexicos: Essays on Regional History, 1876–1911.* Albuquerque, 1984.

Bernstein, Harry. "Regionalism in the National History of Mexico." *Acta Americana* 2 (October–December 1944): 305–14.

Berzunza Pinto, Ramón. *Guerra social en Yucatán.* Mérida, 1965.

———. "Las vísperas yucatecas de la Revolución." *Historia Mexicana* 6 (July–September 1956): 75–88.

Betancourt Pérez, Antonio. "¿Angel, o demonio? Carrillo Puerto y 'Peregrina,'" *Juzgue* 2 (May 1973): 19.

———. *El asesinato de Carrillo Puerto.* Mérida, 1974.

———. *Historia de Yucatán.* Mérida, 1970.

———. *La problemática social: ¿Primera chispa de la Revolución Mexicana?* Mérida, 1983.

———. *Revoluciones y crisis en la economía de Yucatán.* Mérida, 1953.

———. "La verdad sobre el origen de las escuelas rurales en Yucatán." *RUY* 13 (July–August 1971): 34–76.

Bingham, Marie. *Catalog of the Yucatán Collection on Microfilm in the University of Alabama Libraries.* University, Ala., 1972.

Boils Morales, Guillermo. "Las reformas progresistas durante el gobierno de Salvador Alvarado en Yucatán." *YHE* 1 (March–April 1978): 14–21.

Bojórquez Urzáiz, Carlos. "Agitadores subalternos: Duendes, brujos y vampiros en Yucatán." *DdY,* 5 March 1984, p. 7.

———. "Crisis maicera de la comunidad campesina yucateca en la segunda mitad del siglo XIX." *BECA* 6 (March–April 1979): 46–52.

———. "Estructura agraria y maíz a partir de la 'guerra de castas.'" *RUY* 20 (November–December 1978): 15–35.

———. "Milenarismo y crisis política: La Casa del Josué en Campeche." *DdY,* 13 June 1982, p. 7.

———. "Regionalización de la política agraria de Yucatán en la segunda mitad del siglo XIX." *RUY* 21 (May–August 1979): 32–45.

———. "El Yucatán de 1847 hasta 1851: Breves apuntes sobre el trabajo y la subsistencia." *BECA* 5 (November–December 1977): 18–25.

———. "Yucatán: Plantaciones colonialistas y sistema de trabajo a fines del siglo XVIII." *YHE* 6 (September–October 1982): 28–34.

Bolio Ontiveros, Edmundo. *De la cuna al paredón: Anecdotario de la vida, muerte y gloria de Felipe Carrillo Puerto.* Mérida, 1929.

———. *Yucatán en la dictadura y en la Revolución.* Mexico City, 1967.

Bolland, O. Nigel. "The Maya and the Colonization of Belize in the Nineteenth Century." In Jones, *Anthropology and History in Yucatán*, 64–99.

Brading, D. A., ed. *Caudillo and Peasant in the Mexican Revolution.* Cambridge, 1980.

Bricker, Victoria Reifler. "Algunas consecuencias religiosas y sociales del nativismo maya del siglo XIX." *América Indígena* 33 (April–June 1973): 327–48.

————. "The Caste War of Yucatán: The History of a Myth and the Myth of History." In Jones, *Anthropology and History in Yucatán*, 251–58.

————. *The Indian Christ, the Indian King: The Historical Substrate of Maya Myth and Ritual.* Austin, 1981.

Brown, Lyle. "Cárdenas: Creating a *Campesino* Power Base for Presidential Policy." In Wolfskill and Richmond, *Essays on the Mexican Revolution,* 101–36.

Brunhouse, R. L. *Sylvanus G. Morley and the World of the Ancient Maya.* Norman, Okla., 1971.

Burns, Allen F. "The Caste War in the 1970s: Present-Day Accounts from Village Quintana Roo." In Jones, *Anthropology and History in Yucatán,* 259–73.

Bustillos Carrillo, Antonio. *Yucatán al servicio de la patria y la Revolución.* Mexico City, 1959.

Buve, Raymond Th. "Peasant Movements, Caudillos and Land Reform during the Revolution (1910–1917) in Tlaxcala, Mexico." *Boletín de Estudios Latinoamericanos y del Caribe* 18 (June 1975): 112–52.

Cal, Angel. "The Yucatec Maya of Belize, 1847–1900: A Preliminary Overview." Belize College of Arts, Science, and Technology, 1984. Mimeographed.

Cámara Patrón, Alberto, and Ayora Sarlat, Vicente. "Vida y obra de Felipe Carrillo Puerto." In *Memoria de los actos realizados en el quincuagésimo aniversario de la Universidad de Yucatán,* 97–127. Mérida, 1973.

Cámara Zavala, Gonzalo. "Historia de la industria henequenera hasta 1919." In Yucatán, *Enciclopedia Yucatanense* 3 (1947): 657–725.

Canto López, Antonio. *La guerra de castas en Yucatán.* Mérida, 1976.

Carbine, Carol Lee. "The Indian Policy of Porfirio Díaz in the State of Yucatán, 1876–1910." Ph.D. diss., Loyola University of Chicago, 1977.

Cardoso, Fernando Henrique. "The Consumption of Dependency Theory in the United States." *LARR* 12, no. 3 (1977): 7–24.

Cardoso, Fernando Henrique, and Faletto, Enzo. *Dependencia y desarrollo en América Latina.* Mexico City, 1969.

Careaga, Lorena. "Historia contemporánea de Chan Santa Cruz." *YHE* 4 (September–October 1980): 66–75.

Carey, James C. *The Mexican Revolution in Yucatán, 1915–1924.* Boulder, Col., 1985.

Carmack, Robert. "Ethnography and Ethnohistory: Their Application in Middle American Studies." *Ethnohistory* 18 (Spring 1971): 127–45.

Carnegie Institution of Washington. *Reports of the Department of Archaeology.* Yearbooks 50–57. Washington, D.C., 1950–58.

————. *Reports of the Division of Historical Research.* Yearbooks 29–49. Washington, D.C., 1930–50.

Carr, Barry. "Recent Regional Studies of the Mexican Revolution." *LARR* 15, no. 1 (1980): 3–14.

Carrillo Puerto, Acrelio. *La familia Carrillo Puerto de Motul.* Mérida, 1959.

Carstensen, Fred V., and Roazen Parrillo, Diane. "International Harvester, Molina y Compañía, and the Henequen Market: A Comment." *LARR* 18, no. 3 (1983): 197–203.

Casasús, Francisco A. "Ensayo biográfico del Licenciado Olegario Molina Solís." *RUY* 14 (May–June 1972): 68–95.

Castillo Torre, José. *A la luz del relámpago: Ensayo de biografía subjetiva de Felipe Carrillo Puerto.* Mexico City, 1934.

Chacón, Ramón D. "Rural Educational Reform in Yucatán: From the Porfiriato to the Era of Salvador Alvarado, 1910–1918." *The Americas.* Forthcoming.

————. "Salvador Alvarado and the Catholic Church: Church and State in Yucatán, 1914–1918." *Journal of Church and State.* Forthcoming.

————. "Yucatán and the Mexican Revolution: The Pre-Constitutional Years, 1910–1918." Ph.D. diss., Stanford University, 1982.

Chamberlain, Robert S. *The Conquest and Colonization of Yucatán, 1517–1550.* Washington, D.C., 1948.

Chardon, Roland E. P. *Geographical Aspects of Plantation Agriculture in Yucatán.* Washington, D.C., 1961.

————. "Hacienda and Ejido in Yucatán: The Example of Santa Ana Cucá." *Annals of the Association of American Geographers* 53 (1963): 174–93.

Civeira Taboada, Miguel. "Deficiencias de Yucatán: El Archivo General del Estado." *DdY,* 12 July 1984, pp. 3, 7.

Clements, Kendrick A. "'A Kindness to Carranza': William Jennings Bryan, International Harvester, and Intervention in Yucatán." *Nebraska History* 57 (Winter 1976): 479–90.

Cline, Howard F. "The Aurora Yucateca and the Spirit of Enterprise in Yucatán, 1821–1847." *HAHR* 27 (February 1947): 30–60.

————. "The Henequen Episode in Yucatán." *Inter-American Economic Affairs* 2 (Autumn 1948): 30–51.

————. "Introduction: Reflections on Ethnohistory." In Cline, *Guide to Ethnohistorical Sources,* 3–16.

————. "Regionalism and Society in Yucatán, 1825–1847: A Study of 'Progressivism' and the Origins of the Caste War." In Cline, *Related Studies,* pt. 3.

————. *Related Studies in Early Nineteenth Century Yucatecan Social History.* 3 pts. Microfilm Collection of Manuscripts on Middle American Cultural Anthropology, no. 32. University of Chicago Library, 1950.

————. "Remarks on a Selected Bibliography of the Caste War and Allied Topics." Appendix to Villa Rojas, *The Maya of East Central Quintana Roo,* pp. 165–78.

————. "The Sugar Episode in Yucatán, 1825–1850." *Inter-American Economic Affairs* 1 (Spring 1948): 79–100.

————. "The War of the Castes and Its Consequences." In Cline, *Related Studies,* pt. 1, no. 2.

————. "War of the Castes and the Independent Indian States of Yucatán." In Cline, *Related Studies,* pt. 1, no. 1.

————, ed. *Guide to Ethnohistorical Sources.* Austin, 1972.

Coatsworth, John H. *Growth against Development: The Economic Impact of Railroads in Porfirian Mexico.* DeKalb, Ill., 1981.

Collins, Anne C. "The *Maestros Cantores* in Yucatán." In Jones, *Anthropology and History in Yucatán,* 233–47.

Cook, Sherburne F., and Borah, Woodrow. *Essays in Population History: Mexico and the Caribbean.* 3 vols. Berkeley, 1971–79.

————. "The Population of Yucatán, 1517–1960." In Cook and Borah, *Essays in Population History,* 2:1–170.

Córdova, Arnaldo. *La ideología de la Revolución Mexicana: La formación del nuevo régimen.* Mexico City, 1973.

Craig, Ann L. *The First Agraristas: An Oral History of a Mexican Agrarian Reform Movement.* Berkeley, 1983.

Diacon, Todd A. "The Brazilian Contestado Movement and the Caste War of Yucatán: The Social Origins of Millenarian Movements." Ph.D. diss., University of Wisconsin, Madison. Forthcoming.

Domínguez, José Luis. "Situación política en el partido de Sotuta (1911–1916)." In González Rodríguez et al., *Yucatán: Peonaje y liberación,* 178–205.

Domínguez Aké, Santiago. *Aniverisario del fusilamiento de Felipe Carrillo en Muxupib (Bilingüe: Español-Maya).* Mérida, 1982.

Dumond, D. E. "Competition, Cooperation, and the Folk Society." *Southwestern Journal of Anthropology* 26 (Autumn 1970): 261–86.

————. "Independent Maya of the Late Nineteenth Century: Chiefdoms and Power Politics." In Jones, *Anthropology and History in Yucatán,* 103–38.

Eckstein, Salomón. *El ejido colectivo en México.* Mexico City, 1966.

Eckstein, Salomón, and Restrepo, Iván. *La agricultura colectiva de La Laguna.* Mexico City, 1975.

"Editorial." *YHE* 1 (September–October 1977): 2, and 2 (September–October 1978): 2.

Emond, Charles John. *The History of Orange Walk.* Belize City, 1983.

Escoffié, Manuel M. *Yucatán en la cruz*. Mérida, 1957.

Espinosa, Lydia. "Historia regional: El rincón de la fatalidad." *Nexos* 1 (July 1978): 11–13.

Falcón, Romana. *Revolución y caciquismo: San Luis Potosí, 1910–1938*. Mexico City, 1984.

Fallon, Michael J. "El Archivo de la Secretaría del Arzobispado, Calle 58, Núm. 501, Altos, Mérida, Yucatán." *The Americas* 33 (July 1976): 149–54.

Farriss, Nancy M. *Colonial Maya Society: The Collective Enterprise of Survival*. Princeton, 1984.

―――. "Indians of Colonial Yucatán: Three Perspectives." In MacLeod and Wasserstrom, *Indians and Spaniards in Southern Mesoamerica*, pp. 1–39.

―――. "Nucleation versus Dispersal: The Dynamics of Population Movement in Colonial Yucatán." *HAHR* 58 (May 1978): 187–216.

―――. "Propiedades territoriales en Yucatán en la época colonial: Algunas observaciones acerca de la pobreza española y la autonomía indígena." *RUY* 25 (April–June 1983): 37–86.

Ferrer, Adolfo. *El archivo de Felipe Carrillo Puerto: El callismo; la corrupción del régimen obregonista*. New York, 1924.

Franco, Iván C. "Casta divina y monopolio." In González Rodríguez et al., *Yucatán: Peonaje y liberación*, 45–57.

Frank, André Gunder. "The Development of Underdevelopment." *Monthly Review* 17 (September 1966): 17–31.

Franz, David A. "Bullets and Bolshevists: A History of the Mexican Revolution in Yucatán, 1910–1924." Ph.D. diss., University of New Mexico, 1973.

Friedrich, Paul. *Agrarian Revolt in a Mexican Village*. 2d ed. Chicago, 1977.

Frost, Frederick J. T., and Arnold, Channing. *The American Egypt*. New York, 1909.

Gamboa Berzunza, Fernando. "Visión pedagógica de Felipe Carrillo Puerto." *RUY* 3 (January–February 1961): 35–41.

Gamboa Ricalde, Alvaro. *Yucatán desde 1910*. 3 vols. Veracruz and Mexico City, 1943–55.

García Bernal, Manuela Cristina. *La sociedad de Yucatán, 1700–1750*. Seville, 1972.

García Cantón, Alberto. *Memorias de un ex-hacendado*. Mérida, 1965.

García Cantú, Gastón. *El socialismo en México, siglo XIX*. Mexico City, 1969.

García Quintanilla, Alejandra. "La formación de la estructura económica de Yucatán: 1850–1940." *YHE* 2 (November 1978–April 1979): 44–60.

―――. "Historia de la producción en Yucatán, 1850–1915." Departamento de Estudios Económicos y Sociales, Universidad de Yucatán, 1983. Mimeographed.

―――. "Historia y etapas de la producción de una mercancía: Henequén, 1850–1915." *YHE* 5 (July–August 1981): 3–22.

Goldkind, Victor. "Class Conflict and Cacique in Chan Kom." *Southwestern Journal of Anthropology* 22 (Winter 1966): 325–45.

_____. "Social Stratification in the Peasant Community: Redfield's Chan Kom Reinterpreted." *American Anthropologist* 67 (August 1965): 863–84.

González Navarro, Moisés. *La colonización en México.* Mexico City, 1960.

_____. "Las guerras de castas." *RUY* 21 (September–October 1979): 24–53.

_____. *Raza y tierra: La guerra de castas y el henequén.* Mexico City, 1970.

González Padilla, Beatriz. "La dirigencia política en Yucatán, 1909–1925." In Millet Cámara et al. *Hacienda y cambio social,* 103–61.

González Rodríguez, Blanca. "Cuatros proyectos de cambio en Yucatán." In Millet Cámara et al., *Hacienda y cambio social,* 75–102.

_____. "Henequén y población: Dzemul a manera de ejemplo." Tesis de Licenciatura en Antropología Social, Universidad de Yucatán, 1979.

González Rodríguez, Blanca, et al. *Yucatán: Peonaje y liberación.* Mérida, 1981.

González y González, Luis. *Invitación a la microhistoria.* Mexico City, 1973.

_____. *Nueva invitación a la microhistoria.* Mexico City, 1982.

_____. "El oficio de historiar." *Nexos* 6 (September 1983): 31–35.

Goodman, Margaret A. "The Effectiveness of the Mexican Revolution as an Agent of Change in the State of Yucatán, Mexico." Ph.D. diss., Columbia University, 1970.

Graham, Richard, and Smith, Peter H., eds., *New Approaches to Latin American History.* Austin, 1974.

Gruening, Ernest. *Un viaje al estado de Yucatán: Felipe Carrillo Puerto, su obra socialista.* Guanajuato, 1924.

Halperin, Rhoda. "Redistribution in Chan Kom: A Case for Mexican Political Economy." In Halperin and Dow, *Peasant Livelihood: Studies in Economic Anthropology,* 79–85.

Halperin, Rhoda, and Dow, James, eds. *Peasant Livelihood: Studies in Economic Anthropology.* New York, 1973.

Hamilton, Nora. *The Limits of State Autonomy: Post-Revolutionary Mexico.* Princeton, 1982.

Hansen, Asael T., and Bastarrachea M., Juan R. *Mérida: Su transformación de capital colonial a naciente metrópoli en 1935.* Mexico City, 1984.

Hartman, Keith. "The Henequen Empire in Yucatán: 1870–1910." Master's thesis, University of Iowa, 1966.

"History of the International Harvester Company." H. L. Boyle files. International Harvester Company Archives. Chicago, n.d. [1947].

Hu-Dehart, Evelyn. "Development and Rural Rebellion: Pacification of the Yaquis in the Late Porfiriato." *HAHR* 54 (February 1974): 72–93.

Huizer, Gerrit. *The Revolutionary Potential of Peasants.* Lexington, Mass., 1972.

Hunt, Marta Espejo-Ponce de. "Colonial Yucatán: Town and Region in the

Seventeenth Century." Ph.D. diss., University of California, Los Angeles, 1974.

_____. "The Process of the Development of Yucatán, 1600–1700." In Altman and Lockhart, *Provinces of Early Mexico*, 33–63.

Iglesias L., Esther. *Estado y alianza de clases en la reforma agraria cardenista: El campesinado henequenero.* Mexico City. Forthcoming.

_____. "Historias de vida de campesinos henequeneros." *YHE* 2 (May–June 1978): 3–15.

_____. "Yucatán, monocultivo, oro verde y decadencia henequenera: La región y dependencia del mercado norteamericano." Paper presented to the Primer encuentro sobre impactos regionales de las relaciones económicas México-Estados Unidos, Guanajuato, 1981. Mimeographed.

Irabién Rosado, Manuel. *Historia de los ferrocarriles.* Mérida, 1928.

Irigoyen, Renán. "Carrillo Puerto, mártir de la cultura." *RUY* 16 (May–August 1959): 20–23.

_____. "Don Us Escalante, precursor de la industria henequenera." *Revista de Estudios Yucatecos* 1 (February 1949): 17–32.

_____. *Ensayos henequeneros.* Mérida, 1975.

_____. *Felipe Carrillo Puerto: Primer gobernante socialista en México.* Mérida, 1974.

_____. *¿Fué el auge del henequén producto de la guerra de castas?* Mérida, 1947.

_____. "El impulso a la economía de Yucatán durante el gobierno de Alvarado." *RUY* 7 (March–April 1965): 45–71.

_____. "Origen y trayectoria del henequén." *RUY* 15 (March–April 1973): 114–28.

_____. *Salvador Alvarado: Extraordinario estadista de la Revolución.* Mérida, 1973.

Jacobs, Ian. *Ranchero Revolt: The Mexican Revolution in Guerrero.* Austin, 1982.

Jones, Grant D. "La estructura política de los mayas de Chan Santa Cruz: El papel del respaldo inglés." *América Indígena* 31 (April–June 1971): 415–21.

_____. "Levels of Settlement Alliance among the San Pedro Maya of Western Belize and Eastern Petén, 1857–1936." In Jones, *Anthropology and History in Yucatán*, 139–89.

_____. "Maya Intergroup Relations in Nineteenth Century Belize and Southern Yucatán." *Journal of Belizean Affairs* 1 (June 1973): 3–13.

_____. "Mayas, Yucatecans and Englishmen in the Nineteenth Century Fiesta System of Northern Belize." *Belizean Studies* 10, no. 3/4 (1982): 25–42.

_____. "Revolution and Continuity in Santa Cruz Maya Society." *American Ethnologist* 1 (November 1974): 659–83.

————, ed. *Anthropology and History in Yucatán*. Austin, 1977.

Joseph, Gilbert M. "Apuntes hacia una nueva historia regional: Yucatán y la Revolución Mexicana, 1915–1940." *RUY* 19 (January–February 1977): 12–35.

————. "British Loggers and Spanish Governors: The Logwood Trade and Its Settlements in the Yucatán Peninsula." *Caribbean Studies* 14 (July 1974): 7–37.

————. "Caciquismo and the Revolution: Carrillo Puerto in Yucatán." In Brading, *Caudillo and Peasant in the Mexican Revolution*, 193–221.

————. "The Fragile Revolution: Cacique Politics and Revolutionary Process in Yucatán." *LARR* 15, no. 1 (1980): 39–64.

————. "Mexico's 'Popular Revolution': Mobilization and Myth in Yucatán, 1910–1940." *Latin American Perspectives* 6 (Summer 1979): 46–65.

————. "Revolution from Without: The Mexican Revolution in Yucatán, 1910–1940." In Moseley and Terry, *Yucatán: A World Apart*, 142–71.

————. *Revolution from Without: Yucatán, Mexico, and the United States, 1880–1924*. Cambridge, 1982.

Joseph, Gilbert M., and Wells, Allen. "Collaboration and Informal Empire in Yucatán: The Case for Political Economy." *LARR* 18, no. 3 (1983): 204–18.

————. "Corporate Control of a Monocrop Economy: International Harvester and Yucatán's Henequen Industry during the Porfiriato." *LARR* 17, no. 1 (1982): 69–99.

————. "The Crisis of an Oligarchical Regime: Elite Politics, Rural Rebellion, and Patterns of Social Control in Yucatán, 1910–1913." Paper presented to the meeting of the Latin American Studies Association, Albuquerque, N.M., 1985.

Katz, Friedrich. "Labor Conditions on Haciendas in Porfirian Mexico: Some Trends and Tendencies." *HAHR* 54 (February 1974): 1–47.

————. "Peasants in the Mexican Revolution of 1910." In Spielberg and Whiteford, *Forging Nations*, 61–85.

————. *The Secret War in Mexico: Europe, the United States and the Mexican Revolution*. Chicago, 1981.

————. "El sistema de plantación y la esclavitud." *Ciencias Políticas y Sociales* 8 (January–March 1962): 103–35.

————, ed. *La servidumbre agraria en México en la época porfiriana*. Mexico City, 1976.

Kirk, Rodney C. "San Antonio, Yucatán: From Henequen Hacienda to Plantation Ejido." Ph.D. diss., Michigan State University, 1975.

Knight, Alan. "Peasant and Caudillo in Revolutionary Mexico, 1910–1917." In Brading, *Caudillo and Peasant*, 17–58.

Knox, A. J. Graham. "Henequen Haciendas, Maya Peones, and the Mexican

Revolution Promises of 1910: Reform and Reaction in Yucatán, 1910–1940." *Caribbean Studies* 17 (April–July 1977): 55–82.

———. "Regionalism as a Problem in Mexican National History: Yucatán, a Case Study, 1821–1840." University of Calgary, 1973. Mimeographed.

Labrecque, Marie-France. "From Peasantry to Proletariat: The Rural Proletariat in the Henequenera Region of Yucatán, Mexico." Ph.D. diss., City University of New York, 1982.

———. "La herencia maya del proletariado rural de Yucatán." *YHE* 5 (January–February 1982): 25–38.

Lapointe, Marie. "Indigenisme et réforme agraire au Yucatán, 1937–1940." Paper presented to the 44th International Congress of Americanists, Manchester, Engl., September 1982.

———. *Los mayas rebeldes de Yucatán.* Zamora, Michoacán, 1983.

———. "La prolongation de la guerre des castes au Yucatán (1850–1901)." Ph.D. diss., Institut des Hautes Études de l'Amérique Latine de Paris, 1978.

Lee, Rosemary. "The Tourist Industry in Yucatán: A Case Study in the Interaction between Class Structure and Economic Development." Ph.D. diss., University of California, Irvine, 1977.

Lewin, Linda. *Politics and Parentela in Paraiba: A Case Study of Family-based Oligarchy in Brazil's Old Republic.* Princeton. Forthcoming.

Lewis, Oscar. *Life in a Mexican Village: Tepoztlán Restudied.* Urbana, Ill., 1951.

Liga de Acción Social. *Biografía del Señor Licenciado Don Olegario Molina Solís.* Mérida, 1925.

Littlefield, Alice. "The Expansion of Capitalist Relations of Production in Mexican Crafts." *Journal of Peasant Studies* 6 (July 1979): 471–87.

———. *La industria de las hamacas en Yucatán, México.* Mexico City, 1976.

Lockhart, James. "The Social History of Colonial Spanish America." *LARR* 7, no. 1 (1972): 6–45.

Lombardo Toledano, Vicente. *El llanto del sureste.* Mexico City, 1934.

López Amabilis, Manuel. "Yucatán en la estadística antes de la guerra de castas." *RUY* 5 (January–February 1963): 115–29.

López Cárdenas, Fernando. *Revolucionarios contra la Revolución.* Mexico City, 1938.

López Rivas, Luis. "Archivo General del Estado de Yucatán." *Boletín del Archivo General de la Nación,* 3d ser., 1 (October–December 1977).

Loret de Mola, Carlos. *Yucatán en la patria.* 2 vols. Mexico City, 1969.

Love, Joseph L. "An Approach to Regionalism." In Graham and Smith, *New Approaches to Latin American History,* 137–55.

Loveira, Carlos. *El socialismo en Yucatán.* Havana, 1923.

Luna, Jesús. *La carrera pública de Don Ramón Corral.* Mexico City, 1975.

McBride, George M. *The Land Systems of Mexico.* New York, 1923.

McCreery, David. "Debt Servitude in Rural Guatemala, 1876–1935." *HAHR* 63 (November 1983): 735–59.

Macías, Anna. *Against All Odds: The Feminist Movement in Mexico to 1940.* Westport, Conn., 1982.

MacLeod, Murdo J., and Wasserstrom, Robert, eds. *Indians and Spaniards in Southern Mesoamerica.* Lincoln, Nebr., 1983.

Magaña Esquivel, Antonio. *La tierra enrojecida.* Mexico City, 1951.

Manero, Enrique. *La anarquía henequenera de Yucatán.* Mexico City, 1966.

Manzanilla D., Anastasio. *El bolchevismo criminal de Yucatán.* Mexico City, 1921.

Margolies, Barbara L. *Princes of the Earth: Subcultural Diversity in a Mexican Municipality.* Washington, D.C., 1975.

Martín, Manuel. "Acerca del capitalismo en Yucatán (siglo XIX)." *YHE* 1 (November–December 1977): 17–24.

Mediz Bolio, Antonio. "Prólogo." In Alvarado, *Actuación revolucionaria del General Salvador Alvarado en Yucatán.*

Mejía Fernández, Miguel. *Política agraria en México en el siglo XIX.* Mexico City, 1979.

Mena Brito, Bernardino. *Bolchevismo y democracia en México: Pugna entre dos partidos políticos en Yucatán durante de la Revolución Constitucionalista.* Mexico City, 1933.

————. *Reestructuración histórica de Yucatán.* 3 vols. Mexico City, 1969.

Menéndez, Carlos R. *La primera chispa de la Revolución Mexicana.* Mérida, 1919.

Menéndez, Iván. "Aproximación a la historia de Yucatán." *RUY* 22 (May–August 1980): 60–77.

————. *Lucha social y sistema política en Yucatán.* Mexico City, 1982.

Menéndez Rodríguez, Mario. *Yucatán o el genocidio.* Mexico City, 1964.

Meyer, Eugenia. *Conciencia histórica norteamericana sobre la Revolución de 1910.* Mexico City, 1970.

————. "La periodización de la historia contemporánea de México." In Wilkie, Meyer, and Wilkie, *Contemporary Mexico,* 730–46.

Meyer, Jean. *The Cristero Rebellion: The Mexican People between Church and State, 1926–1929.* Translated by Richard Southern. Cambridge, 1976.

————. *Problemas campesinos y revueltas agrarias (1821–1910).* Mexico City, 1973.

————. *La Revolución Mejicana.* Barcelona, 1973.

Meyer, Lorenzo. *Mexico and the United States in the Oil Controversy, 1917–1942.* Austin, 1977.

Meyer, Michael C. "Perspectives on Mexican Revolutionary Historiography." *New Mexico Historical Review* 44 (April 1969): 167–80.

Meyers, William K. "Interest Group Conflict and Revolutionary Politics: A

Social History of La Comarca Lagunera, Mexico, 1888–1911." Ph.D. diss., University of Chicago, 1979.

Michaels, Albert L., and Bernstein, Marvin. "The Modernization of the Old Order: Organization and Periodization of Twentieth Century Mexican History." In Wilkie, Meyer, and Wilkie, *Contemporary Mexico*, 687–710.

Millet Cámara, Luis. "De la estancias y haciendas en el Yucatán colonial." In Millet Cámara et al., *Hacienda y cambio social en Yucatán*, 11–37.

Millet Cámara, Luis, et al. *Hacienda y cambio social en Yucatán*. Mérida, 1984.

Mintz, Sidney W. "The Folk-Urban Continuum and the Rural Proletarian Community." *American Journal of Sociology* 59 (September 1953): 136–43.

Mintz, Sidney W., and Wolf, Eric. "Haciendas and Plantations in Middle America and the Antilles." *Social and Economic Studies* 6, no. 3 (1957): 380–412.

Molina Font, Gustavo. *La tragedia de Yucatán*. Prologue by Luis Cabrera. Mexico City, 1941.

Molina Solís, Juan Francisco. *Historia de Yucatán desde la independencia de España hasta la época actual*. 2 vols. Mérida, 1921–27.

Montalvo [Ferraez], Jorge. "Apuntes sobre el capitalismo y el henequén en Yucatán." *YHE* 1 (September–October 1977): 36–43.

Montalvo Ortega, Enrique. "Caudillismo y estado en la Revolución Mexicana: El gobierno de Alvarado en Yucatán." *Nova Americana* 2 (1979): 13–36.

————. "Historia y política: Los usos de la historia y el Partido Socialista del Sureste." *YHE* 1 (March–April 1978): 22–34.

Montalvo [Ortega], Enrique, and Sierra Villarreal, José Luis. "La transición al capitalismo: El caso Yucatán; apuntes de una investigación." In Centro Regional del Sureste, INAH, *Memoria del Congreso Interno, 1979*, pp. 291–94. Mexico City, 1981.

Morales Valderrama, Carmen. "Delimitación y características de la región sur de Yucatán." *YHE* 5 (September–October 1981): 54–66.

Moseley, Edward H. "From Conquest to Independence: Yucatán under Spanish Rule, 1521–1821." In Moseley and Terry, *Yucatán: A World Apart*, 83–121.

Moseley, Edward H., and Terry, Edward D., eds. *Yucatán: A World Apart*. University, Ala., 1980.

Orosa Díaz, Jaime. *Apuntes elementales de la historia de Yucatán*. Mérida, 1976.

————. "Carrillo Puerto en la historia y en la literatura." *Orbe* 31 (August 1951): 75–77.

————. *Se vende un hombre*. Mérida, 1974. Originally published in 1959.

Ortega Noriega, Sergio. "Archivos históricos regionales y locales—un proyecto de catálogo." *Boletín del Archivo General de la Nación,* 3d ser., 1 (July–September 1977).

Owen, Norman G. *Prosperity without Progress: Manila Hemp and Material Life in the Colonial Philippines.* Berkeley, 1984.

Palerm, Angel. *Modos de producción y formaciones socioeconómicas.* Mexico City, 1976.

Paoli Bolio, Francisco J. "Carrillo Puerto y el PSS." *RUY* 16 (January–February 1974): 75–91.

——. *Salvador Alvarado y la Revolucion en Yucatán.* Mérida, 1981.

——. "Yucatán, embrión del estado mexicano: Gobierno de Salvador Alvarado, 1915–1918." Ph.D. diss., Universidad Ibero-Americana, Mexico City, 1982.

Paoli [Bolio], Francisco J., and Montalvo [Ortega], Enrique. *El socialismo olvidado de Yucatán.* Mexico City, 1977.

Patch, Robert. "Agrarian Change in Eighteenth-Century Yucatán." *HAHR* 65 (February 1985): 21–49.

——. "Apuntes acerca de los orígenes y las características de la hacienda henequenera." *YHE* 2 (September–October 1978): 3–15.

——. "A Colonial Regime: Maya and Spaniard in Yucatán." Ph.D. diss., Princeton University, 1979.

——. "El fin del régimen colonial en Yucatán y los orígenes de la guerra de castas: El problema de la tierra, 1812–1846." *BECA* 10 (May–June 1983): 17–26.

——. *La formación de estancias y haciendas durante la colonia.* Mérida, 1976. Also printed in *BECA* 4 (July–August 1976): 21–61.

——. "El mercado urbano y la economía campesina en Yucatán durante el siglo XVIII." *RUY* 20 (May–August 1978): 83–96.

Patterson, Orlando. *Slavery and Social Death: A Comparative Study.* Cambridge, Mass., 1982.

Peniche Vallado, Leopoldo. "Una tesis histórica rigurosa y racional acerca de la llamada guerra de castas." *RUY* 19 (January–February 1977): 56–70.

Pérez-Mallaina Bueno, Pablo Emilio. *Comercio y autonomía en la Intendencia de Yucatán (1797–1814).* Seville, 1978.

Pérez Martínez, Héctor. *Yucatán: Catálogo de documentos para la historia de Yucatán y Campeche que se hallen en diversos archivos y bibliotecas de México y del extranjero.* Campeche, 1943. Reprinted as *Yucatán, An Annotated Bibliography.* Salisbury, N.C., 1980.

Pintado Cervera, Oscar M. *Estructura productiva y pérdida de la indianidad en Yucatán en el proceso henequenero (dos ensayos).* Mexico City, 1982.

Platt, Robert. "Chichi: An Hacienda in Yucatán." In Platt, *Latin America: Countrysides and United Regions,* 63–67.

_____, ed. *Latin America: Countrysides and United Regions.* New York, 1942.

Pompa y Pompa, Antonio. "Prólogo." In Alvarado, *Antología ideológica,* 7–17.

Press, Irwin. *Tradition and Adaptation: Life in a Modern Yucatán Maya Village.* Westport, Conn., 1975.

Quezada, Sergio. "El origen de la producción y el capital comercial en la provincia de Yucatán, a mediados del siglo XVIII." *BECA* 5 (January–February 1978): 12–29.

Quintal Martín, Fidelio. *Yucatán. Carácter de la guerra campesina en 1847: Una síntesis interpretiva.* Mérida, 1976.

_____. *Yucatán: Un período de historia contemporánea, 1910–1924.* Mérida, 1974.

Raat, W. Dirk, ed. *The Mexican Revolution: An Annotated Guide to Recent Scholarship.* Boston, 1982.

Raymond, Nathaniel C. "The Impact of Land Reform in the Monocrop Region of Yucatán, Mexico." Ph.D. diss., Brandeis University, 1971.

_____. "Land Reform and the Structure of Production in Yucatán." *Ethnology* 7 (October 1968): 461–70.

Redfield, Robert. "Culture Change in Yucatán." *American Anthropologist* 36 (January–March 1934): 57–69.

_____. *The Folk Culture of Yucatán.* Chicago, 1941.

_____. "The Folk Society." *American Journal of Sociology* 52 (January 1947): 293–308.

_____. *The Little Community.* Chicago, 1958.

_____. *A Village That Chose Progress: Chan Kom Revisited.* Chicago, 1950.

Redfield, Robert, and Villa Rojas, Alfonso. *Chan Kom: A Maya Village.* Washington, D.C., 1943.

Reed, Alma. "Felipe Carrillo Puerto." *Boletín de la Universidad Nacional del Sureste,* época 2, 4 (June 1924): 20–21.

Reed, Nelson. *The Caste War of Yucatán.* Stanford, 1964.

Regil, José M., and Peón, Alonso M. "Estadística de Yucatán." *Boletín de la Sociedad Mexicana de Geografía y Estadística* 1, no. 3 (1853): 237–339.

Reina, Leticia. *Las rebeliones campesinas en México.* Mexico City, 1980.

Remmers, Lawrence J. "Henequen, the Caste War, and the Economy of Yucatán, 1846–1883: The Roots of Dependence in a Mexican Region." Ph.D. diss., University of California, Los Angeles, 1981.

Richmond, Douglas W. "Yucatán durante la época carrancista." Paper presented at the Segunda Semana de la Historia de Yucatán, Mérida, February 1980. Mimeographed.

[Rius]. "Felipe Carrillo Puerto: El Salvador Allende Mexicano." *Los Agachados* 5 (June 1974).

Roazen Parrillo, Diane. "American Enterprise, American Government, and the Sisal Industry of Yucatán, Mexico, 1876–1924." Paper presented to the American Historical Association, San Francisco, December, 1978. Mimeographed.

———. "U.S. Business Interests and the Sisal Industry of Yucatán, Mexico, 1876–1924." Ph.D. diss., University of Chicago, 1984.

Rodríguez Losa, Salvador. "El henequén: Hoy, ayer y mañana." Mérida, n.d. Mimeographed.

———. "Población y 'guerra de castas.'" *RUY* 20 (November–December 1978): 123–35.

Ronfeldt, David. *Atencingo: The Politics of Agrarian Struggle in a Mexican Ejido.* Stanford, 1973.

Rosales González, Margarita. "La actividad comercial en el poblado de Oxkutzcab entre 1900 y 1950." *RUY* 25 (April–June 1983): 159–72.

———. "Etapas en el desarrollo regional del Puuc, Yucatán." *YHE* 3 (March–April 1980): 41–53.

Roys, Ralph L. *The Book of Chilám Balám of Chumayel.* Washington, D. C., 1933.

———. *The Indian Background of Colonial Yucatán.* Washington, D.C., 1943.

———. *The Political Geography of the Yucatán Maya.* Washington, D.C., 1957.

———. *The Titles of Ebtún.* Washington, D.C., 1939.

Roys, Ralph L., and Scholes, France V. *The Maya Chontal Indians of Acalán-Tixchel: A Contribution to the History and Ethnography of the Yucatán Peninsula.* Washington, D.C., 1948.

Rubio Mañé, Jorge Ignacio. "La guerra de castas según un escritor angloamericano." *RUY* 2 (January–February 1969): 9–20.

———. *El separatismo de Yucatán.* Mérida, 1935.

Ruibal Corella, Juan Antonio. *Los tiempos de Salvador Alvarado.* Hermosillo, 1982.

Ruz Menéndez, Rodolfo. "Los archivos del estado de Yucatán." *RUY* 22 (March–April 1980): 12–19.

———. *Ensayos Yucatanenses.* Mérida, 1976.

———. *Por los viejos caminos del Mayab: Ensayos históricos y literarios.* Mérida, 1973.

———. "Problemas prioritarios de la historiografía regional." *DdY,* 23 September 1976, pp. 3, 7.

Ryder, James W. "Internal Migration in Yucatán: Interpretation of Historical Demography and Current Patterns." In Jones, *Anthropology and History in Yucatán,* 191–231.

Salamini, Heather Fowler. *Agrarian Radicalism in Veracruz, 1920–38.* Lincoln, Nebr., 1978.

Sanders, Thomas G. "Henequen: The Structure of Agrarian Frustration."

American University Field Staff Reports, North American Series, 5 (July 1977).

Saragoza, Alex M. "The Formation of a Mexican Elite: The Industrialization of Monterrey, Nuevo León." Ph.D. diss., University of California, San Diego, 1978.

Sarkisyanz, Manuel. *Felipe Carrillo Puerto: Säkulare hagiographie aus dem revolutionären Mexiko.* Forthcoming.

Scholes, France V., Adams, Eleanor, Menéndez, Carlos R., and Rubio Mañé, J. Ignacio, eds. *Documentos para la historia de Yucatán.* 3 vols. Mérida, 1936–38.

Shanin, Teodor, ed. *Peasants and Peasant Societies: Selected Readings.* Harmondsworth, 1971.

Shuman, Malcolm K. "The Town Where Luck Fell: The Economics of Life in a Henequen Zone Pueblo." Ph.D. diss., Tulane University, 1974.

Sierra Villarreal, José Luis. "Hacia una economía política de la hacienda henequenera." *YHE* 3 (January–February 1980): 57–63; 4 (July–August 1980): 16–22.

———. "Oro amarillo, oro verde y oro negro: Tres colores y . . . ¿una misma dependencia?" *YHE* 5 (July–August 1981): 23–54.

———. "Prensa y lucha política en Yucatán, 1895–1925." Centro Regional del Sureste, INAH, 1984. Mimeographed.

Smith, Carol A. "Local History in Global Context: Social and Economic Transitions in Western Guatemala." *Comparative Studies in Society and History* 26 (April 1984): 193–228.

Solís, Rosendo. "Vida cotidiana y salud en X-Can." *YHE* 2 (September–October 1978): 16–22.

Sosa Ferreyro, Roque Armando. *El crimen del miedo: Cómo y por qué fue asesinado Felipe Carrillo Puerto.* Mexico City, 1969.

Spalding, Karen. "The Colonial Indian: Past and Future Research Perspectives." *LARR* 7, no. 1 (1972): 47–76.

Spielberg, Joseph, and Whiteford, Scott, eds. *Forging Nations: A Comparative View of Rural Ferment and Revolt.* East Lansing, Mich., 1976.

Stavenhagen, Rodolfo. "Collective Agriculture and Capitalism in Mexico: A Way Out or a Dead End?" *Latin American Perspectives* 2 (Summer 1975): 146–63.

Stephens, John L. *Incidents of Travel in Central America, Chiapas, and Yucatán.* 2 vols. New York, 1841.

———. *Incidents of Travel in Yucatán.* 2 vols. New York, 1843. Reprint. New York, 1963.

Stokes, Eric. "Late Nineteenth Century Colonial Expansion and the Attack on the Theory of Economic Imperialism." *Historical Journal* 12 (1969): 285–301.

Strickon, Arnold. "Hacienda and Plantation in Yucatán: An Historical-Ecological Consideration of the Folk-Urban Continuum in Yucatán." *América Indígena* 25 (January 1965): 35–63.

Suárez Molina, Víctor M. "Espíritu y características de las regiones yucatecas en la primera mitad del siglo XIX." *RUY* 20 (March–April 1978): 69–83.

_____. *La evolución económica de Yucatán.* 2 vols. Mérida, 1977.

_____. "La guerra de castas y el problema de la tierra." *RUY* 19 (January–February 1977): 49–55.

_____. "La industria cordelera en Yucatán en el siglo XIX." *DdY,* 20 February 1972, pp. 3, 11.

_____. "El tobaco en Yucatán en el siglo XIX." *RUY* 16 (May–August 1974): 16–25.

Sullivan, Paul. *A Maya Apocalypse: Contemporary Maya Prophecy in Ethnographic and Historical Context.* Forthcoming.

Tannenbaum, Frank. *The Mexican Agrarian Revolution.* Washington, D.C., 1930.

_____. *Peace by Revolution: Mexico after 1910.* New York, 1933.

Taylor, William B. "Revolution and Tradition in Rural Mexico." *Peasant Studies* 5 (October 1976): 31–37.

_____. "Time and Community Studies: Four Books on Rural Societies in Contemporary Mexico." *Peasant Studies* 4 (April 1975): 13–17.

Terry, Edward D. "Revolution and Social Struggle: Three Plays by Leopoldo Peniche Vallado." Paper presented to the South Eastern Council of Latin American Studies, San Juan, 1983.

Terry, Edward D., et al. "Analyzing a Region: The Interaction of the University of Alabama and the Yucatán." *SECOLAS Annals* 13 (1982): 32–47.

Thompson, Edward H. *People of the Serpent: Life and Adventure among the Mayas.* Boston, 1932.

Thompson, Richard. *The Winds of Tomorrow: Social Change in a Maya Town.* Chicago, 1974.

Turner, John K. *Barbarous Mexico.* Chicago, 1910.

United States. Department of State. Consular Post Records. Correspondence: Progreso, 1916, vol. 1. RG 84. National Archives, Washington, D.C.

_____. National Archives. *Record Group 59, Records of the Department of State Relating to the Internal Affairs of Mexico, 1910–1929.* Washington, D.C., 1959.

Universidad de Yucatán. *Memoria de los actos realizados en el quincuagésimo aniversario de la Universidad de Yucatán.* Mérida, 1973.

_____. *Memorias de la Primera Semana de la Historia.* Mérida, 1980.

Urzáiz R., Eduardo. *Del Imperio a la Revolución, 1865–1910.* Mérida, 1945.

Valadés, Diego. "Ideas políticas y sociales de Salvador Alvarado." *Estudios de Historia Moderna y Contemporánea de México* 5 (1976): 109–18.

Valdés Acosta, José María. *A través de los siglos.* 3 vols. Mérida, 1923–26.

Van Young, Eric. "Mexican Rural History since Chevalier: The Historiography of the Colonial Hacienda." *LARR* 18: 3 (1983): 5–61.

Vaughan, Mary Kay. *The State, Education, and Social Class in Mexico, 1880–1928.* DeKalb, Ill., 1982.

Villa Rojas, Alfonso. *The Maya of East Central Quintana Roo.* Washington, D.C., 1945.

Villanueva Mukul, Eric. *Así tomamos las tierras.* Mérida, 1984.

––––––. "Las causas de la guerra campesina de 1847." *YHE* 1 (March–April 1978): 42–49.

––––––. *Crisis henequenera y movimientos campesinos en Yucatán (1966–1983).* Forthcoming.

––––––. "La lucha de la comunidad de Chemax." *YHE* 8 (July–August 1978): 35–51.

Voss, Stuart F. *On the Periphery of Nineteenth-Century Mexico: Sonora and Sinaloa, 1810–1877.* Tucson, 1982.

Voss, Stuart F., Balmori, Diana, and Wortman, Miles. *Notable Family Networks in Modern Latin America.* Chicago, 1984.

Wallace, Anthony F. C. "Revitalization Movements." *American Anthropologist* 58 (1956): 264–81.

Wallerstein, Immanuel. *The Modern World-System.* New York, 1974.

Wasserman, Mark. *Capitalists, Caciques, and Revolution: The Native Elite and Foreign Enterprise in Chihuahua, Mexico, 1854–1911.* Chapel Hill, 1984.

Weinstein, Barbara. *The Amazon Rubber Boom, 1850–1920.* Stanford, 1983.

––––––. "Brazilian Regionalism." *LARR* 17, no. 2 (1982): 262–76.

Wells, Allen. "Economic Growth and Regional Disparity in Porfirian Yucatán: The Case of the Southeastern Railway Company." *South Eastern Latin Americanist* 22 (September 1978): 1–16.

––––––. "Family Elites in a Boom-and-Bust Economy: The Molinas and Peóns of Porfirian Yucatán." *HAHR* 62 (May 1982): 224–53.

––––––. "Violence and Social Control: Yucatán's Henequen Plantations." In Benjamin and McNellie, *Other Mexicos,* 213–41.

––––––. *Yucatán's Gilded Age: Haciendas, Henequen, and International Harvester, 1860–1915.* Albuquerque. Forthcoming.

Wilkie, James W., Meyer, Michael C., and Wilkie, Edna Monzón, eds. *Contemporary Mexico: Papers of the IV International Congress of Mexican History.* Berkeley, 1976.

Wilkins, Mira. *The Emergence of Multinational Enterprise: American Business Abroad from the Colonial Era to 1914.* Cambridge, Mass., 1970.

Williams, Mary Wilhelmine. "The Secessionist Diplomacy of Yucatán." *HAHR* 9 (May 1929): 132–43.

Williams, Ross. "Yucatán Henequen: A Study in Microeconomics." Master's thesis, University of the Americas, Cholula, Mexico, 1972.

Wolf, Eric. "Aspects of Group Relations in a Complex Society: Mexico." In Shanin, *Peasants and Peasant Societies,* 50–68.

Wolfskill, George, and Richmond, Douglas W., eds. *Essays on the Mexican Revolution: Revisionist Views of the Leaders.* Austin, 1979.

Womack, John, Jr.. "The Mexican Economy during the Revolution, 1910–1920: Historiography and Analysis." *Marxist Perspectives* 4 (Winter 1978): 80–123.

————. *Zapata and the Mexican Revolution.* New York, 1969.

Yucatán. *Enciclopedia Yucatenense.* 8 vols. Mérida, 1944–47. Additional vols. in preparation.

————. *Murales de Fernando Castro Pacheco en el Palacio de Gobierno.* Mérida, 1981.

Zapata Casares, Manuel. *Vía-Crucis del henequén: Colección de escritos sobre el gran problema de Yucatán.* Mérida, 1961.

Zimmerman, Charlotte. "The Cult of the Holy Cross: An Analysis of Cosmology and Catholicism in Quintana Roo." *History of Religions* 3, no. 1 (1963): 50–71.

Index

199

About the Author

Gilbert M. Joseph, who received his Ph.D. from Yale University in 1978, is an associate professor of history at the University of North Carolina at Chapel Hill. He is also the author of *Revolution from Without: Yucatán, Mexico, and the United States, 1880–1924* (Cambridge: Cambridge University Press, 1982). Professor Joseph specializes in the history of social movements and foreign involvement in modern Mexico and Central America.